SPIRITUAL BEINGS

IN THE HEAVENLY BODIES
AND IN THE KINGDOMS
OF NATURE

SPIRITUAL BEINGS

IN THE HEAVENLY BODIES
AND IN THE KINGDOMS OF NATURE

A CYCLE OF TEN LECTURES
HELSINKI • APRIL 3–14, 1912

with Four Additional Lectures: Two Private Addresses
to Russian Members and Two Public Lectures

Rudolf Steiner

Anthroposophic Press

The cycle of ten lectures in this book and the additional lecture "Occultism and Initiation" in the appendix appear in the original German in *Die geistigen Wesenheiten in den Himmelskörpern und Naturreichen* (volume 136 in the Collected Works), 4th edition, 1974. "Address to the Russians / 1," Address to the Russians / 2," and "The Essence of National Epics," which are the additional lectures in the appendix, are published in the original German in *Der Zusammenhang des Menschen mit der elementarischen Welt* (volume 158 in the Collected Works), 3rd edition, 1980. Both of these German titles are published by Rudolf Steiner Verlag, Dornach, Switzerland.

This edition copyright © 1992 by Anthroposophic Press
Introduction © René Querido, 1992

Published by Anthroposophic Press
RR 4 Box 94 A1, Hudson, NY 12534

Library of Congress Cataloging-in-Publication Data

Steiner, Rudolf, 1861–1925.
  [Geistigen Wesenheiten in den Himmelskörpern und
Naturreichen. English]
  Spiritual beings in the heavenly bodies and in the kingdoms of
nature : a cycle of 10 lectures, Helsinki, April 3–14, 1912 : with four
additional lectures, two public lectures and two private addresses,
given to Russian members / Rudolf Steiner.
    Translation of: Die geistigen Wesenheiten in den Himmelskörpern
und Naturreichen.
  ISBN 0-88010-367-1
  1. Anthroposophy. 2. Spirits. 3. Occultism. 4. Initiation rites.
5. Kalevala. I. Title.
BP595.S894G47413   1992   92-26629
299'.935—dc20   CIP

10 9 8 7 6 5 4 3 2

Printed in the United States of America

CONTENTS

Introduction *by René Querido*   7

Lecture One *19*

Lecture Two *33*

Lecture Three *50*

Lecture Four *67*

Lecture Five *80*

Lecture Six *97*

Lecture Seven *117*

Lecture Eight *139*

Lecture Nine *162*

Lecture Ten *187*

Appendix I

Address to the Russian Members /1 .... *215*
April 11, 1912

Address to the Russian Members /2 .... *230*
June 5, 1913

Appendix II

Public Lectures:

The Essence of National Epics
with special reference to the *Kalevala* 243
April 9, 1912

Occultism and Initiation 274
April 12, 1912

Further Reading   *301*

INTRODUCTION

I

With the passage of time, Rudolf Steiner's immense contribution to the renewal of art, science, and religion—and to the practical application of spiritual science—has gained increased significance.

Within less than two decades at the beginning of this century, Steiner laid the foundation for the teaching of anthroposophy in two main endeavors. Firstly, between 1900 and 1909, he wrote the five basic books, of which *Occult Science: An Outline* is the most comprehensive. Secondly, he traveled widely, covering almost every corner of Europe, bringing to larger and sometimes smaller audiences the basic thoughts of the new science of the spirit. During this period of tireless travel, with Berlin as his headquarters, Steiner would often visit eight or nine countries per year.

What came about was virtually a traveling university. He would lecture in Holland, Switzerland, Norway, Austria, Italy, Hungary, England, Czechoslovakia, Finland, Sweden and in many cities of Germany. Apart from addressing local members, a fairly extensive group of friends, having taken time off from their regular activities, would follow him from place to place. Some fifty courses, each comprising about ten lectures each, were held in this manner between 1906 and 1918.

It is within this context that we have to consider the Helsinki cycle of lectures that is here being reprinted.

Rudolf Steiner arrived in the Finnish capital by boat a few days before Easter in 1912. A number of friends from Scandinavia and Germany accompanied him. There was a special sense of expectation in the air, for this was Rudolf Steiner's first visit to Finland. Russian members had hoped that he would visit them in St. Petersburg, but as the Russian authorities had refused him a visa, they came to Helsinki in order to participate in the course. From all accounts there was a festive Easter mood. Rudolf Steiner attended a traditional Russian Orthodox Easter mass. He also shared a typical Easter meal with the Russian friends.

Margarita Woloschin, in *"Die Grüne Schlange"* (*The Green Snake*) vividly describes this event. "After we had taken our seats around the table, Steiner cut the Easter loaf in the form of a hexagon, divided it among us, rose, and held an address. The content of this was as follows: 'The whole history of humankind is the entombment of the Godhead. With our consciousness we can only celebrate the entombment on Good Friday. We cannot understand Easter with our ordinary reasoning powers. We can celebrate Easter only to the extent that we commit ourselves to tread the path of the spirit.' These words were spoken with great earnestness."

A few days later, Rudolf Steiner invited the Russian members to a gathering at the hotel where he was staying in the heart of Helsinki. They crowded into one of the guest rooms and received a special message. This address, unique in Rudolf Steiner's work, is here published for the first time in English. A second address followed a year later on the occasion of Rudolf Steiner's second visit, again only imparted to Russian members. [It is also included, for the first time in English, in the present volume.]

Both lectures contain unusual material, and Margarita
Woloschin reported that she had never heard Steiner speak
with such inwardness. "He spoke so personally to each
one, and it seemed as if each word was imbued with endless
warmth, which he sought to implant in our souls. He spoke
of the young soul of the Russian people, of which one can
become conscious in the spiritual worlds and which was not
able as yet to reveal itself.... He showed us the path to our
own folk soul and how important that was for the future."

When reading these lectures today, we find that they contain an unusually prophetic element. Steiner graphically
describes the role of Russia between two mighty temptations, the material decadence of the West and the vague
mysticism of the East. English-speaking readers will be
interested not only in the many references to both England
and America, but also in the quite remarkable characteriza-
tion of the forces that flow into Russia from Asia. In the second address, we find the following poignant remark: "You
have found it possible, in spite of the great difficulties that
prevail in your country, to assemble here unhindered.
Make use of this opportunity to achieve the greatest possible inward relatedness among you, in order to build the
bridge between each one of you and your folk soul."

Strange as it may seem initially that Rudolf Steiner chose
to speak to the Russians separately, some eighty years later
we are now better able to understand why the particular
and intimate messages contained in these lectures were not
available, even in the original German form, until the late
sixties.

During this first visit to Finland, Rudolf Steiner also gave
a public lecture on the nature of national epics with special
reference to the *Kalevala*, which, too, is included for the first
time in English in the present collection. This particular lecture opens up a very significant aspect in Steiner's work.

He rediscovered the importance of this Finnish epic as one of the great poems, not only of national importance, but for the whole of humanity. The *Kalevala*, which had lived strongly in the oral tradition among the people of Finland, was collected by Elilas Lonnrot (1802-1884), a district physician, on his extended excursions in the rural parts of Karelia. Lonnrot roamed thousands of miles on foot, by boat, and by horse cart carrying with him writing equipment and a flute, which at times he played at weddings or village celebrations. By 1845, he had made eleven long journeys collecting material. In the course of the next few years he continued this activity, gathering incantations and poems from simple people still endowed with great spirituality and a remarkably accurate memory of age-old oral traditions.

Rudolf Steiner commented on the importance of this mythological heritage and showed its relevance for our own time and for the future. To Herbert Hahn, one of the original Waldorf teachers, Rudolf Steiner pointed out that in the future the *Kalevala* would have a cultural influence as profound as the works of Homer have had in the world for over two thousand years.

In 1914, two years after the first Helsinki visit, Rudolf Steiner gave a series of three lectures on the *Kalevala*, thus launching a revival of interest in one of the greatest epics of all humankind [Dornach, November 9, 14, 15, 1914].

It is worthwhile to note that the powerful music of Jean Sibelius and the arresting paintings of Akseli Gallen-Kellela both contributed a great deal to a growing interest in the *Kalevala*. Inspired by creative Finnish anthroposophists, the mighty poem has recently been performed for large audiences in southern Finland in festivals featuring music, recitation, and drama. This has become a major national cultural event.

II

Depending on the location and the nature of the audience, Rudolf Steiner's lectures varied immensely in tone, style, and content. Speaking to Scandinavians and Finnish members, Rudolf Steiner was particularly sensitive to the fact that the people of the north still have an immediate relationship to the weaving and working in nature of elemental beings that has largely been lost in other parts of Europe. The cycle of lectures reprinted here, entitled *The Spiritual Beings in the Heavenly Bodies and in the Kingdoms of Nature*, opens with a sensitive contemplation of various phenomena that are easily accessible to every human being. It begins with a consideration of the blue sky, then describes the green of trees bursting into leaf and the green of the meadows, and finally offers a contemplation of the white snow mantle that covers the earth in winter. Rudolf Steiner guides his listeners to an impression of how such meditative observations of nature can be transmuted into inner moral feelings. This he shows to be a gradual, stage-by-stage path to experience, and he shows how the threshold from the physical to the supersensible is crossed—in order to commune first with the elemental beings and then with the hierarchies in their ascending ranks and functions throughout the cosmos. The ten lectures are permeated by a mighty symphonic sweep leading us from the lowliest to the highest in nature and the universe. In the final lectures the cosmic Christ is revealed in this lofty vision. A culmination is reached at the end of the last lecture, "Thus through true heavenly science, something uniform is brought to the human beings, and this will promote the intellectual and moral understanding of humanity on earth.... We do not wish to consider merely the abstract and theoretical but every such consideration ought to become in us...a source of moral power."

In view of the renewed interest in angelology, it might not be inappropriate to include in this introduction a brief survey on the teachings of the celestial beings throughout history.

The earliest systematic mention is found in the writings of Dionysius the Areopagite, a disciple of St. Paul, who lived in the first century A.D. The authenticity of these documents and their author has been fiercely disputed from the ninth century A.D. right into our own time, some scholars purporting them to be the work of a "Pseudo-Dionysius" who incorporated Neoplatonic, Christian, Gnostic, Judaic, and even ancient Indian elements.

It should be borne in mind that the writings on the Divine Names and the Celestial Hierarchies only appeared at the turn of the fifth and sixth centuries A.D. The question is justified: How could they have been written by Dionysius the Areopagite, the pupil and friend of St. Paul?

Rudolf Steiner offers an elucidation that goes to the very heart of the matter: The teachings of Dionysius the Areopagite were given by word of mouth to a small group of chosen pupils and included the practice of a meditative path leading to "deification"—a path by means of which the neophyte could become, through catharsis and enlightenment, a conscious co-creator with the gods.

These teachings and practices were closely guarded in the first esoteric school of Christianity instituted by St. Paul in Athens and guided by Dionysius the Areopagite for many decades. None of the content was written down; powers of memory were still strong enough to ensure an accurate oral transmission through esoteric circles up to the fifth and sixth centuries. But as these powers began to wane it became necessary to commit these teachings to a written form—except for the meditative path toward deification (becoming like God), which remained closely guarded for centuries. In fact, Rudolf Steiner pointed out that it is only now, since the Age of Light began in 1899, that the truths can and should be fully revealed. One of the tasks of anthroposophy is to make the reality of heavenly beings and the meditative practice leading to actual experience of them available to anyone wishing to tread this path in full consciousness.

To the modern mind, wide open to any and all ideas, it may seem strange that the practice of the path was surrounded by such secrecy. We need to remember that especially since the establishment of the Roman Church in the fourth century A.D., the idea that human beings could become like unto God out of their own inmost striving— without the intercession of the church—was regarded as totally heretical. The concept of deification was to be uprooted energetically; it survived in the heretical and mystical streams of the Middle Ages such as the Grail, the School of Chartres, the Cathars, and the Templar movement, to name but a few.

But who was Dionysius the Areopagite? Legend tells us that this gifted young Athenian, an ardent student of Plato's writings, was in Heliopolis, the ancient Egyptian mystery center, when the events on Golgotha took place. He witnessed the darkening of the sun and experienced the earthquake on Good Friday as the Christ went through death. These events moved him to the core of his being but they remained a riddle to him.

Dionysius returned to Athens and as his surname, "the Areopagite," suggests he was elected to the prestigious circle of judges that conferred regularly on the Hill of Mars. Some fourteen years later, St. Paul preached on this hill, revealing the nature of the Christ who had gone through death and resurrection; Dionysius was present and deeply moved. He now understood what he had experienced from a great distance at the time of the Crucifixion to be a turning point in the development of humanity.

In the Bibliothèque Nationale in Paris, an autobiography in Syriac is preserved which describes these events. It also relates that Dionysius sent to fetch the notes he had made in Egypt regarding the crucifixion which were publicly read and found to agree with St. Paul both as to the day and the hour. The manuscript states that St. Paul's visit to Athens took place fourteen years after Dionysius's experience of the darkening of the sun in Egypt, which would place the conversion of Dionysius in A.D. 44 (see the works of Dionysius the Areopagite, translated by John Parker, 1897).

In the Acts of the Apostles we find mention of Paul's visit to Athens and the reaction it brought forth. "Now when they heard of the resurrection of the dead, some mocked; but others said, 'We will hear you again about this.' But some joined him (Paul) and believed, among them Dionysius the Areopagite, a woman named Damaris, and others with them" (Acts 17: 30-33). (For further details regarding the life of Dionysius see *The Golden Age of Chartres* by R. M. Querido, Hudson, New York, 1987)

As a result of this remarkable meeting between Paul and Dionysius, an esoteric school was founded whose influence flowed through the whole of Christendom for centuries. Whereas St. Paul traveled extensively proclaiming the Christ, Dionysius remained, until past ninety years of age, in Athens teaching small circles of students. Rudolf Steiner pointed out in a cycle of lectures entitled "Theosophy of the Rosicrucian" that the Rosicrucian spiritual path was already prepared in remote, pre-Christian times. "It took on a particular configuration through the great initiate Dionysius the Areopagite, who founded the School of St. Paul in Athens, from which all later esoteric wisdom and training has sprung" (Lecture 14).

The influence of these writings was indeed momentous and shaped much of the deepest thought of the leading scholars and masters of the Middle Ages. In the ninth century, Charles the Bald summoned John Scotus Eriugena to his court in Paris, so that he might translate the works of Dionysius into Latin. As a result, these documents became more readily available. A couple of centuries later the nine-fold Celestial Hierarchies were made visible in sculptural form on the South Porch of Chartres Cathedral. Abundant commentaries began to appear by such masters as John of Salisbury, Bishop of Chartres; Thomas Aquinas; and Albertus Magnus of Paris. It is estimated that in the work of Thomas Aquinas no fewer than 1700 references to Dionysius the Areopagite can be found. Around 1300 A.D. the mystical-religious insight into the working of the Divine Hierarchies is translated into the imagery of Dante's majestic poem *The Divine Comedy*. One has the impression on reading the "Paradise" that not only did Dante know about the hierarchies, but that he had experienced them, in a mighty vision. Pico de la Mirandola, famous as one of the outstanding minds of the Renaissance despite his youth, also held the works of Dionysius the Areopagite in high regard.

However, during the Reformation the fiercest opposition against Dionysius reared its head. Luther and Erasmus looked upon him as an arrogant, idle dreamer. By the sixteenth century, humanity had lost the connection with the guiding spirits of the hierarchies; even the tradition had eroded, and soon materialism was to take over and sweep aside a spiritual view of the universe.

In his work, *The Heavenly Hierarchies*, Dionysius the Areopagite leads us downward from the loftiest spiritual beings of the first hierarchy: Seraphim, Cherubim, and Thrones, through the ranks of the second hierarchy to those of the third—closest yet superior in faculty to the human kingdom. We find many references to Hebrew traditions in Dionysius's work, alluding to the fact that Michael became the leader of the Jewish people so that the providence of God in the incarnation of Christ Jesus might be fulfilled. Each hierarchical being is described in turn with its function and relationship to the whole of the divine world and special mention is accorded the rank of the angels. For as the angels are the celestial beings closest to earthly humanity, presumably we may be able to fathom their influence more readily.

Understandably, Dionysius's treatment of the hierarchies does not include a description of their influences in the kingdoms of nature and in the human being. This work still springs from an earlier clairvoyance, before the time had come for this to be revealed. It fell to Rudolf Steiner, as the first spiritual scientist of the new age of light, to proclaim the relationship between macrocosm and microcosm, the heavenly worlds and the kingdoms of nature. He embarked on this very early, and literally thousands of references are to be found in his work—both in books and lectures—over the course of some twenty-one years (from 1904 to 1925).

Characteristically (as in the present cycle), Steiner usually describes the working of the Hierarchies from below upward—starting with the third hierarchy and its three ranks of angels, archangels, and archai. Modern initiation has its starting point where we are: standing at the threshold between angel and beast.

The diagram on the following page may be helpful. (In view of the fact that the hierarchies were given different names in accordance with the various languages, several of these different forms are included.)

The threefold hierarchical world (each comprising beings of three ranks) interpenetrates the three kingdoms of nature with the human being at the center.

Seraphim *or* Spirits of Love

FIRST
HIERARCHY

Cherubim *or* Spirits of Harmony

Thrones *or* Spirits of Will

Kyriotetes *or* Spirits of Wisdom
also called Dominions (Dionysius)

SECOND
HIERARCHY

Dynamis *or* Spirits of Movement
also called Mights or Virtues (Dionysius)

Exusiai *or* Spirits of Form
also called Powers

Archai *or* Spirits of Personality
also called Principalities (Dionysius)

THIRD
HIERARCHY

Archangels *or* Folk Spirits
also called Fire Spirits

Angels *or* Messengers
also called Sons of Life or of Twilight

THE HUMAN BEING

Animal

THREE
KINGDOMS

Plant

Mineral

The Cosmic Christ, one of the Trinity, descended through the ranks of the Hierarchies to become "Man" on earth as Christ Jesus so that human beings might become co-creators with the Gods for the future kingdoms of nature. But we need to learn step-by-step, gradually, to achieve this goal in full consciousness, with love. We are indeed responsible for the future of our planet.

The idea of deification first formulated by Dionysius the Areopagite can receive a new dimension in our time. We cannot become co-creators with the Gods unless we know the overall plan of the Hierarchies in creating the cosmos, and our planet in particular.

III

A final point: When Rudolf Steiner was asked how one could counter the one-sided mechanistic view of the universe so prevalent today, he indicated that an active understanding of the working of the heavenly hierarchies in the kingdoms of nature, in the human being, and in the universe could act as a powerful corrective (G.A. 193, Berlin, 12 September 1919).

We may also recall that when *Occult Science* was published in 1909, it bore the subtitle *An Outline*. The present cycle of lectures, along with many others given in different parts of Europe, may be considered an elaboration, especially of Chapter 4 "The Evolution of the Cosmos and the Human Being."

Study of the present Helsinki course on the Spiritual Beings is eminently suited to help overcome the Ahrimanic influence that we are all subject to. The publishers should be commended on this new edition. The earnest hope is that many students of spiritual science and groups throughout the English-speaking world will take full advantage of the opportunity to contribute to the healing influence provided in such a powerful way by this cycle of lectures.

Lecture One

WHEN OUR FRIENDS here gave me a warm invitation to come to them, they requested me to speak about the spiritual beings we find in the realms of nature and in the heavenly bodies.

Our theme will compel us to touch upon a realm that is very far removed from all the knowledge humanity is given today by the external world, the intellectual world. From the very beginning we shall have to allude to a domain whose reality is denied by the outer world today. I shall take only one thing for granted, namely, that as a result of the studies you have made in spiritual science, you will meet me with a feeling and perception for the spiritual world; in respect to the manner in which we shall name things, we shall come to a mutual understanding in the course of the lectures. All the rest will, in certain respects, come of itself when, as time goes on, we acquire an understanding born of feeling and of perception for the fact that behind our sense world, behind the world which we as human beings experience, there lies a world of spirit, a spiritual world; and that, just as we penetrate into the physical world by regarding it not only as a great unity, but as specified into individual plants, animals, minerals, peoples, persons, so we can specify the spiritual world into different classes of individual spiritual beings. So that in spiritual science we do not merely speak of a spiritual world, but of quite definite beings and forces standing behind our physical world.

What, then, do we include in the physical world? First, let us be clear about that. As belonging to the physical world, we reckon all that we can perceive with our senses, see with our eyes, hear with our ears, all that our hands can grasp. Further, we reckon as belonging to the physical world all that we can encompass with our thoughts insofar as these thoughts refer to external perception, to that which the physical world can say to us. In this physical world we must also include all that we, as human beings, do within it. It might easily make us pause and reflect when it is said that all that we, as human beings, do in the physical world forms part of that world, for we must admit that when we act in the physical world, we bring down the spiritual into that world. People do not act merely according to the suggestions of physical impulses and passions, but also according to moral principles; our conduct, our actions, are influenced by morals. Certainly when we act morally, spiritual impulses play a part in our actions; but the field of action in which we act morally is, nevertheless, the physical world. Just as in our moral actions there is an interplay of spiritual impulses, even so do spiritual impulses permeate us through colors, sounds, warmth and cold, and through all sense impressions. The spiritual is, in a sense, always hidden from external perception, from that which the external human being knows and can do. It is characteristic of the spiritual that we can only recognize it when we take the trouble, at least to a small extent, to become other than we have been hitherto.

We work together in our groups and gatherings; and not only do we hear there certain truths that tell us that there are various worlds—that the human being consists of various principles or bodies, or whatever we like to call

them—but by allowing all this to influence us, although
we may not always notice it, our soul will gradually
change to something different, even without our going
through an esoteric development. What we learn through
spiritual science makes our soul different from what it was
before. Compare your feelings after you have taken part in
the spiritual life of a working group for a few years—the
way you feel and think—with the thoughts and feelings
you had before, or with the way in which people think and
feel who are not interested in spiritual science. Spiritual science does not merely signify the acquisition of knowledge;
it signifies most preeminently an education, a self education of our souls. We make ourselves different; we have
other interests. When one imbues oneself with spiritual science, the habits of attention for this or that subject which
one developed during previous years, alter. What was once
of interest is of interest no longer; what was of no interest
previously, now begins to be interesting in the highest
degree. We ought not simply to say that only a person who
has gone through esoteric development can attain to a connection with the spiritual world; esotericism does not begin
with occult development. The moment that, with our
whole heart, we make any link with spiritual science, esotericism has already begun; our souls begin at once to be
transformed. There then begins in us something resembling
what would arise, let us say, in a being who had previously
only been able to see light and darkness, and who then,
through a special and different organization of the eyes,
begins to see colors. The whole world would appear different to such a being. We need only observe it, we need only
realize it, and we shall soon see that the whole world
begins to have a new aspect when we have for a time gone
through the self-education we can get in a spiritual scientific circle. This self-education to a perception of what lies

behind physical facts is a fruit of the spiritual scientific movement in the world, and is the most important part of spiritual understanding. We should not believe that we can acquire spiritual understanding by mere sentimentality, by simply repeating continually that we wish to permeate all our feelings with love. Other people, if they are good, wish to do that too. This would only be giving way to a sort of pride. Rather, we should make it clear to ourselves how we can educate our feelings—by letting the knowledge of the facts of a higher world influence us and by transforming our souls by means of this knowledge. This special manner of training the soul to a feeling for a higher world is what makes a spiritual scientist. Above all, we need this under-standing if we intend to speak about the things that are to be spoken of in the course of these lectures.

One who, with trained occult vision, is able to see behind the physical facts, immediately finds—behind all that is spread out as color, sound, warmth, and cold, behind all that is embodied in the laws of nature—beings that are not revealed to the external senses, to the external intellect, but that lie behind the physical world. Then, as one penetrates further and deeper, one discovers, so to speak, worlds with beings of an ever higher order. If we wish to acquire an understanding of all that lies behind the sense world, then, in accordance with the special task that has been assigned to me here, we must take as our real starting point what we encounter immediately behind the sense world as soon as we raise the very first veil that sense perceptions spreads over spiritual happenings. As a matter of fact, the world that reveals itself to trained occult vision as the one lying next to us, presents the greatest surprise to contemporary understanding, to our present powers of comprehension. I am speaking to those who have, to some extent, accepted spiritual science. Therefore I may take it for granted that you know that immediately behind what meets us externally as a human being—behind what we see with our eyes, touch with our hands, and grasp with our understanding, in ordinary human anatomy or physiology—behind what we call the physical body—we recognize the first supersensible human principle. This supersensible principle of the human being we call the etheric or life body.

Today, we will not speak of still higher principles of human nature, but need only be clear that occult vision is able to see behind the physical body and to find there the etheric or life body. Now, occult vision can do something similar with regard to nature around us. Just as we can investigate a human being occultly to see if there is not something more than the physical body, and then find the etheric body, so too we can look with occult vision at external nature in her colors, forms, sounds, and kingdoms—in the mineral, the plant, the animal, and the human kingdoms, insofar as these meet us physically. We then find that, just as behind the human physical body there is a life body, so we can also find a sort of etheric or life body behind the whole of physical nature. Only there is an immense difference between the etheric body of all of physical nature and that of the human being. When occult vision is directed to the human etheric or life body, it is seen as a unity, as a connected structure, as a single connected form or figure. When occult vision, on the other hand, penetrates all that external nature presents as color, form, mineral, plant, or animal structures, it discovers that in physical nature the etheric body is a plurality—something infinitely multiform. That is the great difference; the human etheric or life body is a single unitary being—while there are many varied and differentiated beings behind physical nature.

Now, I must show you how we arrive at such an assumption as that just made, namely, that behind our physical nature there is an etheric or life body, strictly speaking an etheric or life world— that is, a plurality, a multiplicity of differentiated beings. To express how we can arrive at this, I can clothe it in simple words: we are more and more able to recognize the etheric or life world behind physical nature when we begin to have a moral perception of the world lying around us. What is meant by perceiving the whole world morally? What does this imply? First of all, looking away from the earth, if we direct our gaze into the ranges of cosmic space, we are met by the blue sky. Suppose we do this on a day in which no cloud, not even the faintest, silver-white cloudlet, breaks the azure space of heaven. We look upward into this blue heaven spread out above us—whether we recognize it in the physical sense as something real or not does not matter. The point is the impression that this wide stretch of the blue heavens makes upon us. Suppose that we can yield ourselves up to this blue of the sky, and that we do this with intensity for a long, long time. Imagine that we can do this in such a way that we forget everything else that we know in life and all that is around us. Suppose that we are able for one moment to forget all external impressions, all memories, all cares and troubles of life, and can yield ourselves completely to the single impression of the blue heavens. What I am now saying to you can be experienced by every human soul if only it will fulfill these necessary conditions; what I am telling you can be a common human experience. Suppose a human soul gazes in this way at nothing but the blue of the sky. A certain moment then comes, a moment in which the blue sky ceases to be blue—in which we no longer see anything that can in human language be called blue. If at that moment, when the blue ceases to be blue to us, we turn our attention to our own soul, we shall notice quite a special mood in it. The blue disappears and, as it were, an infinity

arises before us, and in this infinity we experience a quite
definite mood in our soul. A quite definite feeling, a quite
definite perception pours itself into the emptiness which
arises where the blue had been before. If we would give a
name to this soul perception, to what would soar out there
into infinite distances, there is only one word for it: it is a
devout feeling in our soul, a feeling of pious devotion to
infinity. All the religious feelings in the evolution of humanity have fundamentally a nuance that contains what I have
here called pious devotion. The impression has called up a
religious feeling, a moral perception. When within our souls
the blue has disappeared, a moral perception of the external
world springs to life.

Let us now reflect upon another feeling by means of
which we can in another way attune ourselves in moral
harmony with external nature. When the trees are bursting
into leaf and the meadows are filled with green, let us fix
our gaze upon the green which in the most varied manner
covers the earth or meets us in the trees; and again we will
do this in such a way as to forget all the external impressions that can affect our souls, and simply devote ourselves
to what in external nature meets us as green. If once more
we are so circumstanced that we can yield ourselves to
what springs forth as the reality of green, we can carry this
so far that the green disappears for us, in the same way that
previously the blue as blue disappeared. Here again we
cannot say, "a color is spread out before our sight," but
(and I remark expressly that I am telling you of things that
each one of us can experience for ourselves if the requisite
conditions are fulfilled) the soul has instead a peculiar feeling that can be expressed thus: "Now I understand what I
experience when I think creatively, when a thought springs
up in me, when an idea strikes me: I understand this now
for the first time. I can only learn this from the bursting

forth of the green all around me. I begin to understand the inmost parts of my soul through external nature when the outer natural impression has disappeared and in its place a moral impression is left. The green of the plant tells me how I ought to feel within myself, when my soul is blessed with the power to think thoughts, to cherish ideas." Here again an external impression of nature is transmuted into a moral feeling.

Or, again, we may look at a wide stretch of white snow. In the same way as in the description just given of the blue of the sky and the green of earth's robe of vegetation, so too can the white of the snow set free within us a moral feeling for all that we call the phenomenon of matter in the world. And if, in contemplation of the white snow mantle, we can forget everything else, and experience the whiteness, and then allow it to disappear, we obtain an understanding of that which fills the earth as substance, as matter. We then feel matter living and weaving in the world. And just as one can transform all external sight impressions into moral perceptions, so too can one transform impressions of sound into moral perceptions. Suppose we listen to a tone and then to its octave, and so attune our souls to this dual sound of a tonic note and its octave that we forget all the rest, eliminate all the rest and completely yield ourselves to these tones. It then comes about at last that, instead of hearing these dual tones, our attention is directed from these and we no longer hear them. Then, again, we find that in our soul a moral feeling is set free. We begin then to have a spiritual understanding of what we experience when a wish lives within us that tries to lead us to something, and then our reason influences our wish. The concord of wish and reason, of thought and desire, as they live in the human soul, is perceived in the tone and its octave.

In like manner we might let the most varied sense perceptions work upon us; we could in this way let all that we perceive in nature through our senses disappear, as it were, so that this sense veil is removed; then moral perceptions of sympathy and antipathy would arise everywhere. If we accustom ourselves in this way to eliminate all that we see with our eyes, or hear with our ears, or that our hands grasp, or that our understanding (which is connected with the brain) comprehends—if we eliminate all that, and accustom ourselves, nevertheless, to stand before the world—then there works within us something deeper than the power of vision of our eyes, or the power of hearing of our ears, or the intellectual power of our brain-thinking. We then confront a deeper being of the external world. Then the immensity of infinity so works upon us that we become imbued with a religious mood. Then the green mantle of plants so works upon us that we feel and perceive in our inner being something spiritually bursting forth into bloom. Then the white robe of snow so works upon us that by it we gain an understanding of what matter, of what substance is in the world; we grasp the world through something deeper within us than we had hitherto brought into play. And therefore in this way we come into touch with something deeper in the world itself. Then, as it were, the external veil of nature is drawn aside, and we enter a world which lies behind this external veil. Just as when we look behind the human physical body we come to the etheric or life body, so in this way we come into a region in which, gradually, manifold beings disclose themselves—those beings that live and work behind the mineral kingdom. The etheric world gradually appears before us, differentiated in its details.

In occult science, what gradually appears before us in the way described has always been called the elemental world;

and those spiritual beings we meet with there, and of whom we have spoken, are the elemental spirits that lie hidden behind all that constitutes the physical sense perceptible world. I have already said that whereas the human etheric body is a unity, what we perceive as the etheric world of nature is a plurality, a multiplicity. How then can we, since what we perceive is something quite new, find it possible to describe something of what gradually impresses itself upon us from behind external nature? Well, we can do so if by way of comparison we make a connecting link with what is known. In the whole multiplicity that lies behind the physical world, we first find beings that present self-enclosed pictures to occult vision. In order to characterize what we first of all find there I must refer to something already known. We perceive self-enclosed pictures, beings with definite outline, of whom we can say that they can be described according to their form or shape. These beings are one class that we first of all find behind the physical-sense world. A second class of beings that we find there, we can only describe if we turn away from what shows itself in set form, with a set figure, and employ the word metamorphosis or transformation. That is the second phenomenon that presents itself to occult vision. Beings that have definite forms belong to the one class; beings that actually change their shape every moment, who, as soon as we meet them and think we have grasped them, immediately change into something else, so that we can only follow them if we make our souls mobile and receptive, such beings belong to the second class. Occult vision actually only finds the first class of beings, those that have quite a definite form, when (starting from such conditions as have already been described) it penetrates into the depths of the earth.

I have said that we must allow all that works on us in the external world to arouse a moral effect, such as has been described. We have brought forward, by way of example, how one can raise the blue of the heavens, the green of the plants, the whiteness of the snow, into moral impressions. Let us now suppose that we penetrate into the inner part of the earth. When, let us say, we associate with miners, we reach the inner portion of the earth, at any rate we enter regions in which we cannot at first so school our eyes that our vision is transformed into a moral impression. But in our feeling we notice warmth, differentiated degrees of warmth. We must first feel the warmth—warmth must be the physical impression of nature when we plunge into the realm of the earth. If we keep in view these differences of warmth, these alternations of temperature, and all that otherwise works on our senses because we are underground, if we allow all this to work upon us, then through thus penetrating into the inner part of the earth and feeling ourselves united with what is active there, we go through a definite experience. If we then disregard everything that produces an impression, if we exert ourselves while down there to feel nothing, not even the differences of warmth which were only for us a preparatory stage, if we try to see nothing, to hear nothing, but to let the impression so affect us that something moral issues from our soul—then there arises before our occult vision those creative nature beings who, for the occultist, are really active in everything belonging to the earth, especially in everything of the nature of metal, and who now present themselves to his imagination, to imaginative knowledge, in sharply defined forms of the most varied kind. If, having had an occult training, and having at the same time a certain love of such things—it is especially important to have this here—we make acquaintance with miners and go down into the mines, and can forget all external impressions when we are down there, we will then feel rising up before our imagination the first class, as it were, of beings that create and weave behind all that is earthy, and especially in all that pertains to metals. I have not yet spoken today of how popular fairy tales and folk legends have made use of all that, in a sense, is actually in existence; I should like first to give you the dry facts that offer themselves to occult vision. For according to the task set me, I must first go to work empirically—that is, I must give an account, first of all, of what we find in the various kingdoms of nature. This is how I understand the topic put before me.

Just as, in occult vision, we perceive in our imagination clearly outlined nature beings, and in this way can have before us beings with settled form, of whom we see outlines that we could sketch, so it is also possible for occult vision to have an impression of other beings standing immediately behind the veil of nature. If, let us say, on a day when the weather conditions are constantly changing, when, for instance, clouds form and rain falls, and when, perhaps, a mist rises from the surface of the earth, if on such a day we yield to such phenomena in the way already described, so that we allow a moral feeling to take the place of a physical one, then we may again have quite a distinct experience. This is especially the case if we devote ourselves to the peculiar play of a body of water tossing in a waterfall and giving out clouds of spray; if we yield ourselves to the forming and dissolving mist and to the watery vapor filling the air and rising like smoke, or when we see the fine rain coming down, or feel a slight drizzle in the air. If we feel all this morally there appears a second class of beings, to whom we can apply the word metamorphosis, transformation. As little as we can paint lightning, can we draw this second class of beings. We can only note a shape, present for a moment, and the moment after everything is again changed. Thus there appear to us as the second class of beings, those who are always changing form, for whom we can find an imaginative symbol in the changing formations of clouds.

But as occultists we become acquainted in yet another way with these beings. When we observe the plants as they come forth from the earth in the spring, just when they put forth the first green shoots—not later, when they are getting ready to bear fruit—the occultist perceives that the same beings that he or she discovered in the pulverizing, drifting, gathering vapors, are surrounding and bathing the beings of the budding plants. So we can say that when we see the plants springing forth from the earth, we see them everywhere bathed by such everchanging beings as these. Then occult vision feels that what weaves and hovers unseen over the buds of the plants is in some way concerned with what makes the plants push up out of the ground, draw forth from the ground. You see, ordinary physical science recognizes only the growth of the plants, knows only that the plants have an impelling power that forces them up from below. The occultist, however, recognizes more than this in the case of the blossom. The occultist recognizes—around the young sprouting plant—changing, transforming beings who have, as it were, been released from the surrounding space and penetrate downward; they do not, like the physical principle of growth, merely pass from below upward, but come from above downward, and draw forth the plants from the ground. So in spring, when the earth is robing herself in green, to the occultist it is as though nature forces, descending from the universe, draw forth what is within the earth, so that the inner part of the earth may become visible to the outer surrounding world, to the heavens. Something that is in unceasing motion hovers over the plant. It is characteristic that occult vision acquires a feeling that what floats around the plants is the same as what is present in the rarefied water, tossing itself into vapor and rain. That, let us say, is the second class of nature forces and nature beings. In the next lecture we shall pass on to the description of the third and fourth classes, which are much more interesting; and then all this will become clearer. When we set about making observations such as these, which lie so far from present human consciousness, we must always bear in mind that "All that meets us is physical, but permeated by the spiritual."

As we have to think of the individual human being as permeated by what appears to occult sight as the etheric body, so must we think of all that is living and weaving in the world as permeated by a multiplicity of spiritual living forces and beings.

The course to be followed in our considerations shall be such that we shall first describe simply the facts that an occultly trained vision can experience in the external world; facts that are evident to us when we look into the depths of the earth or the atmosphere, into what happens in the different realms of nature, and in the heavenly spaces filled by the fixed stars. And only at the end shall we gather the whole together in a kind of theoretical knowledge that is able to enlighten us as to what lies, as spirit, at the foundations of our physical universe and its different realms and kingdoms.

LECTURE TWO

Y ESTERDAY, I TRIED first of all to point out the way that
leads the human soul to the observation of the spiritual
world hidden directly behind our material physical world,
and then to draw attention to two classes or categories of
spiritual beings, perceptible to occult vision when the veil
of the sense world has been drawn aside.

Today, we shall speak of two other forms or categories of
nature spirits. The one is disclosed to trained occult sight
when we observe the gradual fading and dying of the
plant world in late summer or autumn, the dying of nature
beings in general. As soon as a plant begins to develop
fruit in the blossom, we can allow this fruit to work upon
the soul in the manner described in our last lecture. In this
way, we receive in our imagination the impression of the
spiritual beings concerned with the fading and dying of
the beings of nature. We were able to describe yesterday
that in spring the plants are, so to speak, drawn out of
the earth by certain beings that are subject to perpetual
metamorphosis, and likewise we can say that when, for
instance, the plants have finished this development, and
the time has come for them to fade, other beings then work
upon them—beings of whom we cannot even say that they,
too, continually change their forms, for, strictly speaking,
they have no form of their own at all. They appear flashing

up like lightning, like little meteors; now flashing up, now disappearing; they really have no definite form, but flit over our earth, flashing and vanishing like little meteors or will-o'-the-wisps.

These beings are primarily connected with the ripening of everything in the kingdoms of nature; the ripening process comes about because these forces or beings exist. They are only visible to occult vision when it concentrates on the air itself, indeed, on the purest air possible. We have described the second sort of nature beings by saying that to perceive them we must allow falling water, or water condensed into cloud formations, or something of a like character to work upon us. Now air, as free from moisture as possible, played upon by the light and warmth of the sun, must work upon the soul if we are to visualize in our imagination these meteor-like, flashing, and disappearing beings that live in air free from moisture, and eagerly drink in the light which permeates the air and causes them to flash and shine. These beings then sink down into the plant world or the animal world, and bring about their ripening and maturity. In the very way we approach these beings, we see that they stand in a certain relation to what occultism has always called the elements.

We find what we described in the last lecture as the first class of such beings when we descend into the depths of the earth and penetrate the solid substance of our planet. Our imagination is then confronted with beings of a definite form, and we may call these the nature spirits of solid substance, or the nature spirits of the earth. The second category we then described are to be found in water that collects and disperses, so that we may connect these spiritual beings with what in occultism has always been called the fluid or watery element. In this element they undergo metamorphoses, and at the same time they do the work of drawing

forth from the earth everything that grows and sprouts. The
flashing, disappearing beings of whom we have just spoken
stand, not in connection with the watery element but in connection with the element of air, air when it is as free from
moisture as possible. Thus we may now speak of nature
spirits of earth, water, and of air. There is a fourth category
of such spiritual beings with which occult vision can
become familiar. For this, occult vision must wait until a
blossom has brought forth fruit and seed, and then observe
how the germ gradually grows into a new plant. Only on
such an occasion can such a vision be achieved with ease—
in other conditions it is difficult to observe this fourth kind
of being, for they are the protectors of the germs, of all the
seeds in our kingdoms of nature. As guardians these beings
carry the seed from one generation of plants or other nature
beings to the next. We can observe that these beings, the
protectors of the seeds or germs, make it possible that the
same beings continually reappear on our earth, and that
these beings are brought into contact with the warmth of
our planet—with what from early times has been called the
element of fire or heat. That is why the forces of the seed are
also connected with a certain degree of heat, a certain temperature. If occult vision observes accurately enough, it
finds that the necessary transmutation of the warmth of the
environment into such heat as is needed by the seed or
germ in order to ripen—that the changing of lifeless
warmth into a living heat—is provided for by these beings.
Hence they can also be called the nature spirits of fire, or of
heat. So that, to begin with (more details will be given in the
subsequent lectures), we have become acquainted with four
categories of nature spirits, having a certain relation to what
are called the elements of earth, water, air, and fire.

It is as though these spiritual beings had their jurisdic-
tion, their territory, in these elements, just as we human

beings have as ours the whole planet. Just as the Planet Earth is our home in the universe, so these beings have their territory in one or another of the elements mentioned. We have already drawn attention to the fact that for our earthly physical world, for the earth as a whole with its various kingdoms of nature, these different beings signify what the etheric body or life body signifies for individual human beings. Only we have said that in the human being this life body is a unity, whereas the etheric body of the earth consists of many, many such nature spirits, which are, moreover, divided into four classes. The living cooperation of these nature spirits is the etheric or life body of the earth. Thus it is not unity, but multiplicity, plurality.

If we wish to discern this etheric body of the earth with occult vision, then—as was previously described—we must allow the physical world to influence us morally, thereby drawing aside the veil of the physical world. Then the etheric body of the earth which lies directly behind this veil becomes visible. Now, how is it, when one also draws aside this further veil, described as the etheric body of the earth? We know that behind the etheric body is the astral body, the third principle of the human being—the body that is the bearer of desires, wishes, and passions. Thus, if we disregard the higher principles of human nature, we may say that in a human being we have first of all a physical body, behind which is an etheric body, and behind that an astral body. It is just the same in external nature. If we draw aside the physical, we certainly come to a plurality. This represents the etheric body of the whole earth, with all its kingdoms of nature. Now, can we also speak of a sort of astral body of the earth, something that, in relation to the whole earth and to all its kingdoms, corresponds to the astral body of a human being? It is certainly not as easy to penetrate to the earth's astral body as to its etheric body. We have seen that we can reach the etheric body if we allow the phenomena of the world to work upon us not merely through sense impressions but morally as well. If we wish, however, to penetrate further, then deeper occult exercises are necessary, such as you will find described in part—insofar as they can be in an open publication—in my book *Knowledge of the Higher Worlds and How to Attain It*. At a definite point of esoteric or occult development—as you may read there—a person begins to be conscious, even at a time when he or she is usually unconscious, namely during the time between falling asleep and waking.

We know that the ordinary unconscious condition, the ordinary human condition of sleep, is caused by our leaving our physical and etheric bodies lying in the bed, and by our drawing out our astral bodies and the rest of what belongs to them; but the ordinary person is unconscious when this occurs. If, however, we devote ourselves more and more to those exercises that consist of meditation, concentration, and so on, and further strengthen the slumbering hidden forces of our soul, then we can establish a conscious condition of sleep. In that case, when we have drawn our astral bodies out of our physical and etheric bodies, we are no longer unconscious, but have around us—not the physical world, not even the world just described, the world of the nature spirits—but another and still more spiritual world. When, after having freed ourselves from our physical and etheric bodies, the time comes that we feel our consciousness flash up, we then perceive quite a new order of spiritual beings. The next thing that strikes the occult vision thus far trained, is that the new spirits we now perceive have, as it were, command over the nature spirits. Let us be quite clear as to how far this is the case. I have told you that those beings—whom we call the nature spirits of water—work especially in the budding and sprouting plant world. Those—that we may call the nature spirits of the air—play their part in late summer and autumn, when the plants prepare to fade and die. Then these meteor-like air spirits sink down over the plant world and saturate themselves, as it were, with the plants, helping them to fade away in their spring and summer forms. The disposition that at one time the spirits of the water and at another the spirits of the air should work in this or that region of the earth changes according to the different regions of the earth—in the northern part of the earth it is naturally quite different from what it is in the south. The task of directing, as it were, the appropriate nature spirits to their activities at the right time is carried out by those spiritual beings whom we learn to know when occult vision is so far trained that, when we have freed ourselves from our physical and etheric bodies, we can still be conscious of our environment. There are spiritual beings, for instance, working in connection with our earth, with our Planet Earth, who allot the work of the nature spirits to the seasons of the year, and thus bring about the alternations of these seasons for the different regions of the earth, by distributing the work of the nature spirits. These spiritual beings represent what we may call the astral body of the earth. We plunge into this with our own astral bodies at night when we fall asleep. This astral body, consisting of higher spirits that hover around the Planet Earth and permeate it as a spiritual atmosphere, is united with the earth; and into this spiritual atmosphere our astral bodies plunge during the night.

Now, to occult observation, there is a great difference between the first category of nature spirits—the spirits of earth, water, and so on—and those beings that, on the other hand, direct these nature spirits. The nature spirits are occupied in causing the beings of nature to ripen and fade, in bringing life into the whole planetary sphere of the earth.

The situation is different with regard to those spiritual beings who, in their totality, can be called the astral body of the earth.

These beings are such that when we can become acquainted with them by means of occult vision, we perceive them as beings connected with our own souls—with our own astral bodies. They exert such an influence upon the human astral body—as also upon the astral bodies of animals—that we cannot speak of a mere life-giving activity; their activity resembles the action of feeling and thought upon our own souls. The nature spirits of water and air can be observed; we may say they are in the environment; but we cannot say of the spiritual beings of whom we are now speaking that they are in our environment; we are in fact always actually united with them, as if poured into them, when we perceive them. We are merged into them, and they speak to us in spirit. It is as though we perceived thoughts and feelings from the environment—impulses of will, sympathy and antipathy come to expression in what these beings cause to flow into us as thoughts, feelings, and impulses of will. Thus, in this category of spirits, we see beings already resembling the human soul. If we turn back again to what has been stated, we may say that all sorts of regulations in time—of divisions in the relations of time and space—are also connected with these beings. An old expression has therefore been preserved in occultism for these beings, whom in their totality we recognize as the astral body of the earth, and this in English would be, "spirits of the periods or cycles of time." Thus, not only the seasons of the year and the growing and the fading of the plants, but also the regular alternation which, in relation to the Planet Earth, expresses itself in day and night, is brought about by these spirits, which are to be classed as belonging to the astral body of the earth. In other words, everything connected with rhythmic return, with rhythmic alternation, with repetitions of happenings in time, is organized by spiritual beings who collectively belong to the astral body of the earth and to whom the name "spirits of the periods or cycles of time of our planet" is applicable. What the astronomer ascertains by calculation about the cycle of the earth on its axis is perceptible to occult vision, because the occultist knows that these spirits are distributed over the whole earth and are actually the bearers of the forces which rotate the earth on its axis. It is extremely important that one should be aware that in the astral body of the earth is to be found everything connected with the ordinary alternations between the blossoming and withering of plants and also all that is connected with the alternations between day and night—between the various seasons of the year and the various times of the day, and so on. Everything that happens in this way calls up—in the observer who has progressed so far as to be able to go out of the physical and etheric bodies in the astral body and still remain conscious—an impression of the spiritual beings belonging to the spirits of the cycles of time.

We have now, as it were, drawn aside the second veil, the veil woven of nature spirits. We might say that, when we draw aside the first veil, woven of material physical impressions, we come to the etheric body of the earth, to the nature spirits, and that then we can draw aside a second veil and come to the spirits of the cycles of time, who regulate everything that is subject to rhythmical cycles. Now, we know that what may be called the higher principle of human nature is embedded in our astral body. At first we understand this to be the I, embedded in the astral body. We have already said that our astral body plunges into the region of the spirits of the cycles of time; that it is immersed in the surging sea, as it were, of these spirits; but

as regards normal consciousness our I is still more asleep
than the astral body. One who is developing occultly and
progressing esoterically becomes aware of this, because it is
in the spiritual world into which one plunges—which consists of the spirits of the cycles of time—that one first learns
to penetrate into the perceptions of the astral body. In a certain respect, this perception is really a dangerous reef in
esoteric development, for the human astral body is, in
itself, a unity; but everything in the realm of the spirits of
the cycles of time is, fundamentally, multiplicity, plurality.
And since, in the way described, we are united with, and
immersed in, this plurality, if we are still asleep in our I and
yet awake in our astral body, we feel as if we were dismembered in the world of the spirits of the cycles of time. This
must be avoided in a properly ordered esoteric development. Hence those who are able to give instruction for such
development see that the necessary precautions are taken
that one should not, if possible, allow the I to sleep when
the astral body is already awake, for one would then lose
inner cohesion and would, like Dionysius, be split up into
the whole astral world of the earth, consisting of the spirits
of the cycles of time. In a regular esoteric development precautions are taken that this should not occur. These precautions consist in care being taken that the student, who
through meditation, concentration, or other esoteric exercises is to be stimulated to clairvoyance, should retain two
things in the whole sphere of clairvoyant, occult observation. In every esoteric development it is specially important
that everything should be so adjusted that two things we
possess in ordinary life should not be lost—things we
might, however, very easily lose in esoteric development if
not rightly guided. If rightly guided, however, we will not
lose them. First, we should not lose the recollection of any
of the events of our present incarnation, as ordinarily

retained in our memory. The connection with memory must not be destroyed. This connection with memory means very much more in the sphere of occultism than it does in the sphere of ordinary life. In ordinary life we understand memory only as the power of looking back and not losing consciousness of the important events of one's life. In occultism, a right memory means that we value with our perceptions and feelings only what we have already accomplished in the past, so that we apply no other value to ourselves or to our deeds than the past deeds themselves deserve. Let us understand this quite correctly, for this is extremely important. If, in the course of one's occult development, one were suddenly driven to say to oneself "I am the reincarnation of this or that spirit"—without there being any justification for it through any action of one's own—then one's memory, in an occult sense, would be interrupted. An important principle in occult development is that of attributing no other merit to oneself other than what comes from one's actions in the physical world in the present incarnation. That is extremely important. Any other merit must come only on the basis of a higher development, which can be attained only if one first of all stands firmly on the ground that one esteems oneself for nothing but what one has accomplished in this incarnation. This is quite natural if we look at the matter objectively; for what we have accomplished in the present incarnation is also the result of earlier incarnations; it is that which karma has, so far, made out of us. What karma is still making of us we must first bring about; we must not add that to our value. In short, if we would set a right value on ourselves, we can do so only at the beginning of esoteric development, if we ascribe merit only to what is inscribed in our memory as our past. That is the one element we must preserve, if our I is not to sleep while our astral body is awake.

The second thing that we as people of the present day must not lose is the degree of conscience we possess in the external world. Here again is something that it is extremely important to observe. You must have often experienced that someone you know has gone through an occult development, and if it is not guided and conducted in the right way you find that, in relation to conscience, your friend takes things much more lightly than before the occult training. Before such training, education and social connection were the guides to whether one did this thing or that, or dared not do it. After beginning an occult development, however, many people begin to tell lies who never did so before, and as regards questions of conscience, they take things more lightly. We ought not to lose an iota of the conscience we possess. As regards memory, we must value ourselves only according to what we have already become; not according to any reliance on the future, or on what we are still going to do. As regards conscience, we must retain the same degree of conscience as we acquired in the ordinary physical world. If we retain these two elements in our consciousness—a healthy memory that does not deceive us into believing ourselves to be other than our actions prove us to be, and a conscience that does not allow us morally to take things more lightly than before (indeed, if possible, we should take them more seriously!)—if we retain these two qualities, our I will never be asleep when our astral body is awake.

If we can, as it were, remain awake in our sleep and preserve our consciousness and carry it with us into the condition wherein, with our astral body, we are freed from the physical and etheric bodies—if we can do this—then we shall carry the connection with our I into the world in which we awaken with our astral body. Then, if we awake with our I, not only do we feel our astral body to be connected with all the spiritual beings we have described as the spirits of the cycles of time of our planet, but we feel in a quite peculiar way that we actually no longer have a direct relation to the individual who is the bearer of the physical and etheric bodies in which we usually live. We feel, so to speak, as if all the qualities of our physical and etheric bodies were taken from us. Then, too, we feel everything taken from us that can only live outwardly in a particular territory of our planet. For what lives on a particular territory of our planet is connected with the spirits of the cycles of time. Now, however, when we waken with our I, we feel ourselves not only poured out into the whole world of the spirits of the cycles of time, but we feel ourselves one with the whole undivided spirit of the planet itself; we awaken in the undivided spirit of the planet itself.

It is extremely important that we should feel ourselves as belonging to the whole of our planet. For example, when our occult vision is sufficiently awakened, and we are so far advanced that we can awaken our I and our astral body simultaneously, then our common life with the planet expresses itself in such a way that, just as during our waking hours in the sense world we can follow the sun as it passes over the heavens from morning till night, so now the sun no longer disappears when we fall asleep. When we sleep the sun remains connected with us; it does not cease to shine but takes on a spiritual character, so that while we are actually asleep during the night, we can still follow the sun. We human beings are of such a nature that we are connected with the changing conditions of the planet only insofar as we live in the astral body. When, however, we become conscious only of our I, we have nothing to do with these changing conditions. But when we awaken our astral body and our I simultaneously then we become conscious of all the conditions which our planet can go through. We then pour ourselves into the whole substance of the planetary spirit.

When I say that we become one with the planetary spirit, that we live in union with this planetary spirit, you must not suppose that this implies an advanced degree of clairvoyance; this is but a beginning. For when we awaken in the manner described, we really only experience the planetary spirit as a whole, whereas it consists of many, many differentiations—of wonderful, separate, spiritual beings—as we shall hear in the following lectures. The different parts of the planetary spirit, the special multiplicities of this spirit, of these we are not yet aware. What we realize first of all is the knowledge: "I live in the planetary spirit as though in a sea, which spiritually bathes the whole Planet Earth and itself is the spirit of the whole earth." One may go through immensely long development in order further and further to experience this unification with the planetary spirit; but, to begin with, the experience is as has been described. Just as we say of ourselves as human beings: "behind our astral body is our I"—so do we say that behind all that we call the totality of the spirits of the cycles of time is hidden the spirit of the planet itself, the planetary spirit. Whereas the spirits of the cycles of time guide the nature spirits of the elements in order to call forth the rhythmic change and repetitions in time—the alterations in space of the Planet Earth—the spirit of the earth has a different task. It has the task of bringing the earth itself into mutual relation with the other heavenly bodies in the environment, to direct it and guide it, so that in the course of time it may come into the right relations to the other heavenly bodies. The spirit of the earth is, as it were, the earth's great sense apparatus, through which the Planet Earth enters into right relationship with the cosmos. If I were to sum up the succession of those spiritual beings with whom we on our earth are first of all concerned, and to whom we can find the way through a gradual occult development, I must say: As the first external veil, we have the sense world, with all its multiplicity, with all we see spread out before our senses and which we can understand with our human mind, then, behind this sense world, we have the world of nature spirits. Behind this world of nature spirits we have the spirits of the cycles of time, and behind these the planetary spirit.

If you wish to compare what normal consciousness knows about the structure of the cosmos with the structure of the cosmos itself, you may make that clear in the following way. We will take it that the most external veil is this world of the senses, behind which is the world of the nature spirits, and behind that the spirits of the cycles of time and behind that the planetary spirit. Now, we must say that the planetary spirit in its activity in a certain respect penetrates through to the sense world, so that in a certain way we can perceive its image in the sense world. This also applies to the spirits of the cycles of time, as well as to the nature spirits. So, if we observe the sense world itself with normal consciousness, we can see in the background, as it were, the impression, the traces, of those worlds that lie behind—as if we drew aside the sense world as the outermost skin, and behind this we had different degrees of active spiritual beings Normal consciousness realizes the sense world by means of its perceptions; the world of nature spirits expresses itself from behind these perceptions as what we call the forces of nature. When science speaks of the forces of nature, we have there nothing that is actually real; to the occultist the forces of nature are not realities but *maya*, imprints of the nature spirits working behind the world of sense.

PLANETARY SPIRIT				I
SPIRITS OF THE CYCLES OF TIME				ASTRAL BODY
WORLD OF NATURE-SPIRITS				ETHERIC BODY
SENSE WORLD			*Perceptions*	PHYSICAL BODY

Meaning of Nature · Laws of Nature · Nature Forces

Again, the imprint of the spirits of the cycles of time is what is usually known to ordinary consciousness as the laws of nature. Fundamentally, all the laws of nature are in existence because the spirits of the cycles of time work as the directing powers. To the occultist, the laws of nature are not realities. Whereas the ordinary natural scientist speaks of the laws of nature and combines them externally, the occultist knows that these laws are revealed in their reality when, in his awakened astral body, he listens to what the spirits of the cycles of time say, and hears how they order and direct the nature spirits. That is expressed in *maya*—in external sem-blance—as the laws of nature, and normal consciousness, as a rule, does not go beyond this. It does not usually reach the imprint of the planetary spirit in the external world. The normal consciousness of contemporary humanity speaks of the external world of perception, of the facts that can be perceived. It speaks of the forces of nature, light, warmth, magnetism, electricity, and so on; of the forces of attraction and repulsion, of gravity, and so forth. These are the beings of *maya*, semblance, behind which, in reality, lies the world of nature spirits—the etheric body of the earth. External science also speaks of the laws of nature, but that again is *maya*. Underlying these laws is what we have described as the world of the spirits of the cycles of time. Only when we penetrate still further do we come to the stamp or imprint of the planetary spirit itself in the external sense world. Science today does not do this. Those who still do so are no longer quite believed. The poets, the artists do—they seek for a meaning behind things. Why does the plant world blossom? Why do the different species of animals arise and disappear? Why do human beings inhabit the earth? If we thus inquire into the phenomena of nature and wish to analyze their meaning and to combine the external facts as even a deeper philosophy still sometimes tries to do, we then approach the imprint of the planetary spirit itself in the external world. Today, however, nobody really believes any longer in this seeking after the meaning of existence. Through feeling, one still believes a little, but science no longer wishes to know what could be discovered about the laws of nature by studying the passage of the phenomena.

If we still seek a meaning as to the laws of nature in the things of the world perceptible to our senses, we should be able to interpret this meaning as the imprint of the planetary spirit in the sense world. That would be the external *maya*. In the first place, the sense world itself is an external *maya* or semblance, for it is what the etheric body of the earth, the substance of the nature spirits, drives out of itself. A second *maya* is what appears to us of the nature spirits in the forces of nature. A third *maya* is what appears as the laws of nature, coming from the spirits of the cycles of time. A fourth *maya* is something that, in spite of its *maya* nature, speaks to the human soul because, in the perception of the purpose of nature, we at any rate feel ourselves united with the spirit of the whole planet, with the spirit that leads the planet through cosmic space and gives meaning, in fact, to the whole planet. In this *maya* lies the direct imprint of the planetary spirit itself.

Thus we may say that we have today ascended to the undivided spirit of the planet. If again we wish to compare what we have now discovered about the planet with the human being, we may say: "The sense world corresponds to the human physical body; the world of nature spirits to the human etheric body, the world of the spirits of the cycles of time to the human astral body, and the planetary spirit to the human I." Just as the human I perceives the physical environment of earth, so does the planetary spirit perceive everything in the periphery and in cosmic space as a whole outside the planet; it adjusts the acts of the planet and also the feelings of the planet, of which we shall speak tomorrow, according to these perceptions of cosmic space. For what a planet does outside in space, when it passes on its way in cosmic distances, and what it effects in its own body, in the elements of which it consists, that again is the result of the observations of the planetary spirit with regard to the external world. Just as the individual human soul lives in the world of the earth side by side with other human beings, and adjusts to them, so does the planetary spirit live in its planetary body, which is the ground on which we stand; but this planetary spirit lives in fellowship with other planetary spirits, other spirits of the heavenly bodies.

LECTURE THREE

I N THE COURSE of the two preceding lectures, we have
become acquainted with certain spiritual beings that occult
vision can encounter when it is directed toward the spiritual life of our planet. Today, in order to ascend into the
spiritual world, it will be necessary for us to follow another
path, for we can only form a correct conception of the
nature of the spiritual beings of whom we have spoken,
even of the planetary spirit itself, when we have observed
them from another side. It is always extremely difficult to
describe in the words of any language these spiritual
beings visible to occult perception, because human languages—at least those of the present day—are only suited
to the facts and phenomena of the physical plane. It is
therefore only by a description from various aspects that
one can hope to arrive at anything approaching what is
meant when allusion is made to spiritual beings. It will be
necessary for this purpose to begin today from the nature
of human beings themselves and to make clear certain
attributes of human nature, and we can then proceed to
describe the higher beings we meet with in the higher
worlds. One attribute of human nature shall be brought
into very special prominence today, and that can be
described in the following way. As human beings we are
endowed with the possibility of leading inner lives that are

quite independent of our outer lives. This possibility confronts us every hour of our waking life. We know that as regards what we see with our eyes or hear with our ears, we have something in common with all other beings that also use their senses. As human beings we also have a common life with other human beings, and perhaps with other beings too. People, as we know only too well, have their own special sorrows, their special joys, their troubles and cares, their hopes and ideals. In a sense, these form a special kingdom not immediately visible to the physical sight of others, a kingdom we carry through the world as an independent inner life. When we are in the same space with other people, we know what they see with their eyes and hear with their ears. We may even perhaps have an idea of what takes place in their souls by what is expressed in their faces, by their gestures, or their speech. But if a person wishes to keep his or her inner life as a special world for themselves alone, then we can penetrate no further.

Now, if we look with occult vision into the world hidden behind the first veil of the external world, we meet there with beings quite differently organized, particularly with respect to these qualities. We meet with beings unable to lead such an independent inner life as we human beings lead. We meet as a first group with those who, when they lead an inner life, are immediately transferred by this inner life into a different state of consciousness from the one they possess in the life they lead in and with the external world. Let us try to understand this. Suppose we lived in such a way that should we desire to live in our inner being and not direct our gaze to the external world, we would, simply by means of our will, immediately have to pass over into another state of consciousness. We know that, without our will, we human beings do pass over into a different state of consciousness in normal life when we are asleep. We also know that sleep is the result of our astral bodies and our I separating from our physical and etheric bodies. Thus we know that something has to take place in a human being if he or she is to pass over into another form of consciousness. For instance, if one says: "Here before me is a meadow covered with flowers; when I look at it, it gives me joy," one does not simply on that account enter another state of consciousness; one experiences one's joy in the meadow and the flowers together with one's association with the outer world. Now those beings that occult vision meets as the next category in a higher world change their state of consciousness each time they turn their perception and their action from the external world to themselves. Thus, in them, there need be no separation between the different principles of their being. They simply bring about in themselves—just as they are—by means of their will, another condition of consciousness. Now, the perceptions of these beings of the next category above humanity are not like our human perceptions. Human beings perceive because an external world appears before their senses. They surrender themselves, so to speak, to this external world. The beings I am speaking of do not perceive an external world in the same way as we do with our senses. They perceive it (though this is only a comparison) rather as we perceive when, for instance, we speak, or make a movement of the hand, or in any way externalize our inner being in a kind of miming—when, in short, we give expression to our own nature. Thus, in a certain sense, in the case of these beings of a higher world of whom we are speaking, all their perceptions are at the same time a manifestation of their own being. I want you to bear in mind that when we ascend to the higher category of beings who are no longer perceptible by us externally, we have before us beings who perceive whenever they manifest, when they express what they themselves are; and they actually perceive their own being only as long as they wish to manifest it, as long as in any way they express it outwardly. We might say they are only awake when they are manifesting themselves. And when of their own will they are not manifesting themselves, not entering into connection with the world around them, another condition of consciousness arises for them—in a certain sense they sleep. Only, their sleep is not unconscious sleep like that of human beings. Sleep, for them, signifies a sort of diminution, a sort of loss of their feeling of self. They have their feeling of self so long as they manifest themselves externally, and in a certain sense they lose it when they cease to manifest. They do not sleep then as we sleep, but something arises in their own being like a manifestation of spiritual worlds higher than themselves. Their inner being is then filled by higher spiritual worlds.

Therefore please take note: When we direct our gaze outward and observe, we live with the outer world; we lose ourselves in it. In our planet, for instance, we lose ourselves in the various kingdoms of nature. But when we divert our gaze from what is outside, we enter our own inner being and live an independent inner life, and then we are free from this external world. When these beings—of whom we speak as a first category above humanity—are active externally, then they manifest themselves; they have their feeling of self, their actual self-expression in this manifestation; and when they enter their inner being they do not enter into an independent inner life, as do human beings, but into a life in common with other worlds. Just as we enter such a life when we perceive the external world, so they perceive other spiritual worlds above them when they look into themselves; they enter this other condition of consciousness in which they find themselves filled with other beings higher than themselves. So, with regard to human beings, we may say that when they lose themselves in the external world, they have their perceptions, and that when they withdraw from the external world, they have their independent inner lives. The beings belonging to the next higher category above humanity—we call them, generally speaking, the beings of the so-called third hierarchy—these beings, instead of perception have manifestation, and in this manifestation or revelation they experience themselves. Instead of an inner life, they have the experience of higher spiritual worlds, that is to say, they are filled with spirit. This is the most essential difference between human beings and the beings of the next higher category.

Third Hierarchy: Manifestation: Spiritfilled
Humanity: Perception: Inner Life.

We might define the difference between these beings and human beings by means of a crude comparison from life. When someone is in a position of having inner experiences that do not coincide with what he or she experiences or perceives externally—in the crudest case, the result is a lie. In order to make this clearer, we can express a possible human peculiarity by saying: As human beings we are capable of perceiving something and yet of arousing contrary ideas in our inner being and even of giving vent to them externally, although they do not coincide with our perceptions. Through this peculiarity a person can contradict the external world by means of an untruth. This is a possibility that—as we shall hear later in the course of these lectures—had to be given to humanity, in order that human beings might come to the truth by their own free will. When we consider ourselves as we really are in the world we must fix our attention on this quality namely, that we can form ideas in our inner life—and externalize them—that do not coincide with our perceptions or with facts. So long as they retain their nature, this quality is not a possibility for the beings of the higher category spoken of here. If they retain their nature, the possibility of untruth does not exist in the beings of the third hierarchy. For what would result if a being of this hierarchy wished to lie? In its inner being, it would experience something in a different way than it transmitted it to the external world. Then, however, this being of the next highest category would no longer be able to perceive this, for everything these beings experience in their inner life is revelation and immediately passes over into the external world. These beings must live in a kingdom of absolute truth if they wish to experience themselves at all. Suppose these beings were to lie, that is, had something in their inner being that they would so transform in their revelation that it would no longer coincide with their experience—they would then not be able to perceive it, for they can only perceive their inner nature. They would, under the impression of an untruth, immediately be stupefied, transferred into a state of consciousness that would be a darkening down, a lessening of their ordinary consciousness—which can only live in the realm of absolute truth and sincerity. Every deviation from truth would render these beings less conscious. If they are to be observed by occult vision, the occultist must first of all find the right way in which he can meet them. Therefore I will try to describe how an occultist can find them.

The first inner experience which one who goes through an occult development must have, is the striving, in a certain sense, to subdue the inner life of ordinary normal consciousness. We can designate what we experience in our inner being as egotistic experience—as what we wish to have from the world for ourselves alone, so to speak. The more students who are developing on the occult path can bring themselves to be passive with regard to what only concerns themselves, the nearer they are to the entrance to the higher worlds. Let us take an obvious case. We all know that certain truths, certain things in the world, simply please or do not please us; that certain things affect us sympathetically or antipathetically. Such feelings with regard to the world that we only cherish for our own sake, must, by one who would develop himself or herself occultly, be rooted out of the heart; one must, in a certain sense, be free from all that concerns only oneself. This is a truth that is often emphasized, but which, in fact, is more difficult to observe than one usually thinks; for in normal consciousness we have extremely few footholds through which we can become free from ourselves and overcome what concerns only ourselves. Let us consider for a moment what it actually means "to be free from oneself." Probably to become free from what we usually call egoistic impulses is not so difficult; but we must remember that in the one incarnation in which we live, we are born at a certain time and at a certain place; and that when we direct our gaze to what surrounds us, our eyes rest upon quite different things from those seen by someone, for instance, who lives in a different part of the world. There must be quite different things in this other person's surroundings to interest him or her. Thus, just because we are born as physically embodied human beings at a certain time and at a certain place, we are surrounded by all sorts of things that call forth our attention, our interest—things which actually concern us and are different for other people. Because we, as human beings, are differently distributed over our planet, we are, in a certain sense, placed under the necessity of each having our separate interests, our special home upon the earth. In what we are able to learn from our direct environment we can never, therefore, in the highest sense, experience that which sets us free from our special human interests and attractions. Thus, because we are human beings in physical bodies, and insofar as we are such, we cannot possibly through our external perception reach the portal leading into a higher world. We must look away from all that our senses can see externally, all that our intellect can connect with the things of the external world, everything that belongs to our own special interests. But now, if we look at what we generally have in our inner being, our sorrows and joys, our worries and cares, our hopes and aims, we shall very soon become aware how dependent our inner world is on what we experience externally, and how, in a certain way, it is colored by our experiences. Nevertheless, a certain difference exists.

We shall be willing to admit that each one of us carries his or her own world in their inner being. The fact that one person is born in one part of the earth at one time, and another person elsewhere at a different time does in a sense color our inner world—but we also experience something else quite different in regard to this inner world. It is certainly our special—in a sense, our differentiated—inner world. It bears a certain coloring, but we can also experience something quite different. If we leave the place where we are accustomed to be active through our senses for a distant place, and there meet someone who has had quite different experiences and perceptions from our own, we can nevertheless understand that person, because he or she has passed through certain troubles which we ourselves have similarly passed through—or because he or she can take pleasure, in a certain sense, in the things that please us. Many people have experienced that they may perhaps find it difficult to understand someone they encounter in a distant region or to agree with them about the external world to which they both belong—and yet it may be easy for these people to sympathize with one another concerning what the heart feels and longs for. Through our inner world, we human beings are much nearer one another than we are through the external world, and truly there would be little hope of carrying our spiritual science to the whole of humanity were it not for the consciousness that in the inner being of all people, no matter to what part of the earth they may belong, something lives that can bring them into sympathy with us. Now, however, in order to arrive at something quite free from our own egotistic inner life, we must lay aside even that coloring of inner experience which is still influenced by the external world. That can only be when a person is able to experience something in his or her own inner being that does not in any way come from the external world; something that corresponds to what we may call inner suggestions, inspirations, and which grows and thrives only within the soul itself. We can so transcend our special inner life that we feel something revealed in our inner being that is independent of our special egotistic existence. This is felt by those who assert again and again that, throughout the whole sphere of the earth, there can be mutual understanding of certain moral ideals, or certain logical ideals that no one can doubt. These can illuminate everyone, for they are imparted not by the outer world but by the inner world of humanity.

We all have one province—to be sure an arid, prosaic province—in common as regards such inner manifestation. This is the province of numbers and their relation—in short, of mathematics, numbers, and calculation. We can never experience from the external world the fact that three times three makes nine: it must be revealed to us through our inner being. Hence, there is no possibility of disputing this in any part of the globe. Whether a thing is beautiful or ugly can be very greatly disputed all over the world; but if the fact has once been revealed to our inner being that three

times three is nine, or that the whole is equal to the sum of
its parts, or that a triangle has 180 degrees as the sum of its
angles, we know that it is so, because no external world can
reveal this, only our own inner being. In dry, prosaic mathematics begins what we may call inspiration. Only, as a
rule, people do not notice that inspiration begins with dry
mathematics, because most people take dry mathematics
for something dreadfully tedious, and are therefore not
very willing to let anything be revealed to them by this
means. Fundamentally, however, the same thing applies to
the inner revelation of moral truths. If we have recognized
something as right, we say, "This is right and the contrary
is wrong, and no external power on the physical plane can
make us see that what is revealed to us as right could be
wrong in our inner being." Moral truths also reveal themselves in the highest sense through our inner being. If we
direct our spiritual gaze with feeling and receptivity
toward this possibility of inner manifestation we can educate ourselves in this way. Indeed, education through sheer
mathematics is very good. For instance, if one constantly
devotes oneself to the thought: "I may have my own opinion as to whether a thing is good to eat, but someone else
may be of a different opinion. That depends upon the free
will of the individual, but mathematics and moral obligations do not depend on such free will. I know of these that
they may reveal something to me by which, if I refuse to
accept it as true, I prove myself unworthy of humanity."
This recognition of a revelation through one's inner being—
if we devote ourselves to it in meditation, if we accept it as
feeling, as an inner impulse—is a powerful educative force
in the inner life of human beings. If, to begin with, we say to
ourselves, "In the sense world there is much that can only
be decided by free will, but out of the spirit, things are
revealed to me about which my free will has nothing to say,

and which yet concern me and of which I, as a human being, must prove myself worthy." And if we allow this thought to become stronger and stronger, so that we feel overpowered by our own inner being, then we grow beyond mere egotism. A higher self, as we call it, gains the upper hand—a higher self that recognizes itself as one with the spirit of the world overcomes the ordinary, arbitrary self. We must develop something of this sort as a mood if we wish to succeed in reaching the portal that leads into the spiritual worlds. For if we frequently devote ourselves to such moods as have just been described, they will prove fruitful. They prove especially fruitful if we bring them as concretely as possible into our thoughts and especially if we cherish and accept the thoughts that reveal themselves to us as true, and are yet nevertheless in contradiction to the external sense world. Such thoughts may at first be nothing but pictures, but such pictures can be extremely useful for our occult development.

I will tell you of one such picture. I will show you by such a picture how one can raise one's soul above oneself.

Take two glasses—in the one is water, in the other none. The glass with water should be only half-full. Suppose you observe these two glasses in the external world. If you now pour some of the water from the half-filled into the empty glass, the latter will be partly filled while the other then has less water in it. If you pour water from the glass which was half-filled into the glass which was at first empty a second time, the first glass will have still less water in it; in short, through the pouring-out there is always less and less water in the glass which was at first half-full of water. This is a true picture or representation as regards the external physical sense world.

Now, let us form a different representation or picture. By way of experiment, let us form the contrary idea. Imagine yourself again pouring water from the half-filled glass into the empty one. Into this latter there comes water, but you must imagine that in the half-filled glass, by means of this pouring out of water, there is more instead of less, and that if you poured from it a second time, so that again something passed over into the previously empty glass, there would again be more and not less water left in the glass that was at first half-filled. As the result of the out-pouring, more and more water would be in the first glass. Imagine yourself picturing this idea. Naturally, everyone who counts themselves today among the thoroughly intelligent would say: "Why, you are picturing an absolute delusion! You imagine that you are pouring out water, and that by so doing more water comes into the glass from which you are pouring!" Certainly, if one applies this idea to the physical world, then, naturally, it is an absurd idea. But—marvelous to relate—it can be applied to the spiritual world. It can be applied in a singular manner. Suppose someone has a loving heart, and out of this loving heart he or she performs a loving action for another who needs love. One person gives something to another person, but that person does not thereby become emptier when performing loving actions for another. One receives more, becomes fuller, and has still more, and if that person performs the loving action a second time he or she will again receive more. One does not become poor, nor empty, by giving love or doing loving actions—on the contrary, one becomes richer, one becomes fuller. One pours forth something into the other person, something which makes one fuller oneself. Now, if we apply our picture (which is impossible, absurd, for the ordinary physical world), if we apply our picture of the two glasses to the outpouring of love, it becomes applicable. We can grasp it as an image, as a symbol of spiritual facts. Love is so complex a thing that no one should have the arrogance to attempt to define it, to fathom the nature of love. Love is complex—we perceive it, but no definition can express it. But a symbol, a simple symbol—a glass of water which, when it is poured out becomes ever fuller—gives us one quality of the workings of love. If we imagine the complexity of loving actions in this way we really do nothing else than what a mathematician does in his or her dry science. Nowhere is there an actual circle, nowhere an actual triangle, we must only imagine them. If we draw a circle and examine it a little through a microscope, we see nothing but chalk or small specks; it can never have the regularity of a real circle. We must turn to our imagination, our inner life, if we wish to imagine the circle or the triangle or something of that kind. Thus, to imagine something like a spiritual act—such as love, for instance—we must grasp the symbol and hold fast to an attribute. Such pictures are useful for occult development. In them, we perceive that we are raised above ordinary ideas, and that if we wish to ascend to the spirit, we must form ideas just the opposite of those applicable to the sense world. Thus we find that the forming of such symbolical conceptions is a powerful means for ascending to the spiritual world. You find this treated fully in my book, *Knowledge of the Higher Worlds and How to Attain It.* By this means we succeed in recognizing something like a world above us, a world which inspires us, one that we cannot perceive in the external world, but which penetrates us. If we devote ourselves more and more to these conceptions, we finally recognize that in us, in every human being, there lives some spiritual being higher than we ourselves, human beings with our egotism in this one incarnation. When we begin to recognize that there is something above us ordinary human beings, that there is a being guiding us, we have the first form in the ranks of the beings of the third hierarchy, those beings we call angels, or *angeloi*. When we go out beyond ourselves in the manner described, we first experience the working of an angelic being in our own being. If we now consider this being independently, with the qualities that have been described as revelation, and spiritfilled: if we consider this being which inspires us, as an independent being, we rise to an idea of the beings of the third hierarchy who stand immediately above humanity. We may therefore describe these beings as those who lead, guide, and direct each individual human being.

Thus I have given you a slight description of the way in which we can raise ourselves to begin with to the first beings above us, so that we can gain an idea of them. Just as each individual in this manner has his or her guide—and when we rise above ourselves, above our egotistic interests, occult vision draws our attention to the fact "You have your guide"—so it is now possible to direct our vision to groups of human beings, tribes and peoples. Such groups who belong together likewise have a guidance or leadership, just as individual persons have theirs in the manner described above. These beings, however, who lead whole peoples or tribes, are even more powerful than the leaders of individual human beings. In Western esotericism, these guides of whole peoples or tribes—who live in the spiritual world and have revelation as their perception, and permeation with the spirit as their inner life, and who find expression in the actions performed by peoples or tribes—in Western esotericism these spiritual beings are called archangels or *archangeloi*. As individuals progress in occult development, not only may the angel who leads them be revealed to them, but also the archangel who leads the common group to which they belong may also be revealed. And then as our occult development advances still further, we find beings as leaders of humanity who are no longer concerned with individual tribes and peoples, but are leaders in successive epochs. If those who are occultly-developed study, for instance, the period when the ancient Egyptian or Chaldean lived, they will see that the whole stamp, the whole character of the period is under a definite leadership. If they then look with occult vision upon what follows the Egyptian-Chaldean period, and direct their vision to the age in which Greece and Rome gave the tone to the Western intellectual world, they will see that this leadership changes and that above the individual peoples, there rule spirits, mightier than the archangels who are leaders of the peoples, who direct whole groups of peoples connected with each other at a particular time. They will see, too, that these beings are then relieved after a definite period by other time-leaders. Just as the individual realms of the *archangeloi* who guide contemporary, but individual, groups of people are distributed in space, so do we find, if we allow our vision to sweep over passing time, that the different epochs are guided by their definite spirits of the age, more powerful than the archangels and under whom many different peoples stand at the same time. We call this third category of the third hierarchy the spirits of the age, or *archai* in the terminology of Western esotericism.

All the beings belonging to these three classes of the third hierarchy have the attributes described today; they all have the characteristic of what has here been described as manifestation or revelation and of being inwardly filled with the spirit. Occult vision becomes aware of this when it is able to raise itself to these beings. Thus, we may say that when we observe what surrounds us in the spiritual world, and is, as it were, around each one of us as our own individual leader; when we there observe what lives spiritually and rules invisibly, instigating us to impersonal actions and impersonal thinking and feeling, when we see this, we have there first of all the beings of the third hierarchy. Occult vision perceives these beings. To the occultist they are realities, but normal consciousness also lives under their sovereignty. Although it does not perceive the angel, it is under the angel's leadership, even though unconsciously. And so do groups of people stand under their archangel, just as an age and the people of an age stand under the leadership of the spirit of the age.

Now these beings of the third hierarchy described today are found in the spiritual environment nearest to us. If, however, we went back in the evolution of our planet to a definite point of time, about which we shall learn more in the following lectures, we should find more and more that these beings—who really only live in the process of human culture—are continually bringing forth other beings from themselves. Just as a plant puts forth seed, so do the beings of the third hierarchy, which I have just described, bring forth other beings. There is, however, a certain difference between what the plant brings forth as seed—if we may use this comparison—and the beings that separate themselves off from the beings of the third hierarchy. When the plant brings forth a seed, it is, in a sense, of as much value as the complete plant; for out of it can arise again a complete plant of the same species. These beings put forth others who are separated from them as the seed is from the plant—they have offspring, so to speak—but the offspring are, in a sense, of a lower order than themselves. They have to be of a lower order because they have other tasks that they can only accomplish if they are of a lower order. The angels, archangels, and spirits of the age in our spiritual environment have put forth from themselves certain beings who descend from the human environment into the kingdoms of nature; and occult vision teaches us that the beings we learned about yesterday as the nature spirits, are detached from the beings of the third hierarchy whom we have learned to know today. They are offspring, and to them has been allotted other service than service to human-kind, namely, service to nature. Indeed, certain offspring of the *archai* are the beings we have learned to know as the nature spirits of the earth; those separated from the archangels and sent down into nature, are the nature spirits of water; and those detached from the angels we have recognized as the nature spirits of the air. With the nature spirits of fire or heat we have still to become acquainted. Thus we see that in a sense, through a division of the beings who represent, as the third hierarchy, our union with the world immediately above us, certain beings are sent down into the kingdoms of the elements, into air, water, earth—into the gaseous, fluid, and solid—in order to perform service there, to work within the elements, and in a sense to function as the lower offspring of the third hierarchy—as nature spirits. Thus we can speak of a relationship between the nature spirits and the beings of the third hierarchy.

LECTURE FOUR

I F WE WISH TO KNOW the nature of the spiritual forces and powers active in the different kingdoms of nature and in the heavenly bodies, we must first become acquainted with these spiritual beings themselves, as we have already begun to do in the three lectures that have already been given. In these we tried to characterize the so-called nature spirits, and then ascended to the beings who stand immediately above humanity and whom we can find in the next higher world to our own. We will continue these considerations today, and must therefore link them to what has already been said about the way in which we can raise ourselves to the beings of the third hierarchy. As shown in the last lecture, it is possible for human beings to rise above themselves, to subdue all their own special egoistic interests in order, by that means, to rise into a sphere where they first of all find their own guide, who can give them some idea of those beings called angels or *angeloi* in Western esotericism.

We then pointed out how further progress along this path leads to knowledge of the folk- or nation-spirits, whom we spoke of as archangels or *archangeloi*. We spoke of how, in the course of cultural civilizations, we find the so-called spirits of the age or *archai*. Now, if we follow the path roughly indicated yesterday, we gain a certain feeling for what is meant by these beings of the third hierarchy—and yet, even if we go through an occult development, we will for a long time have only a sort of feeling for this. Only if we go patiently and with perseverance through all the feelings and perceptions mentioned yesterday, can we pass over to what may be called clairvoyant vision of the beings of the third hierarchy. If, therefore, we progress further along this way, we shall find that gradually we educate ourselves, developing in ourselves a different state of consciousness, and then we can begin to have a clairvoyant consciousness of the beings of the third hierarchy. In other words, when we follow this way further we will find that we gradually train ourselves to another condition of consciousness and that then a clairvoyant perception of the third hierarchy can begin.

This other condition of consciousness can be compared with human sleep, because in this condition a person feels the I and astral body freed from the physical and etheric bodies. We must have a perception of this feeling of freedom. We must gradually learn what it means not to see with our eyes, hear with our ears, or think with our intellect, which is connected with the brain. Again, we must distinguish this condition from that of ordinary sleep, inasmuch as in it we are not unconscious, for we have perceptions of the spiritual beings in our environment—at first, only dimly sensing them, until, as has been described, clairvoyant consciousness lights up within us, and we get a living view of the beings of the third hierarchy and of their offspring, the nature spirits. If we wish to describe this condition more accurately, we may say that whoever raises themselves through occult development to this condition actually perceives a sort of demarcation between ordinary consciousness and this new condition of consciousness. Just as we can distinguish between waking and sleeping, so to one who has gone through occult development, there is at first a distinction between the consciousness in which one sees with one's ordinary eyes, hears with one's ordinary ears, and thinks with the ordinary intellect—and that clairvoyant condition in which there is nothing at all around one of what one perceives in normal consciousness, but rather another world, the world of the third hierarchy and its offspring. The first achievement is learning to remember in ordinary consciousness what one has experienced in this other condition of consciousness. This enables us to distinguish accurately a certain stage in human occult development—the stage when we can live alternately in ordinary consciousness, seeing, hearing, and thinking like other people, and the other condition of consciousness that we can, in a sense, produce voluntarily, and in which we perceive what is around us in the spiritual world of the third hierarchy. And, in this case, just as we remember a dream, so we can remember, in ordinary consciousness, what we experienced in the other, clairvoyant condition. We can talk about it—we can translate into ordinary conceptions and ideas what we experience in the clairvoyant state. Thus a seer who, in the ordinary condition of consciousness, wishes to know something of the spiritual world, or to relate something about it, must call to mind what was experienced in the other, the clairvoyant conditions of consciousness. A clairvoyant having reached this stage of development can only know something of those beings whom we have described as the beings of the third hierarchy and their offspring. A clairvoyant can at first know nothing of higher worlds. A clairvoyant who wishes to know of these must attain a still higher stage of clairvoyant vision.

This higher stage is reached by continually practicing the exercises described in my book *Knowledge of the Higher*

Worlds and How to Attain It—especially by going through the exercises described there as the observation, for instance, of a plant or an animal, and so forth. If one continues the exercises in this way, one attains a higher stage of clairvoyance. This stage consists not only in having two alternate conditions of consciousness and being able to remember clairvoyant experiences in the normal condition; but also—having attained this higher stage of clairvoyance—of perceiving spiritual worlds, spiritual beings, and spiritual facts when looking at the things of the external world through one's eyes in one's ordinary condition of consciousness. One can then, so to speak, carry one's clairvoyant vision over into one's ordinary consciousness, and can see, behind the beings around one in the external world, the spiritual beings and forces everywhere more deeply concealed, as though behind a veil.

We may ask: What has happened to a clairvoyant who is able not merely to remember the experiences of another condition of consciousness, but who can have clairvoyant experiences in his or her own everyday consciousness? If someone has ascended only to the first stage, they can only make use of their astral body in order to look into the spiritual world. Thus the body which a person makes use of at the first stage of clairvoyance is the astral body; at the second stage of clairvoyance which has just been described, the person learns to make use of the etheric body. By means of this one can even in ordinary, normal consciousness, look into the spiritual world. If one learns to use one's etheric body in this way as an instrument for clairvoyance, one gradually learns to perceive everything in the spiritual world belonging to the beings of the second hierarchy.

But a person must not remain at this stage, only perceiving his or her own etheric body, so to speak. On attaining this second stage of clairvoyance, one has a very definite experience. One has the experience of seeming to go out of oneself, and, as it were, of no longer feeling enclosed within one's skin. When, let us say, one encounters a plant or an animal, or even another human being, one feels as if a part of oneself were within the other being; one feels as if immersed in the other being. In normal consciousness, and even when we have reached the first stage of clairvoyance, we can still say, in a certain sense, "I am here; and that being which I see is there." At the second stage of clairvoyance, we can no longer say this. We can only say, "Where the being is that I perceive, there I myself am." It is as though our etheric body stretched out tentacles on all sides and drew us within the beings into whom we—perceiving them—plunge our own being. There is a feeling belonging to our ordinary normal consciousness that can give us an idea of this clairvoyant experience—except for the fact that what the clairvoyant of the second stage experiences is infinitely more intense than a feeling, for it amounts to a perception, an understanding of, an immersion in, another being. The feeling I refer to—which can be compared to this experience of the clairvoyant—is sympathy, love. What does it really imply when we feel sympathy and love in ordinary life? If we ponder more closely on the nature of sympathy and love—this was slightly touched upon yesterday—we find that sympathy and love cause us to detach ourselves from ourselves and to pass over into the life of another being. It is truly a wonderful mystery of human life that we are able to feel sympathy and love. There is scarcely anything among the ordinary phenomena of normal consciousness that can so convince us of the divinity of existence, as the possibility of developing love and sympathy. As human beings, we experience our existence in our own selves; and we experience the world by perceiving it with our senses or grasping it with our reason. It is not possible for any intellect, for any eye, to look into the human heart, to gaze into the human soul; for the soul of another keeps enclosed in its innermost chamber what it contains of joy or sorrow, and truly it should appear as a wonderful mystery to anyone, that we can, as it were, pour ourselves into the being of other souls—live in their life and share their joys and sorrows. So just as we with our normal consciousness can by means of sympathy and love plunge into the sorrows and joys of conscious beings, so clairvoyants learn, at the second stage of clairvoyance, not only to plunge into everything conscious, into everything that can suffer and rejoice in a human way or in a manner resembling the human, but to plunge into everything that is alive. Notice that I say everything living—for at this second stage one only learns to plunge into living things, not yet into what is without life or appears lifeless, dead, and which we see around us as the mineral kingdom. But this immersing oneself into living things is connected with a view of what goes on in the inner nature of those beings. We feel ourselves there, within the living beings. At this second stage of clairvoyance, we learn to live with plants, animals, and with other human beings. But not only this; we also learn to recognize behind all living things a higher spiritual world, the beings of the second hierarchy. It is necessary that we should form a clear idea of these connections, for if one only enumerated what sort of beings belonged to the various hierarchies that would seem just a dry theory. We can only gain a living idea of what lives and weaves behind the sense world if we know the path by which clairvoyant consciousness penetrates it.

Now, beginning once more from the human being, we will try to describe the beings of the second hierarchy. We saw yesterday that the beings of the third hierarchy are characterized by the fact that instead of human perception, they have the manifestation of their own being, and instead of human inner life they have what we may call "being filled with the spirit." When we plunge into the beings of the second hierarchy we experience that not only is their perception a manifestation of their being, not only do they manifest their own being, but that this manifestation remains, as something independent that separates from these beings themselves. We can gain an idea of what we thus perceive if we think of a snail, which separates off its own shell. The shell—we understand—consists of a substance that is at first contained in the body of the snail. The snail then detaches it. Not only does the snail manifest its own being externally, but it detaches something which then becomes objective and remains. So it is with the actual nature, with the selfhood of the beings of the second hierarchy. Not only do they manifest their selfhood as do the beings of the third hierarchy, but they detach it from themselves, so that it remains as an independent being. This will be clearer to us if we picture, on the one hand, a being of the third hierarchy and, on the other hand, a being of the second hierarchy. Let us direct our occult vision to a being of the third hierarchy. We recognize this being as such because it manifests its selfhood, its inner life, externally, and in this manifestation it has its perception; but if it were to change its inner perception, its inner experience, the outer manifestation would also be different. As the inner condition of these beings of the third hierarchy change, and their experiences vary, so do the external manifestations continually change. But if you look at a being of the second hierarchy with occult vision, it is quite different. These beings also perceive and experience inwardly; but what they experience is detached from them like a sort of shell or skin; it acquires independent existence. If a being of the second hierarchy then passes on into another inner condition, has a different perception and manifests in a new way, the old manifestation of the being will still exist; it still remains and does not pass away, as happens in the case of a being of the third hierarchy. We can call what appears instead of manifestation in a being of the second hierarchy: a self-creation, a sort of shell or skin. It creates, as it were, an impression of itself, makes itself objective, in a sort of image. That is what distinguishes the beings of the second hierarchy. And if we ask ourselves what appears in these beings—in the place where the beings of the third hierarchy are "filled with the spirit"—it is shown to occult vision that every time a being detaches such a picture or image of itself, life is stimulated. The stimulation of life is always the result of such a self-creation.

Thus, we must distinguish—in the beings of the third hierarchy—their external life in their manifestation, and their inner life in their "being filled with spirit." In the beings of the second hierarchy, we must distinguish their external side as a creating of themselves, a making of themselves objective in images, in pictures; and their inner activity as the stimulation of life—as if fluidity continually rippled in itself and congealed as it detached its image externally. This approximately represents to occult vision the external and internal fulfillment of the beings of the second hierarchy. While the "being filled with the spirit" of the beings of the third hierarchy appears to occult vision in picture and imagination as a sort of spiritual light, so is the fluidic life, the stimulation of life that is connected with an external separation, perceived in such a way that occult perception hears something like spiritual tone, the music of the spheres. It is like spiritual sound, not like spiritual light as in the case of the third hierarchy.

We can distinguish several categories among these beings of the second hierarchy, just as we did among the

beings of the third hierarchy. To distinguish between these
categories will be more difficult, however, for the higher
we ascend the more difficult it becomes. In the course of
our ascent, we must first of all gain some idea of all that
underlies the world surrounding us, insofar as the world
around us has forms. I have already said that, as regards
this second stage of clairvoyance, we need only consider
what is living, not what appears lifeless to us. What lives
comes into consideration, but what lives has, in the first
place, form. Plants have form, animals have form, human
beings have form. If clairvoyant vision is directed, with all
the qualities we have described today, to everything around
us in nature that has form, and if we look away from all the
other parts of the beings and only see the forms, considering the multiplicity of the forms among plants, as also
among animals and human beings, this clairvoyant vision
then perceives from the totality of the beings of the second
hierarchy those which we call the spirits of form—the *exusiai*. We can, however, turn our attention to something
besides the form in the beings around us in nature. We
know indeed, that everything that lives changes its form, in
a certain respect, as it grows. This change, this alteration of
form, this metamorphosis, strikes us more particularly in
the plant world. Now, if we direct, not ordinary vision but
clairvoyant vision of the second stage, to the growing plant
world, we see how the plant gradually gains its form, how
it passes from the form of the root to the form of the leaf, to
the form of the flower, to the form of the fruit. If we look at
the growing animal, at the growing human being, we do
not merely consider a form as it exists at a given moment,
we see the growth of the living being. If we allow ourselves
to be stimulated by this contemplation of the growth of the
living being; reflecting on how the forms change, on how
they are in active metamorphosis, then clairvoyant vision of

the second stage becomes aware of what we call the category of the spirits of motion, the *dynamis*.

It is still more difficult to consider the third category of beings of the second hierarchy. For we must consider neither the form as such, nor the changes of form, nor the movement; but what is expressed in the form. We can describe how we may train ourselves to this. Of course, it does not suffice to train our ordinary, normal consciousness in the way that has been described—one must be helped by the use of the other exercises that raise one to occult vision. We must perform such exercises; educating ourselves not with ordinary consciousness but with clairvoyant consciousness. Clairvoyant consciousness must first educate itself in the way a human being becomes, in outer form, the expression of the inner being. As we have said, this can also be done by the normal consciousness, but in normal consciousness one would attain to nothing but conjecture, a supposition of what may lie behind the bearing, gestures, and facial expressions of a human being. But when clairvoyant vision that has already been trained to the second stage of clairvoyance allows the human physiognomy, gestures, and facial expressions to work upon it, this produces impulses through which one can gradually train oneself to observe the beings of the third category of the second hierarchy. But this cannot take place—please note—if one merely observes the gestures, imitative expression, and physiognomy of human beings; if one remains at this stage very little can really be gained. One must pass on—occult education is carried on most rationally in this realm—one must pass over to the plants. The animals can be left out, it is not very important to study them, but after one has trained oneself a little in clairvoyance to learn the inner being of a person's soul from his or her physiognomy and gestures; then it is important to turn to the plant world and educate oneself further by means of this. Here someone clairvoyantly trained can have very remarkable experiences. They will feel profoundly the difference between the leaf of a plant that—let us say—runs to a point (a) and the leaf of a plant that has the form (b); between a blossom that grows upward in this way (c) and one which opens outward (d). A whole world of difference appears in inner experience if one directs occult vision of the second stage to a lily or to a tulip—or if one lets an oat panicle or a wheat or barley stalk work upon one.

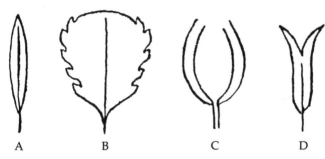

A   B   C   D

All this becomes as living and speaking as the physiognomy of a human being. And when this speaks as livingly as human physiognomy and gestures, when we feel how the blossom that opens outward has something of the character of a hand that turns outward with the inner surface below and the outer surface above, and when we find another blossom that closes its petals above, like the two hands folded—if we feel the gestures, the physiognomy, and the colors of the plant world to be something like a human physiognomy—then the inner vision, occult perception, and understanding are stimulated and we recognize a third category of the beings of the second hierarchy, whom we call the spirits of wisdom. This name is chosen by way of comparison, because when we consider a human being in his or her mimicry, physiognomy, and gestures, we see their spiritual part, which is filled with wisdom, springing forth externally, manifesting itself. In this way we feel how the spiritual beings of the second hierarchy permeate all nature and find expression in the physiognomy, collective gestures, and collective mimicry of nature. Flowing wisdom passes full of life through all beings, through all realms of nature—and not merely a general flowing wisdom, for this flowing wisdom is differentiated into a profusion of spiritual beings, into the profusion of the spirits of wisdom. When occult consciousness raises itself to these spirits, it is at first the highest stage of those spiritual beings whom we can reach in this manner.

But just as we could say that the beings of the third hierarchy—the angels, archangels, and spirits of the age—have offspring who separate from them, so, too, the beings of the second hierarchy likewise have offspring. In the course of time, there are detached from the beings of the second hierarchy, in the same way as we were able to describe yesterday with regard to the beings of the third hierarchy, other beings of a lower order who are sent down into the kingdoms of nature, just as the nature spirits by the third hierarchy who then become, as it were, the master-builders and overseers in miniature in the kingdom of nature. Now the spiritual beings who are detached from the beings of the second hierarchy, and sink down into the kingdoms of nature, are those designated in occultism as the group-souls of the plants and animals, the group-souls of the individual beings. So that occult vision of the second stage finds in the beings of the plant and animal kingdoms, spiritual beings who are not, as in humanity, individual spirits in individual human beings; but we find groups of animals, groups of plants that are of like form, ensouled by a common spiritual being. The form of the lion and tiger and other forms are, for instance, ensouled by a common soul being. These we call group-souls, and these group-souls are the detached offspring of the beings of the second hierarchy, just as the nature spirits are the offspring of the third hierarchy.

Thus when we penetrate from below upward into the higher worlds, we find when we look at the elements—which are of importance to all the beings of the plant, animal, and human kingdoms—that in these elements, in solid, fluidic, and gaseous matter, nature spirits rule who are the offspring of the beings of the third hierarchy. If we ascend from the elements of earth, water, and air, to what lives in the nature kingdoms by the aid of these elements, we find the spiritual beings, group-souls, who animate and interpenetrate the beings of these nature kingdoms, and these group-souls are spiritual beings detached from those we call the beings of the second hierarchy.

You can realize from this that those beings that we call the group-souls are actually perceptible only to occult vision of the second stage. Only for those occultly developed individuals who can extend their own etheric body as tentacles is it possible to know the beings of the second hierarchy and also the group-soul beings who exist in the various kingdoms of nature. Still more difficult is the ascent to the beings of the first hierarchy, and to those beings who are their offspring in the kingdoms of nature. We shall speak further about these in the next lecture.

Lecture Five

W<small>E HAVE COME</small> in our studies to the so-called second hierarchy of the spiritual beings. In the last lecture we described what the human soul must do if it would penetrate to the nature of this second hierarchy. A yet more difficult path leads to a still higher rank of spiritual beings belonging to the first, uppermost, rank of the hierarchies to which we can attain. It has been emphasized that by means of a special enhancement of the experiences we have in ordinary life in feelings of sympathy and love—by raising these feelings to the occult path—we may succeed in pouring forth our own being, coming out of ourselves, as it were, and plunging into the being we wish to observe. Note well that the characteristic of this immersion in another consists in extending our own being like tentacles, and pouring it into the other being. In so doing, we must, however, always retain our own consciousness, we must be consciously present in our own inner life beside the other being. That is the characteristic feature of the second stage of clairvoyance that has been described. At this second stage, where we feel ourselves one with other beings, we must realize that we ourselves are still there, as it were, beside the other being. But even this last remains of egoistic experience must cease if we wish to ascend to the highest stage of clairvoyance.

There we must completely lose the feeling that we exist as a separate being in any one part of the world. We must reach the point not only of pouring ourselves into the other being and standing beside it, retaining our own separate experience, but we must actually feel the foreign being as ourself. We must completely pass out of ourselves and lose the feeling that we are standing beside the other being. If we thus dive down into a foreign being, we succeed in looking upon ourselves as we were previously, as we are in ordinary life—as another being. For example, suppose we, as students at the higher stage of clairvoyance, plunge down into some being of the kingdom of nature. We do not then look upon this being from within ourselves; we do not merely immerse ourselves in it as in the second stage of clairvoyance. Instead, we know ourselves to be one with this being, and we look back upon ourselves from within it. Just as, formerly, we looked upon a foreign being as outside ourselves, so now at the higher stage of clairvoyance we look out from within the foreign being and see ourselves as a foreign being. That is the difference between the second and the higher stages. Only when this third stage is reached do we succeed in perceiving other beings in our spiritual environment besides those of the second and third hierarchies. The spiritual beings of whom we are then aware also belong to three categories. The first category we perceive chiefly when, in the manner described, we plunge down into the being of other human beings or of the higher animals, and by that means educate ourselves. The essential thing is not so much what we perceive in other human beings or in the higher animals, as that we should educate ourselves by that means and perceive behind the human beings and animals the spirits belonging to one of the categories of the first hierarchy: the spirits of will, or, according to Western esotericism, the thrones. For we then perceive beings we cannot describe otherwise than by saying that they do not consist of flesh and blood, nor even of light and air; but of what we can only observe in ourselves when we are conscious that we have a will. Insofar as their lowest substance is concerned, they consist only of will. If we educate ourselves in the manner described and also fix our gaze on the lower animals and their life; or if we plunge into the plant world, considering it not merely according to its gestures or its mimicry, as described yesterday—but become one with the plant, and from the plant look out upon ourselves—then indeed we attain an experience for which there is no real comparison within the world as we know it.

At most, we can attempt to find a comparison for the qualities of those beings to whom we then ascend—the beings of the second category of the first hierarchy—if we allow such feelings to work upon our soul as may be aroused by earnest people of great worth; people who have applied the many experiences of their lives to the gaining of wisdom. These are people who after many applied years of rich experience have gathered so much wisdom that we say to ourselves: "When they express an opinion, it is not their personal will speaking, but that life which they have accumulated for decades and by means of which they have, in a certain sense, become quite impersonal." They make upon us the impression that their wisdom is impersonal, and is the blossom and fruit of a mature life. Such persons call forth in us a feeling, though but a faint one, of what influences us from our spiritual environment when we press forward to the stage of clairvoyance of which we must now speak. In Western esotericism this category of beings is called the cherubim. It is extremely difficult to describe the beings of this higher category, for the higher we ascend the more impossible does it become to make use of any qualities of ordinary life wherewith to arouse an idea of the loftiness, greatness, and sublimity of the beings of this hierarchy. We can perhaps to some slight extent describe the spirits of will—the lowest category of the first hierarchy—by saying: "We become familiar with will, for will is the lowest substance of which they consist." But this would be impossible if we were only to regard the will that we encounter in human beings or animals in normal life, or ordinary human feelings and thoughts. And it would be impossible to describe the beings of the second category of the first hierarchy by what is usually accepted as human thought, feeling, and will. To do so, we must turn to the life of special persons who, in the way described, have built up an overwhelming power of wisdom in their souls. When we realize this wisdom of theirs, we feel somewhat as occultists feel when they stand before the beings we call the cherubim. Wisdom, not acquired in decades, as is the wisdom of eminent men, but such wisdom as is gathered in thousands, nay, in millions of years of cosmic growth, this streams towards us in sublime power from the beings we call the cherubim.

Still more difficult to describe are those beings called the seraphim who form the first and highest category of the first hierarchy. It would only be possible to gain some idea of the impression the seraphim make upon occult vision, if we take the following comparison from life. We will pursue the comparison just made. We will consider a person who for decades has built up experiences that have brought them overwhelming wisdom, and we will imagine that such a wise one speaks from his or her most impersonal life wisdom—that out of this most impersonal wisdom this person's whole being is permeated as if with inner life—so that he or she need say nothing, but just appear before us. The wisdom of those decades, that life-long wisdom, will be apparent in this wise person's countenance, so that his or her look can tell us of the sorrows and experiences of decades; and this look can make such an impression on us that it speaks to us as the world which we experience itself does. If we imagine such a look or imagine that such a wise person does not speak to us in words alone; but that in the tone and in the peculiar coloring of their words they can give us such an impression of all this rich life of experience that we hear in what they say something like an undertone, conveying the nature of their experiences, then again we gain something of the feeling that the occultist has when ascending to the seraphim. It is just like a countenance matured by life which tells of the experience of decades, or like a phrase which is so expressed that we hear not merely the thoughts, but realize: "This phrase expressed with resonance, has been acquired in pain and by the expression of life. It is no theory, it has been attained by struggles and suffering. It has passed through the battles and victories of life, and has sunk into the heart." If we hear all this as in an undertone, we gain an idea of the impression which trained occultists receive when lifting themselves to the beings we call the seraphim.

We might describe the beings of the third hierarchy by saying: What, in human beings, is perception, is, in the beings of the third hierarchy, manifestation of self. What in us is inner life or waking consciousness is in them being filled with spirit. The beings of the second hierarchy we might describe by saying: What, in the beings of the third hierarchy, is manifestation of self, is, in the beings of the second hierarchy, self-realization, self-creation, a stamping of impressions of their own being. What in the beings of the third hierarchy is being filled with spirit, is in these beings of the second hierarchy stimulation of life—which consists in severance, in objectifying themselves. Now, what in the beings of the second hierarchy is self-creation, we also encounter in the beings of the first hierarchy when we look at them with occult vision; but there is a difference. What the beings of the second hierarchy make objective, what they create from themselves, exists only so long as these beings remain connected with their creations. Thus—note well—the beings of the second hierarchy can create something like an image of themselves, but it remains connected with them and cannot be separated from them. The beings of the first hierarchy can also objectify themselves, they can also stamp their own being—it is separated from them as in a sort of skin or shell, but it is an impression of their own being. When this is detached from them, however, it continues to exist in the world though they sever themselves from it. They do not carry their own creations about with them, these creations remain in existence even if they go away from them. Thus a higher degree of objectivity is attained by them than by the second hierarchy. When the beings of the second hierarchy create, if their creations are not to fall into decay, they must remain connected with them. The creations would become lifeless and disintegrate, if they themselves did not remain connected with them. What they create has an independent objective existence, but only so long as they remain linked with it. On the other hand, what is detached from the beings of the first hierarchy can be disconnected from them, and yet remain in existence, self-acting, and objective.

In the third hierarchy we have manifestation and being filled with spirit. In the second hierarchy, we have self-creation and stimulation of life. In the first hierarchy—which consists of the thrones, cherubim, and seraphim—we have a form of creation in which the part created is detached. We have there not only self-creation, but world-creation. What proceeds from the beings of the first hierarchy is a detached

world, such an independent world that this world-phe-
nomenon is a fact, even when the beings are no longer
there.

Now we may ask: What then is the actual life of this first
hierarchy? The actual life of this first hierarchy is such that
when such objective, independent, detached beings proceed from it, it realizes itself. For the inner condition of consciousness, the inner experience of the beings of the first
hierarchy, lies in creation, in forming independent beings.
We may say that they contemplate what they create which
becomes a world, and it is not when they look into themselves, but when they look out of themselves upon the
world, which is their own creation, that they possess themselves. To create other beings is their inner life. To live in
other beings is the inner experience of these beings of the
first hierarchy. Creation of worlds is their outer life, creation of beings is their inner life.

In the course of these lectures we have drawn attention to
the fact that these various beings of the hierarchies have
offspring—beings split off from themselves which they
send down into the kingdoms of nature—and we have
learned that the offspring of the third hierarchy are the
nature spirits, while the offspring of the second hierarchy
are the group-souls. The beings of the first hierarchy likewise have offspring split off from them, and as a matter of
fact I have already described from a different aspect these
beings that are the offspring of the first hierarchy. I
described them at the beginning of this course, when we
ascended to the so-called spirits of the cycles or rotation of
time, the spirits governing and directing what goes on in
the kingdoms of nature in rhythmic succession and repeti-
tion. The beings of the first hierarchy detach the beings
governing the alternation of summer and winter from
themselves, so that the plants spring up and fade away

again. This is that rhythmical succession through which, for instance, the animals belonging to a certain species have a definite period of life in which they develop from birth to death. Everything too which takes place in the kingdom of nature rhythmically and in recapitulation, such as day and night, alternations of the year, the four seasons of the year, everything which thus depends upon repeated happenings, is regulated by the spirits of the cycles of time, the offspring of the beings of the first hierarchy. These spirits of the cycles of time can be described from one aspect, as we did some days ago, and we can now describe them according to their origin, as we have done today.

Thus we can comprehensively represent the beings of these three hierarchies as follows:

First Hierarchy: World-creation. Creation of Beings. Spirits of the Cycles of Time.
Second Hierarchy: Self-creation. Stimulation of Life. Group-Souls.
Third Hierarchy: Manifestation. Being filled with Spirit. Nature Spirits.

If we want to proceed further in the task before us, we must now become familiar with the conceptions to which the trained vision of the occultist gradually rises—conceptions which, when one first becomes acquainted with them, are somewhat difficult. Today we will place these concepts and ideas before us. This will enable us, when in the following lectures the whole life and being of the kingdoms of nature and of the heavenly bodies is to appear before us, to accustom ourselves more and more to the form and manner in which the beings described are connected with the kingdoms of nature and with the heavenly bodies. In this way we shall be able to acquire more definite conceptions concerning them.

My books *Theosophy, Occult Science,* amongst others, describe human beings as they reveal themselves to occult vision. In considering human beings, then, we say first of all that the most external part, the part perceptible to human eyes and senses is the physical body. Thus we look upon the physical body as the first human principle. The second, the etheric body, we already regard as something supersensible, invisible to the normal consciousness, and the astral body we regard as the third principle. These three principles approximately comprise the human sheaths. Then we rise to yet higher principles. They are of a soul nature. In ordinary life we regard them as the inner soul-life and, just as we speak of a threefold external covering, so can we speak of a threefold soul—the sentient soul, the intellectual soul or mind-soul, and the consciousness soul. These principles of human nature, from the physical body to the consciousness soul, are already present today in every human being. To these may also be added a shining-in of the next principle, which we designate the spirit-self—or, as perhaps some are accustomed to call it, manas. The next principle, which will only really be fully formed in humanity in the future, we call the life-spirit, or budhi. Then comes that which we designate as the actual spirit-human, or atma, which is, in fact, the innermost part of human nature, but which, as far as human consciousness today is concerned, is still asleep within us. It will only light up as the real center of consciousness in future earthly days. These principles of human nature are such that we speak of them as separate unities. In a certain sense, the human-physical body is one unity; the human etheric body is another; and so likewise are the other principles of human nature. The whole human being is a unity, consisting of the union and combined working of these various principles.

If we wish to go further, you must picture to yourselves that there are beings so far exalted above human nature that they do not consist of principles that we could call physical body, etheric body, etc., but that the principles of these beings are themselves beings. Thus while human beings have their individual principles which we cannot look upon as beings, but merely as separate principles, we must ascend to beings possessing no physical body as part of themselves, but who, corresponding with the physical body of the human being, have something which in our study we have called the spirits of form. When we say that there are beings of a higher category, not having a physical body as one of their principles, but having among their principles a being itself—a spirit of form—we may then gain an idea of a being not yet described, but which we will now proceed to describe. If we wish to do this we must make use of those concepts to which we have risen in the course of these lectures. I have already said that it is difficult to come to these ideas, but you may be able to raise yourselves to such thoughts by means of an analogy.

Let us consider a beehive or an anthill. Take the individual entities, the individual bees in a beehive. It is clear that the beehive possesses a real common spirit, a real collective being, and that this being has its various parts in the individual bees, just as you have yours in your separate principles. Here you have an analogy for still higher beings than those we have already considered, beings having among their principles nothing that we can compare with the human physical body, but instead something we must designate as itself a being, a spirit of form. Just as we live in our physical body, so does the life of those beings of a higher eminence consist in their having the spirits of form, or a spirit of form as their lowest principle. Then, instead of the etheric body we human beings have, these beings have as their second principle, spirits of motion. Instead of what is to us our astral body, these beings have a spirit of wisdom. Instead of the sentient-soul we as human beings have, these beings have as their fourth principle, the thrones, or spirits of will. Instead of the intellectual soul, these beings have the cherubim as their fifth principle; and as the sixth, as we have the consciousness soul, they have the seraphim. Just as we look up to what we shall only gradually attain in future earthly lives, so do these beings look up to that which towers above the nature of the hierarchies. Just as we speak of our manas, buddhi, atma—or spirit-self, life-spirit and spirit-human—so, as it were, do these beings look up from their seraphic principle, as we out of our conscious soul, to a primal spirituality. Only then have these beings something analogous to our inner spiritual life. It is extremely difficult to arouse concepts within us concerning what exists above the hierarchies as the spiritual nature of the highest spirits themselves. Hence, in course of the evolution of humanity, the various religions and world-concepts have, as we might say, with a certain reverent caution refrained from speaking in the concise concepts pertaining to the sense-world of what exists above the hierarchies.

In order to call forth such a concept as lives in the soul of the occultist when he looks up to the seraphim, we tried to grasp such means as can only be found in analogy—we considered people with a rich experience of life. We find, however, that even in such persons nothing in their lives can in the very least help one to characterize the Trinity, which, as it were, appears above the seraphim, as their highest being—as their manas, budhi and atma.

Unfortunately, in the course of human evolution, there has been much dispute over the cautious surmises with which the human mind has ventured to approach what is above in the spiritual worlds. Unfortunately, we may say, for it would be much more seemly if the human mind were not to try to describe beings of such sublimity with concepts taken from ordinary life, nor by means of all sorts of analogies and comparisons. It would be more seemly for us to desire in deepest reverence to learn ever more fully, so that we might be able to form more approximate concepts. The various religions of the world have tried to give approximate concepts of what is "above" in many significant and speaking ideas—ideas which, to a certain extent, do provide something special in that they reach out beyond individual human life in the external sense world. Naturally, we cannot by means of such ideas describe, even approximately, these exalted beings to whom we refer, but we can, to a certain extent, call up a conception of what is inexpressible, and should be veiled in holy mystery. For one ought not to approach these matters with mere human intellectual concepts obtained from the external world. Hence, in the successive religions and conceptions of the world, it was sought to characterize these things approximately and by faint indications. Human beings thus drew near to what is so far above humanity and in its very nature mysterious, by an attempt to characterize what lies above, or rather, by giving names to it.

The ancient Egyptians have, in their giving of names, made use of the concepts of child or son, father, and mother, and so of concepts that rise beyond the individual human being. Christianity endeavoured in the succession of Father, Son, and Holy Spirit, to find a name for this Trinity. We may therefore say: In the seventh place we should have to put the Holy Spirit, in the eighth place the Son and in the ninth the Father. Therefore when we look up to a being whose highest content disappears as in a spiritual mystery we can say allusively—Spirit, Son, and Father.

And when we look up to such a being with occult vision we say: Just as when we look at the human being externally, regarding the physical body as the lowest principle, so among such beings, if we are to regard them as in any sense analogous, we have before us as their lowest principle the spirit of form, a spirit that gives itself form, a spirit having form. We must therefore look upon what in this being is analogous to, or resembles, the human physical body; as something which has form. Just as we have something of form in this human physical body as the lowest principle and as, in this form—which, in truth, as we encounter it, is obviously *maya*—there lives a spirit of form, so what appears to us when we direct our gaze into cosmic space and perceive there a planet—Mercury, Venus, Mars or Jupiter—is the external form of the spirit of form. It is what belongs to the being of whom we have just spoken, as the human physical body belongs to the human being. When we see human beings before us, their form expresses what lives in them as higher principles—etheric body, astral body, sentient soul, and so forth. When we look at a planet its form expresses to us the work of the spirits of form. Just as behind the human form, behind the physical body, are the etheric body, astral body, sentient soul, and so forth, so, behind the planet, belonging to it, are what we know as the spirits of motion, wisdom, will; cherubim and seraphim etc. If we wish to visualize the complete being of a planet in the sense of spiritual science, we must say: The planet meets our perception in cosmic space when its physical being, given by the spirit of form shines forth; and it conceals from us, just as we conceal our higher principles from the physical gaze, all that rules within and around it, as beings of the higher hierarchies. Thus we rightly imagine such a planet as Mars, or Mercury, only when we first of all picture it in its physical form, and then

think of it as surrounded and permeated by a spiritual
atmosphere stretching out into infinity and having in the
physical planet its physical form, the creation of the spirit
of form—and as its spiritual environment the beings of the
hierarchies. Only when we consider it thus do we conceive
of the complete planet, as having the physical as a kernel in
the center, and around it the spiritual sheaths consisting of
the beings of the hierarchies. This will be considered in
greater detail in the following lectures, but today, in order
to some extent to indicate the direction of our observations,
we may give the following information revealed by occult
investigation.

We have already pointed out that what we observe as the
physical form of the planet is a creation of the spirits of
form. The form of our earth is also a creation of the spirits
of form. Now, with regard to our earth, we know that it is
never at rest; we know that this earth is in a state of perpetual inner change and movement. It will be remembered
from the description given in the Akashic Chronicle that
the external aspect of our earth today is quite different from
what it presented, for example, at the time we call the
Atlantean epoch. In this primeval Atlantean epoch, the surface of the globe of the earth that is today covered by the
Atlantic ocean was a mighty continent; while where
Europe, Asia and Africa are now situated, scarcely any con-
tinents were as yet formed. Thus the solid matter, the substance of the earth, has been transformed by its inner
motion. The planet earth is in a continual state of inner
motion. Consider, for instance, that what we know today as
the island of Heligoland is but a small part of that land
which in the ninth and tenth centuries still projected out
into the sea. Although the periods during which inner
changes alter the earth's surface are comparatively great,
yet without going deeply into these matters, we can all see

that our planet is in perpetual inner motion. Indeed, if we do not merely include the solid earth in the planet, but also the water and the air, then daily life teaches us that the planet is in inner motion. In the formation of clouds and rain, in all the phenomena of atmospheric conditions, in the rise and fall of the water, in all these we see the inner mobility of the planetary substance. That is one life of the planet. Just as the etheric body works in the life of the individual, so do what we designate as the spirits of motion work in the life of the planet. Therefore we may say: The external form of the planet is the creation of the spirits of form. The inner livingness is regulated by the beings we call the spirits of motion.

Now, to the occultist, such a planet is in every way an actual being, a being regulating what goes on within it, according to thought. Not only is what has just been described as inner vitality present in the planet but the planet as a whole has consciousness, for it is indeed a being. This consciousness which corresponds to human consciousness, to the lower form of human consciousness—the subconsciousness in the astral body—is regulated in the planet by the spirits of wisdom. We may therefore say: The lowest consciousness of the planet is regulated by the spirits of wisdom. In thus describing the planet, we still refer to the planet itself. We look up to the planet saying: It has a definite form that corresponds to the spirits of form; it has an inner mobility that corresponds to the spirits of motion. All this is permeated by consciousness, which corresponds to the spirits of wisdom.

Let us follow the planet further. It passes through space; it has an inner impulse that drives it through space, just as a human being has an inner impulse of will causing him or her to take steps, to walk along in space. What leads the planet through space and governs its movement through space and causes it to revolve around the fixed star corresponds to the spirits of will, or the thrones. Now, if these spirits of will were to give only the impulse of motion to the planet, every planet would go its own way through the universe; but this is not the case, for every planet acts in conformity with the whole system. The motion is not only so regulated that the planet moves, but it is brought into due order with the whole planetary system. Just as due order is brought, let us say, to a group of people, of whom one goes in one direction and another in another to reach a common goal—the movements of the planets are also so arranged that they harmonize. The harmony of movement between one planet and another corresponds to the activity of the cherubim. The regulation of the combined movements of the system is the work of the cherubim. Each planetary system with its fixed star, which is in a sense the commander-in-chief under the guidance of the cherubim, is again related to the other planetary systems to which other fixed stars belong. These systems mutually arrange their positions in space with due regard to the neighboring systems, just as individual persons agree together, deliberate with one another regarding their common action. Just as people found a social system by virtue of this reciprocity, so also there is a reciprocity in the planetary systems. Mutual understanding prevails between one fixed star and another. By this means alone does the cosmos come into existence. That which, so to speak, the planetary systems discuss with one another in cosmic space in order to become a cosmos is regulated by the beings we call the seraphim. We have now, as it were, exhausted what we find in human beings, as far as the consciousness soul. Just as in human beings we ascend to higher spirit-nature, to what alone gives meaning to the whole system up to the consciousness soul, so if we ascend above the seraphim we come to what we tried to describe today as the Highest Trinity of Cosmic Being; we come to that in the universe which governs as the all-pervading, divine, Threefold Divine Life. This creates for Itself sheaths in the different planetary systems. Just as what lives in human beings as spirit-self, life-spirit, and spirit-human (manas, budhi, atma) creates sheaths in the consciousness soul, intellectual soul, sentient soul, astral, etheric, and physical bodies, so do the fixed stars of planetary systems move through space as the bodies of divine beings. Inasmuch as we contemplate the life of the world of stars, we contemplate the bodies of the gods, and finally of the Divine as such.

LECTURE SIX

I N OUR LAST LECTURE, we tried to consider a planetary system as it depends on the various spiritual beings of the three hierarchies, ranged, as it were, one above the other. We gained an idea of all that participates in forming a planet, and we saw how a planet receives its form, its enclosed form, as a result of the activity of the spirits of form. We saw, further, that the inner life, the inner mobility of the planet, is the result of the activity of the spirits of motion. What we may call the lowest consciousness of the planet, which can be compared with the consciousness present in the human astral body, we then assigned to the spirits of wisdom. And the impulse by which the planet, instead of remaining stationary changes its place in space, we allotted to the spirits of will, or the thrones. The organizing of the planet in such a way that it does not follow an isolated course in space but moves in such a way that its impulses of motion are in harmony with the whole planetary system to which it belongs—the regulating of the individual movements of the planet in harmony with the whole system—we saw to be an activity of the cherubim. Finally, we ascribed to the seraphim what we may call the inner soul-life of the planet, whereby the planet comes, as it were, into connection with the other heavenly bodies, as a person by means of speech enters into relation with other people.

Thus we must see a sort of coherence in the planet; and in this, what comes from the spirits of form is but a sort of kernel. On the other hand, every planet has something like a spiritual atmosphere—we might even say something like an aura—in which the spirits work who belong to those two higher hierarchies that are higher than the spirits of form. Now, however, if we want to understand all this rightly, we must make ourselves acquainted with yet other concepts than those I have just recalled to you—concepts to which we shall most easily attain if we begin with the beings of that hierarchy which stands, so to speak, nearest to humanity in the spiritual world, namely the beings of the third hierarchy.

We have said that characteristic of the beings of the third hierarchy is the fact that what is perception in human beings is manifestation in them, and that what is inner life in human beings, is being filled with spirit in them. We already find this characteristic even in those beings who start immediately above humanity in the cosmic order, the angels or *angeloi*—namely, that they are actually conscious of what they manifest from out of themselves. When they return to their inner being, they have nothing independent, nothing self-enclosed like the inner life of human beings. Rather, they then feel the forces and beings of the higher hierarchies above them shining and springing forth in their inner being. In short, they feel themselves filled and inspired by the spirit and its beings immediately above them. Thus, what we call our independent inner life really does not exist in them. If they wish to develop their own being, if they wish to feel, think and will somewhat as a human being does, it is all immediately manifested externally—not like we humans, who can shut up our thoughts and feelings within ourselves, and allow our will impulses to remain unfulfilled. What lives as thought in these beings, insofar as they themselves bring forth these thoughts, is also and simultaneously revealed externally. If they do not wish to manifest externally they have no other means of returning into their inner being but by once again filling themselves with the world above them. Thus, the world above them dwells in the inner life of these beings, and when they live a life of their own, they project themselves externally, objectively.

Thus, as we have seen, these beings can hide nothing within them as the product of their own thought and feeling, for whatever they bring about in their inner being must show itself externally. As we mentioned in one of the earlier lectures, these beings cannot lie, they cannot be untrue to their nature in such a way that their thoughts and feelings do not harmonize with the external world; they cannot have an idea within them that does not agree with the external world. For any ideas they have in their inner being are perceived by them in their manifestation. Let us just suppose that these beings had a desire to be untrue to their own nature, what would be the result? Well, in the beings we have designated as angels, archangels, and spirits of the age or *archai*, we find throughout that everything that reveals itself to them, everything that they can perceive is, so to speak, their own being. If they were to wish to be untrue, they would be obliged to develop something in their inner being that would not be consistent with their own nature. Every untruth would be a denial of their nature. That would mean nothing less than a deadening, a damping-down of their own being. Now suppose that these beings had nevertheless the desire to experience something in their inner nature which they did not manifest externally. To do this, they would have to take on another nature.

What I have just described as the denial of their own nature by beings of the third hierarchy, the taking on of another nature, did actually take place. It did occur in the course of the ages. We shall see, as these lectures go on, why this had to happen; but to begin with we will confine our attention to the fact that it did happen; that, as a matter of fact, among the beings of the third hierarchy there were some possessed with this desire to have experiences in their inner nature which they need not manifest externally. That is, they had the wish to deny their own nature. What did this bring about in these beings? Something entered that the other beings, those of the third hierarchy which retained their own nature, cannot have. The beings of the third hierarchy can have no inner independence such as we have. If they wish to live in their inner being, they must immediately be filled with the spirit world above them. A certain number of the beings of the third hierarchy had the desire to develop something within their inner being that they would not immediately encounter in the external world as perception or as the revelation of their own being. Hence the necessity arose of denying their own nature and taking on another. To develop an inner life of their own, to attain inner independence, a number of beings of the third hierarchy had to give up their own nature, to deny it. They had, so to speak, to bring about in themselves the power not to manifest certain inner experiences externally. Now let us ask: What then were the reasons that moved these beings of the third hierarchy to develop such a desire within them? If we fix our attention upon the nature of the beings of the third hierarchy, with their manifestation and their being filled with spirit, we see that these beings are in reality wholly at the service of the beings of the higher hierarchies. Angels have no life of their own—their own life is manifestation, which is for the whole world. As soon as they do not manifest themselves the life of the higher hierarchies radiates into their inner being. What induced a number of them to deny their nature was a feeling of power, of independence and freedom. At a certain time, a number of beings of the third hierarchy had an impulse, an urge, to be dependent not merely upon the beings of the higher hierarchies, but to develop within themselves an inner life of their own. The result of this was very far-reaching for the whole evolution of the planetary system to which we belong, for these beings, whom we may call the rebels of the third hierarchy, brought about nothing less than humanity's actual independence—making it possible for human beings to develop an independent life of their own, one that does not immediately manifest externally, but can be independent of external manifestation.

I am intentionally using many words to describe this circumstance, because it is extremely important to grasp accurately what is in question here, namely, that an impulse arose in a number of the third hierarchy to develop an inner life of their own. Everything else was simply the result, the consequence of this impulse. What, then, was this result? It was, in fact, a terrible one—the betrayal of their own nature, that is, untruth, falsehood. You see, it is important that you should understand that the spirits of the third hierarchy who had this impulse did not do what they did for the sake of lying but in order to develop an independent life of their own; but in so doing they had to take the consequence, they had to become "spirits of untruth"—spirits who betrayed their own being—in other words, spirits of lies. It is as though someone were to take a journey on foot and meet with a wet day. Such a person must of necessity make the best of it and put up with getting wet, which they did not at all intend. In the same way, the spirits of whom we are speaking had no intention of doing something in order to sink into untruth. Their action arose from their wish to develop an inner life, an inner activity; but the result, the consequence, was that at the same time they became spirits of untruth. Now, all the spiritual beings who, by betraying their own nature, arose in this way as a second category beside the spirits of the third hierarchy occultism calls luciferic spirits.

The concept of the luciferic spirits consists essentially in the fact that these beings wish to develop an inner life. Now, the question is, What have these spirits to do, to attain their goal? We have already seen what they had to develop as a result, and we shall now inquire further what they had to do in order to attain this goal of an inner independent life. What did these spirits wish to surmount? They wished to prevent themselves from being filled wholly with the substance of the higher hierarchies. They wished to be filled not only with the beings of the higher hierarchies, but with their own being. They could only accomplish this in the following way. Instead of filling themselves with the spirit of the higher hierarchies, and, as it were, leaving themselves open to looking freely outward toward the higher hierarchies, they cut themselves off and detached themselves from the higher hierarchies in order in this way to create substance of their own from the substance of the higher hierarchies. We can gain a correct idea of what is here in question if we think of the beings of the third hierarchy thus. We think of them represented symbolically, graphically, in such a way that they manifest their own being outwardly, as it were, as though it were their skin. Hence each time they develop inner thought or feeling, a manifestation arises, like a shining-forth of their own being. The moment they do not manifest themselves, they take up the light of the higher hierarchies flowing into them; they fill themselves with the spirit of the higher hierarchies and, as it were, open their whole being to them.

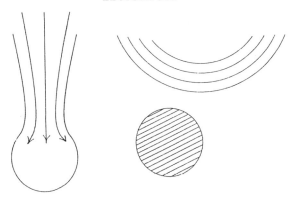

Those (luciferic) spiritual beings of the third hierarchy of whom we have just spoken did not wish to be filled with the spirit nor to be connected with the spiritual substance of the hierarchies. They wanted an independent spiritual life. Therefore they cut themselves off, they detached themselves, so that the being of the higher hierarchies was above them. They cut the connection and detached themselves as independent beings, retaining the actual light in their inner being. Thus, as it were, they stole what should only have filled them, and then returned to the higher hierarchies. They stole it for themselves, filled their own inner being with it, and thereby developed an independent side of their nature. This concept can provide an explanation of events in the cosmos, without which we should be quite unable to grasp a stellar system or the constitution of the stars in general as we know them with our human physical consciousness. Without these concepts one cannot possibly grasp the life of the stars, the life of the heavenly bodies.

I have now tried to indicate to you how certain beings of the third hierarchy have become quite different beings—luciferic spirits. What took place in these beings of the third hierarchy cannot, of course, take place in the same way in the beings of the other hierarchies, but something similar takes place even with these. If we apply what takes place in the beings of the other hierarchies to a consideration of the spirits of form, it will give us an idea of how a planetary system is actually formed. At the conclusion of the last lecture it was said that what our vision first perceives in the planets proceeds from the spirits of form, but it is not quite accurate to represent it thus. If you consider the planets—Mars, Saturn, or Jupiter for instance—that are outside in cosmic space as you see them with your physical eyes, or with the telescope, you have the form revealed to you, not merely the spirits of form. Let us take, for example, the planet that for a long period of time, has been reckoned as the outermost one in our system, Saturn. Uranus and Neptune were added later, as we shall see—but to begin with we will consider Saturn as the outermost. If we look at Saturn with physical vision we find it outside in cosmic space, a sort of luminous globe (leaving the rings out of the question). To the occultist who follows the spiritual events in the cosmos, this globe which we see out there is not what the occultist calls Saturn; to an occultist, Saturn is what fills the whole space that is bounded by the apparently elliptical orbit of Saturn.

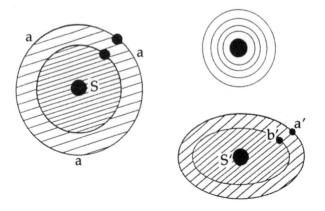

You know that astronomy describes an orbit of Saturn that it interprets as the path of Saturn round the sun. We will not now discuss the accuracy of that statement, but if you take this accepted concept and here in the center imagine the sun (S), and the outer circle as the orbit of Saturn, as astronomy conceives it, then everything that is within this orbit of Saturn, within the ellipse of Saturn, is Saturn to the occultist. For, to an occultist, Saturn is not only what the external eye sees as the most external physical matter—not only what gleams in the heavens—for the occultist knows, as occult vision teaches, that, as a matter of fact, a sort of accumulation exists extending from the sun to the orbit of Saturn (a, a, a, in the diagram). So if we regard this orbit of Saturn with occult vision, we have a sort of etheric filling-in of the whole space (the wide cross lines). We must think of what lies within this orbit as filled with matter, not however in the form of a globe, for we have to do with a very flattened ball, a lens. Looked at from the side, if we had the Sun at (S'), we would have to draw the Saturn of the occultist thus: as a much-flattened ball, and at (a'), we would have what is designated physical Saturn. We shall understand still better what is in question if we add an idea regarding Jupiter that we can gain in a similar way from occult science. External, physical astronomy knows as Jupiter that shining body revolving round the sun as the second planet (the inner circle). To the occultist, that is not Jupiter: to the occultist, Jupiter is all that lies within the orbit of Jupiter (narrow sloping lines). Looked at from the side, we would have to draw Jupiter in such a way that if we put wide sloping lines for Saturn, we put narrow sloping lines for Jupiter. What astronomy describes is only a body (b') which is, so to speak, on the outermost limits of the true occult Jupiter.

What I am here saying is not a mere theoretical idea or fancy. The fact actually is that matter, not coarse physical matter but fine etheric matter, fills the space within the orbit of Saturn in its lenticular, flattened, ball-like form, as drawn here. It is just as much a fact that the second smaller space for Jupiter is filled with a different etheric substance that permeates the first, so that there is simple etheric substance only between the two orbits. Within, the two etheric substances permeate one another, mutually permeate one another.

Now let us ask: What is the task of the spirits of form in this whole disposition? The spirit of form that forms the basis of Saturn sets a boundary and gives a form to the etheric substance we call, in an occult sense, Saturn. Thus the outermost line in the formation of Saturn has been shaped by the spirit of Saturn, who is also a spirit of form. In the same way, the line of Jupiter was formed by the spirit of form allotted to Jupiter; the line of Mars by the spirit of Mars, who is a spirit of form. Now, we may ask: Where then does the spirit of form corresponding to Saturn, Jupiter, or Mars actually dwell? If we can speak of a place in which these beings are, where is this place? In the ordinary sense of the word, however, we cannot so do; we can only say: The spiritual beings, whom we call the spirits of form, work as forces within the etheric substance we have just mentioned; but they all have a common center, and this center is none other than the sun. Thus, if we seek for the actual place whence the spirits of form work, the spirits of Saturn, Jupiter, Mars, and so forth, as well as the spirit of form belonging to our earth—if we seek for the center, the starting point from which the spirits of form work—we find it in the sun. This means that the spirits of form corresponding to our planets comprise, as it were, a synod or council of spirits, having its seat in the sun, and from there set boundaries to certain etheric substances, certain masses of ether, so that what we call, for instance, occult Saturn or occult Jupiter comes into being. Now, let us ask: How would it be if only the spirits of form were to work?

The whole meaning of these observations can show you that the physical planets would not be in existence if only the spirits of form were to work. They would indeed have, as it were, their abode in the sun, where they form a sort of college; and we should have around us the planetary spheres as far as the orbit of Saturn. For concentric globes, flattened balls, so to speak, would exist as the occult planets—the most external of these flattened globes being of the finest etheric matter, the next somewhat denser, and the innermost of the densest etheric matter. Therefore the physical planets would not be in existence if only the spirits of form were to work. There would be globe-shaped, accumulated masses bounded by what the physical astronomy today calls the orbits of the planets. But within the cosmos there are certain other spiritual beings corresponding to the spirits of form, but who, as it were, are rebels against those of their own class. Just as we find luciferic spirits among the beings of the third hierarchy who, in order to set up their own independent life, cut themselves off from the spiritual substance of the higher hierarchies, so we also find, within the category of the spirits of form, that some separated and would not go through the usual development of a spirit of form, but went through an evolution of their own. These oppose the normal spirits of form—they are in opposition to them. What then happens is as follows.

Let us suppose that we had, at point (S*), the center-point of the spiritual council of the spirits of form. The spirit of form working upon Saturn would call forth this etheric globe, so that by the agency of this spirit a flattened globe would arise, as in the following diagram. At an outermost

point of this etheric globe—in opposition to the spirit of
form working from the center of the sun—the rebel, the
luciferic spirit of form, works. He works from without
inward; in opposition. Thus we have the normal spirit of
form working centrifugally outward from the sun, bringing
about the occult Saturn, which is then to be seen as a
mighty etheric globe with its center-point in the sun. At the
periphery, working inward from cosmic space, is an abnormal spirit of form that has cut itself off from the normal
evolution of the others. Then at point (a*)—through the
combined working of the forces working inward from cosmic space and those working outward from the sun—there
occurs an "inturning" that finally becomes detached and
that is the physical planet Saturn.

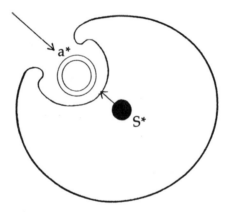

Thus we have to imagine that there are two forces working together where our physical eyes see the planet Saturn:
one is the normal force of the spirit of form working outward from the sun; the other is the detached spirit of form
that at a definite point works in opposition. This produces
an "inturned" structure; the ether is notched, and this
notch appears to the physical eye as the physical planet

Saturn. The same occurs with the physical Jupiter, and with the physical Mars. Hence, by this example, you see how in individual cases there actually arises what we call *maya*, the great illusion. Where physical astronomy places a planet, there is in truth a combined working of two forces. The appearance of the physical planet arises only because a great and mighty etheric heavenly body is truly there which, through the contact of these opposing forces, is dented in and has a notch formed in one place.

For truly here we have actually to do with a turning-in, and to be really accurate the matter must in the first place be described in this way. The spirits of form, working from the sun, extended the etheric substance a certain distance. The abnormal spirits of form working in opposition, caved the substance in, so that in reality a hollow was made in the etheric substance. As regards the original etheric substance of the planet, where the physical eye believes it sees the planet—there is really nothing. The actual planet is where the physical eye sees nothing. That is the peculiarity of *maya*. Where the physical planet is seen, there is a hollow. It may perhaps be said, asking about our earth: "It is a very strange idea that where the physical planet is to be seen, there is a hollow." According to what we have been saying, our earth too must be a sort of flattened ball having its central point in the sun. It must likewise be such a notch, such a sort of hollow on the outermost rim. "A fine thing that!" you can say, "We know quite well that we are walking on firm, solid earth!" Similarly, we might take for granted that where Saturn, Jupiter or Mars is, there would naturally have to be solid filling, not hollow. Yet nevertheless where you walk about on our earth—where, in the sense of *maya*-perception you believe yourselves to be walking on solid, firm ground—even then, in reality, you are walking about on a hollow. Our earth itself, insofar as it is an accumulation of matter, is a hollow in cosmic space, something bored into cosmic space. All physical matter comes into being through the meeting together of forces coming from the spirits of form. In the present case we have the meeting of the forces of the normal spirits of form and those of the abnormal spirits of form. These collide with one another and in reality an indentation is produced and consequently at this point a simultaneous breaking-up of the form, but only of the form. The form breaks up and this hollow space is bored. Now broken spiritual form, crushed form, is in reality matter. In a physical sense, matter only exists when spiritual forms are broken up. Thus the planets out there are also broken-up forms.

In our planetary system the spirits of form have helpers, as our previous considerations have made evident. The spirits of form themselves determine the boundaries, as we have described. But above the spirits of form stand the spirits of motion; above these the spirits of wisdom; above these the spirits of will; above them the cherubim and the seraphim. In all ranks of these spiritual beings there are those who can be likened to what we have described as luciferic spirits. So, wherever a planet is formed, on its outermost border, the spirits of form do not simply cooperate—for what goes out from the sun, from the activities of the normal hierarchies who work from within outward, is always being opposed by the forces that come from the abnormal, the rebellious hierarchies.

The cherubim and seraphim are those hierarchies that take part in the whole working of the forces as much as do the spirits of form. The cherubim and the seraphim have the task of bearing the power of light outward from the center-point of the planetary system, the center of the sun. Inasmuch as the beings of the higher hierarchies—the seraphim and cherubim—become the bearers of light, they then have

the same relation to the light as the forces of the spirits of
form have to the etheric substance. Just as the forces of the
normal spirits of form pass outward and encounter the
forces of the abnormal spirits working in opposition, and by
that means a notch is hollowed out, so also do the forces
work which carry the light, filling the whole etheric space,
meet with opposition. In opposition to them work the
abnormal forces (point a), with the result that the planet
arrests the light. Just as the planet arrests the forces of the
spirits of form, so does it also arrest the light and throw it
back; hence it appears as a reflector, as a thrower-back of the
light that the spirits we call the cherubim and seraphim
carry to it from the sun.

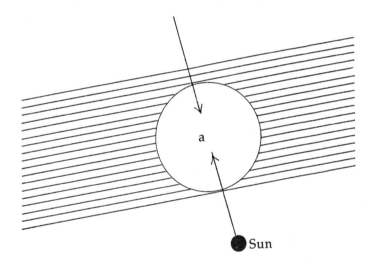

Thus the planets have no light of their own, because they
claim for themselves the force of the light that would be
due to them as beings if they were to open themselves to
the normal cherubim and seraphim, and because they veil
themselves, cut themselves from the whole. Hence every

planet has a cut-off, separated light. It is incorrect to say that the planets only have light borrowed from the sun; every planet has its own light, but it has cut it off, keeps it hidden within itself, and develops it for its own independent inner life of light. We shall see that each planet only shares this light with its own beings, belonging to the kingdoms of nature on the planet in question. The light to which they ought to open themselves, which they ought to take up from outside, is brought to them by the cherubim and seraphim from the sun, but to this light they close themselves, and throw it back. Seen in cosmic space, they are stars that have no light of their own. Thus, as it were, a notch is formed with the light that flows in from the sun and the planet throws itself against the light that flows in from the sun, arresting it and throwing it back.

For occult vision, therefore, what we observe in the stellar world is absolutely different from what it appears to physical astronomy. What exists for the latter is nothing but a description of a *maya*, and only behind this *maya* does the truth lie; for the truth behind the material world is the spiritual world. In reality, the material world does not exist at all. What is called the material world is the interplay of the forces of the spiritual world.

Today we have tried to describe how a planetary system such as ours actually arises. Very little is really known in the external world, in the world of physical science, of the origin of such a system; for though physical science imagines that a planetary system arises from a sort of massing of etheric substance, the first fundamental principle, which ought to hold good in all natural science, is omitted. How often are children told at school—I do not know whether it is done here, but at least in Central Europe they are always told—that, according to the Kant-Laplace system of the origin of the world, a mass of original matter was in rotation and from this then the separate planets split off. (There may be some little improvement in that today, but the principle is the same.) And, in order that this may be quite clear and comprehensible, the children are shown by means of a little experiment how easily a planetary system can be formed. A large drop of some oily substance that floats on water is taken, and a circle ingeniously made in the line of the equator that is pierced through with a card. Then a needle is passed through from pole to pole, and one begins to turn, and behold, a pretty little planetary system arises out of the drop of oil. Quite in accord with the Kant-Laplace theory of the origin of the world, little drops separate off and rotate, while the big drop, the sun, remains in the center. What is more natural than to represent this to young people as a visible proof that this was also once enacted in the great cosmic spaces. But in so doing an important error is made, one which ought never to be made in natural science. There are certain conditions that ought never to be forgotten in making experiments. A scientist who forgets conditions without which no experiment can come about does not describe it accurately even according to natural science. If you omit any essential condition you are not describing it correctly according to natural science. The essential condition in the origin of this planetary system is that the teacher should stand there and make it revolve, otherwise the whole system could not originate! The Kant-Laplace theory would thus only be possible if those who believe in it could at the same time supply a gigantic teacher in cosmic space who would revolve the whole etheric mass. Perhaps not always, but often, people notice even small errors in logic, but capital errors, such errors as those that, in their effects, extend to the whole conception of the cosmos, are not remarked.

Now, there is no great teacher outside, making the axis of the world revolve, but there are the individual beings of the various hierarchies who, through the interplay of their forces, bring about the distribution and regulation of the movements of the different heavenly bodies. This should be the answer to those who would believe that the ordinary materialistic theory—as expressed in Kant-Laplace, or in later hypotheses—is sufficient to explain the cosmic system, and that it is unnecessary to consider anything else, as do the occultists. To those people who from a materialistic standpoint object to this living interplay of the hierarchies, we must again reply: with the capital error in logic that must be made by all materialistic cosmic hypotheses we cannot reach our goal; for it is impossible to explain a planetary system without calling to one's aid what occult vision can actually see. It is certainly abundantly proved to occult vision that what must be described with the physical senses is indeed, considered in its reality, something quite different. What the eye sees is really nothing but the reflected light, which is thrown back, because, when the seraphim and cherubim carry the light of the sun into cosmic space, the luciferic cherubim and seraphim throw themselves against them, so to speak, and insert darkness into the substance of the sunlight, cutting off the light within and claiming for each of the planets a light of its own.

These thoughts, now given out on the basis of occult observation and occult investigation, were first expounded in the post-Atlantean period in a sublime way by the great Zarathustra to his pupils. Everything that is rayed down by the beings of the higher hierarchies centered in the sun—rayed down from the sun into cosmic space in the way just described—all this was ascribed by Zarathustra to the Spirit whom he named Ahura Mazda, or Ormuzd. This Spirit, who carried the forces of his being from the center-point of the sun into the periphery, was everywhere opposed by the abnormal spirits of the different hierarchies, which in their totality, form the kingdom of Ahriman. We shall see, however, that—with regard to the planetary system—we must separate the kingdom of Ahriman from that of Lucifer. We shall have more to say about this; but at the conclusion of this lecture, attention must be drawn to the fact that Zarathustra in his own way symbolically pointed out to his pupils this connection of the Light of Ahura Mazda, or Ormuzd, streaming out from the Sun, and of the kingdom of Ahriman embedded within it. Zarathustra said: "What proceeds from the sun we represent symbolically by what the seraphim and cherubim carry, that is, by the light. What is hurled against the light in opposition by all the abnormal spirits of the higher hierarchies, the notch thus hollowed out, we represent by what is accepted as darkness." (That is, an individual light imprisoned within, manifesting externally as darkness.) This darkness, Zarathustra represented as a kingdom of Angramanyu, or Ahriman. Thus we see how this teaching that originated in Asia Minor and is in a sense given to us once more today was met first in the civilization of Zarathustra. What always fills us with such significant feelings with regard to the evolution of humanity is that we ourselves come upon certain things which, even if they are not traditional and may not be observed in the akasha chronicle, are furnished by the results of contemporary occult investigations and by what we can rediscover in the great teachings of antiquity. And only when we permeate ourselves with the truth to be found today in occult investigation—and when this same truth shines toward us from the old teachers and leaders of humanity—only then do we acquire a right relation to these leaders of humanity. Only then do they become living to us, only then do we understand them rightly. Then the evolution of humanity reveals itself to us as a mighty discourse held by the spirits who now not only resound forth to one another in space, but also interpret one another in the successive periods of time, completing one another and leading the stream of civilization on into the future.

LECTURE SEVEN

Y OU WILL HAVE UNDERSTOOD from the former lectures that when we gaze at the planetary system, at the starry heavens, our physical vision only perceives *maya*, the great illusion. We reach reality, actual reality, only when we gradually attain knowledge of the spiritual beings at work in the various heavenly bodies. We began these studies by making the attempt to learn about the individual spiritual beings at work in cosmic space, in the stellar system. We sought to know these spiritual beings as such—in other words, we had to become acquainted with the various beings of the three hierarchies standing above humanity. You will have noticed that we approached the beings of these hierarchies by pointing out the ways in which occult consciousness actually penetrates to a sort of perception of the beings in the supersensible world who are directly or even indirectly exalted above humanity. We tried to follow an inner, a mystic-esoteric path in order to gain some idea—a purely spiritual-psychic idea—of the character of the beings of the higher hierarchies. Only in the last lecture did we try to turn a little from the inner to the outer, so to speak, and try to show how, by means of a working-together of a duality in the hierarchies—a duality of normal and luciferic beings—the actual external forms of the stars visible to the senses came into being. Before proceeding further with our occult, esoteric, mystical considerations I should now like to approach from another side, namely, the side that is connected with ordinary consciousness. This brings us again to the paths we followed earlier. In considering this more external path—which starts from facts known to normal consciousness—we shall in any case have to refer to much in the earlier lectures.

When we look out into cosmic space with our ordinary, normal consciousness, we discover first of all heavenly bodies of various kinds. These have indeed been differentiated and described by external, materialistic astronomy. Today, we will devote our attention to what in a planetary system is, to a certain extent, visible to external consciousness. We have there the planets themselves, with the fixed star, the sun, as their ruler; and circling the planets we have their moons (speaking of our earth, we have our own moon). But within the planetary system we also have those remarkable stars that are so difficult for external consciousness to place in the collective picture of the system—the meteoric and cometary bodies. We will, to begin with, look away from everything else in the stellar systems and fix our attention upon the following quaternary in a planetary system: the planets, the fixed stars, the moons, and the comets. Let us be quite clear concerning the obvious fact that, to ordinary consciousness, only the planet itself—and, indeed, only the particular planet on which ordinary consciousness functions—is perceptible. Thus to the Earth-dweller the Earth is the planet. All the rest is at first only observable in its most external nature to normal consciousness. With the hypotheses given us by occult-esoteric methods we will now pass on to the external classification normal consciousness provides. We have already classified the human being in the ranks of the beings who stand, as it were, above us, as on the lowest step of the ladder of the hierarchies. We then ascended to the three categories of the third hierarchy, and described the beings known to Western esotericism as angels or *angeloi*, archangels or *archangeloi*, and spirits of the age *or archai*. Standing above these, as the second hierarchy, we have those beings we have described as spirits of form, spirits of motion, spirits of wisdom; and, above these again, the spirits of will or thrones, the cherubim, and the seraphim. Only when we fix our attention in this way upon the ranks of the spiritual beings—the steps, as it were, of the ladder of the different beings of the hierarchies—are earthly relationships brought into esoteric consciousness. Indeed, as we have seen, if we wish fully to consider humanity and everything that pertains to us on this planet, we must think of ourselves in relation to all these beings. We saw, in the last lecture, that the phenomena of humanity and our planet are not to be explained spiritually unless we fix our attention on these beings. We have seen that, from human beings to the spirits of the age, we are concerned with beings who, in the first instance, play their part in the human, historical process of civilization. Thus we must regard the beings of the third hierarchy as bringing humanity forward, step by step, in its earthly development—as leading the evolution of civilization. Further, we have seen that, while these beings of the third hierarchy remain above, certain of their offspring, whom we have called nature spirits, descend into the world of nature and work there. We have also seen that when we turn our attention to the planets themselves, they cannot be explained unless we think of their forms as determined by the spirits of form; their inner mobility and activity by the spirits of motion, and their consciousness by the spirits of wisdom. This only refers to the inner part of the planet, the inner part of the earth, the part which belongs to humanity.

Seraphim
Cherubim

Thrones
Spirits of Wisdom

Spirits of Motion
Spirits of Form

Spirits of the Age
Archangels

Angels
Humanity

We have seen, too, that the planet would be still if only beings up to the rank of the spirits of wisdom were active. We must ascribe to the spirits of will the fact that it moves and has an impulse to movement; and the regulation of movement in the whole planetary system we must ascribe to the cherubim. We have in this way put together the whole planetary system, for while the movements of the individual planets are so ordered that together they comprise the system, it must be presumed that the whole is directed from the fixed stars. And what speaks from the planetary system to cosmic space—to the neighboring planetary system—we have in the seraphim. We could compare this with the fact that people do not live only for themselves, or simply in a social connection—this could be compared with the directing of the spirits of will—but rather understand one another by their speech. So there is similarly mutual understanding between one planetary system and another by means of the seraphim. The seraphim are to the whole system what corresponds to language that draws and holds people together, and leads them to agreement. The seraphim carry messages from one planetary system to another, and give information of what takes place in one planetary system to the other system. By this means the world of planetary systems is integrated and forms a whole.

We were obliged to instance these successive grades of the beings of the hierarchies, for all the forces and activities proceeding from these hierarchies are perceptible in the collective phenomena of humanity on its planet. Occult vision teaches us that just as this whole system of beings has to do with the Planet Earth, so a similar system likewise belongs to other planets. When, with all the means at our disposal, we direct our occult vision to the other planets of our own planetary system, we find that we have the same experiences approaching the planets as we do when we approach the cherubim, seraphim, or thrones. In other words, everything I have described as necessary in order to raise ourselves to a being of the rank of the cherubim, seraphim, or thrones—insofar as they cooperate in events on earth—all this we find when we direct our spiritual vision to Saturn, or to other planets of our system. We must proceed exactly in the same way as far down as the spirits of motion. Seraphim, cherubim, thrones, spirits of wisdom— the results for occult vision are the same as for all the individual planets of our planetary system. Whether we direct our observation to Mars, Jupiter, Mercury, or Venus, we find the same results as when we fix our attention on the activities of these particular beings. On the other hand, we no longer find the same results for the other planets of our system as regards the activity of the spirits of motion and the spirits of form. In other words, if we try to direct our occult vision to another planet, to Mars, for instance, and ask, How do the seraphim, cherubim, thrones, and spirits of wisdom work upon Mars? The answer is: They work on Mars just as they do on Earth. But if we ask the same question with regard to the spirits of motion and form, this is no longer the case. The activities of these two categories of higher hierarchies differ from one another as regards the individual planets. We must make this distinction: Every planet of our planetary system has its own spirit of form, its own spirit of motion.

Now we can also direct our occultly developed vision to the sun itself, the fixed star. If we wish to know the fixed star in its own being, we must take care that in our observation of it we do not confuse it with what chiefly has significance not for the fixed star but for its surrounding planets. Let us understand correctly. In a previous lecture I stated that all these beings of the higher hierarchies, down to the spirits of form, actually work together in the cosmic system as a sort of council having its residence in the sun. I said that the sun is actually the center of activity of all these spirits. Now, when we state that Mars, for instance, has its own spirit of form, as has Jupiter, and also the Earth, we must imagine—if we wish to speak in pictures (and in relation to these exalted conditions everything is more or less a picture)—that although the sun is always actually the seat, the center, of the activities of the spirits of form of Mars and Jupiter and so on, and although they work from there, from the fixed star, their sphere of action on Mars is, so to speak, allotted to the spirits of form from the sun. They work upon Mars from the sun; other spirits of form work upon the Earth, others upon Jupiter. What they perform is an activity for the benefit of the whole system. We will not ask what is accomplished from the sun, from the fixed star, for the benefit of the planets, but rather what takes place in the realm of the fixed star itself for its own beings, for the actual evolution of the beings belonging to the fixed star.

We can best understand this matter if we compare it with what one does as one human being for another; we cannot regard this activity as directly meaning something for one's own development—it is done for the benefit of others. This particular activity of the spirits of form and the spirits of motion benefits the planetary system. But if we ask, Apart from the fact that the fixed star is surrounded by planets, how does evolution take place upon the fixed star itself as a separate entity? What contributes to the evolution of the beings of the fixed star itself? Then we actually come to the same boundary. If we direct our occult vision to the fixed star—in our system, to the sun—we have to say that only those spiritual beings of the higher hierarchies from the seraphim down to the spirits of wisdom have a certain power over the nature of the sun; only they work for the development of the fixed star itself and its beings, whereas the spirits of motion and form can, so to speak, do nothing for the evolution of the beings of the fixed star itself. To them is apportioned the planets that surround the fixed star in the planetary system.

Thus, if we direct our gaze to the fixed star, we must conclude: Life upon the fixed star is so exalted, so grand and mighty, that the beings developing there can associate only with beings of the sublimity of the seraphim, cherubim, thrones, and spirits of wisdom. Those spirits—the spirits of motion and the spirits of form—who are going through their evolution upon the fixed star itself are powerless to do anything for its evolution. They are not of sufficiently exalted rank; they, who are of such immense importance for planetary humanity are of no importance to the fixed star; they are powerless to work upon its development. Hence if we fix our attention on the being of the planet, and look away from the humanity dwelling upon it—on our Earth—we can say: Insofar as the planet has its place in the solar system, all ranks of beings down to the spirits of form have an influence on its development. We must reckon the sphere of influence that works upon the fixed stars as extending down to the spirits of wisdom; the sphere of influence upon the planets we have to reckon down to the spirits of form.

Now, within the planetary system there still remain two cosmic bodies, the moon and the comets, and the question now is: How do these cosmic bodies present themselves to occult vision? If directed to the moon, revolving around our Earth, what forms of activity does occult vision find there?

Occult vision finds nothing upon the moon similar to what is developed as human life upon the Earth. An evolution resembling the human is not to be found upon the moon. Nor is there any evolution to be found there that can be compared to our animal kingdom. Neither of these is to be found by occult vision upon our moon. It would, of course, be trivial and superfluous to say that no human beings incorporated in flesh walk upon the moon, nor such animals as are to be met with upon the Earth; when an occultist uses such expressions he or she means something essentially different. It certainly might be possible for something resembling the higher principles of human nature (the human I or astral body) to exist under other conditions on a cosmic body, and pass through a development there without being incarnated in a human fleshly or etheric body. That is conceivable— such conditions really do exist. It is conceivable that an evolution in a spiritual sense might take place upon the moon without the external embodiment, the external stamp of the beings resembling those of human beings; but that does not happen to be the case. Nothing like human history, like a development of beings who might even psychically resemble human beings or earthly animals, exists upon the moon. Even if we

ascend from humanity to the beings we have called the first
spiritual leaders of humanity, whom we have described as
angels in the ranks of the hierarchies—we do not find their
evolutions upon the moon. We find there no form of activity, no forces such as those that proceed from the intervention upon earth of the angels or *angeloi*. We have described
with some precision what these beings have to do for
humanity upon the earth. No such intervention takes place
on the moon. Nowhere do we find traces of any human or
animal activity, or any activity such as we could attribute to
the angels. But if we go further and fix our attention on the
forces by means of which the archangels forward human
evolution, and if we then turn our occult sight to the moon,
strange to say we find the following forces existing there.
Occult vision finds as active, existing forces on the moon
the same forces that it encounters when, contemplating
earthly evolution, it contemplates the development of a
people through its folk soul or archangel. The archangel
who guides the lives of nations spiritually is present in its
special characteristic as forces and speaks to us when we
focus our spiritual sight upon the moon. When we fix our
attention upon the nature of those spiritual beings whom
we designate as the *archai* or spirits of the age—those
beings who take charge of and lead earthly evolution from
one epoch to another: for instance, from the Egyptian civilization to the Greek, or from the Greek to our own—if we
acquire an occult vision of the forces ruling in the guidance
of evolution by the spirit of the age, we find these same distinctive forces again when we look upon what meets our
gaze from the moon. So, just as we could in the case of the
planet designate for its sphere the beings of the higher hierarchies as far as the spirits of form, so can we also set limits
to the sphere of the moon and say: The sphere of the moon
extends as far as the archangels.

Now, before we continue to study the results of occult investigation as we have done before, it will be useful for our further consideration if, from the point of view of occultism, we further compare the moon, the planets, and the fixed star. In undertaking such a comparison, it is necessary, in the first place, to acquire a true idea of what exists in us as human beings—especially in our physical bodies—in a way not taken into account by the ordinary materialistic anatomy and physiology. What does the ordinary anatomist of today do when investigating a physical body? Well, the anatomist takes a piece of the liver, let us say, then a piece of nerve or brain substance as contiguous substances and investigates them side by side, comparing the one with the other in a purely external way. The ordinary materialistic anatomist or physiologist does not take into consideration the fact that when we have before us a piece of brain substance and a piece of liver substance, we have absolutely different things. We have in one part of the human body something upon which the higher bodies, the supersensible principles, work quite differently from the way they do on another part. Thus, for instance, a portion of brain substance is so constituted that the whole structure, the whole formation could not arise if this substance had not been worked upon, not only by an etheric body, but also by an astral body. The astral body permeates and works upon the brain substance, and there is nothing in the brain substance or the nerve substance upon which the astral body, in cooperation with the etheric body, does not work. Take, on the other hand, a portion of the liver. You must imagine that the liver is also permeated by the astral body, but that this permeation does nothing for the liver, takes no part in the inner organization of the liver. On the other hand, the etheric body takes a very essential part in the organization and structure of the liver. The different human organs are in reality very different from each other. We can only study the liver when we know that in it the etheric body with its forces plays the chief part, and that the astral body, though it certainly permeates the liver as water does a sponge, has no special share in its formation or inner configuration. We can only picture the brain substance as something in which the astral body has essentially the largest share, and the etheric body only a lesser one. Again, in the whole structure of the blood system, even to the framework of the heart, the I has its essential part, while in the organization of nerve substance as such for instance—not to mention the other organs—the I takes no part at all. Thus, when we consider the human physical body in the occult sense, not in the sense of mere formulae, we have in its various organs, things, beings of quite different value, of quite different essence, altogether of quite different natures. We may say that what in human beings is the liver or the spleen depends upon higher principles at work within it. Liver and spleen are very different organs; the astral body has, in a very special manner, a strong share in the spleen, while it has hardly any share in the liver. All these things will at some time have to be studied—and indeed at no very distant date—by the physiologists and anatomists. Gradually facts will come to light in materialistic descriptions of human, animal, and plant organs which will make no sense at all if only compared as though they were peas and beans—as external anatomy and physical science do today. How something in the world and in the human being stands in relation to the spirit represents its true nature. And as it is in the human being, so it is in the heavenly system. A moon is quite different from a planet or fixed star. We have already seen that the relation of the beings of the higher hierarchies to the sun is different than it is to the moon or the planets. Consequently, in order to describe these differences, we must fix our attention on the following.

Suppose we could take out of a planetary system—as it were, peel off—all the moons of the individual planets—think away for a moment the fixed star itself and the planets, till we have only the moons remaining in the planetary system. If occult vision were so directed that it observed only what it now had before it—the moons, everything that is "moon" within the planetary system, everything in which the forces, as far down as the archangels, are the same as upon our earth in the successive evolution of humanity—if we were to do this, we should then gain a very definite impression; we should have a very definite occult experience. We can then repeat this occult experience a second time.

Now, anyone with trained occult vision can, with sufficient willpower—that is to say, having prepared oneself—think away the fixed star and the planets from the planetary system so that only the moons remain. Having done so, one must then seek for something else that gives the same impression as that connected with all the moons of a planetary system. Now, precisely the same impression is made on a person who visualizes all the moons as is made on one who looks at a human corpse, a physical body, the bearer of which has recently passed through the gate of death. Although these things appear externally as absolutely different, what appears to natural science as an external difference is *maya*. The impression made upon our occult vision when we, as human beings, stand thus with regard to all the moons of a planetary system on the one hand, and on the other stand before a physical body left behind, deserted by the astral and etheric bodies, is one and the same. From this arises the occult knowledge that the planetary system in the moons that are continually coming into existence is gradually forming its own corpse within itself. All the moons of a system which are continually being formed will constitute the corpse of a planetary system. The difference with regard to humans is that at the moment when we, with our being, pass into the condition in which the planetary system is when it forms its moons, we reject our corpse; while the planetary system keeps the corpse within itself, binds it together, and condenses the dying matter into moons. Thus it is as though we humans, when we go through the gates of death, were not to lay aside our physical body, but were to form it into some sort of organ and, by a certain power within ourselves, drag it about with us. A planetary system actually drags about its own corpse—a continually changing corpse, a corpse in the process of becoming, an evolving corpse—in its moons.

Let us now go further and try to describe the impression occult sight has when it thinks away all the moons of the planetary system as well as the fixed star and the possibly existing comets. If we fix our attention in this way upon the whole system of the planets themselves, completely concentrate ourselves upon this system of planets—make the impression clear to ourselves and imprint it upon our memory in order to describe it—we must once more, at a later moment, compare this impression with something that differs from the impression we received from the individual planets. If we search for something in our immediate earthly environment that gives us the same impression as all the planets of a system we find none other than that made on us if we allow the various animal forms to work on us. This impression is extremely difficult to gain completely; but it can be partially gained by allowing various animal forms to work upon us. One cannot in a single moment have an occult impression of all the animals on the earth—that would be too complicated—but a compromise can be made by letting a number of characteristic animal forms so work upon us that we take into consideration only the occult forces at work in those forms; then, comparing them by means of occult vision, we can gain from the form something that produces a similar impression upon us to that produced by the totality of the planets of a system. Thus, as the animal kingdom lives on earth (and insofar as we human beings have an extract of the animal body in our living body we can also draw this comparison with the living human body) and as the impression of all the forms working in the animal kingdom resembles the forces proceeding from the individual planets, we can say the following: The actual living body, the body with which a living, conscious being is endowed as in primitive humanity, or in the animals, corresponds to the system of planets of a planetary system. In other words, we have in a complete planetary system all that we call the totality of the planetary mass, the living body—the body permeated by the principle of life and of consciousness. The totality of the planets of a system is therefore the living body of the planetary system. If we consider all the spiritual beings we have described as contained in the planetary system as the spirit and soul of the system, we must then consider the totality of the planets as its living body, and the totality of the moons as the corpse of the planets, which they drag about with them.

Let us now direct our occult vision to the fixed star—in our case, the sun—and try to gain an impression of the fixed star in the way described for the totality of the moons and planets. Once we notice the impression made by the forces active in the fixed star, we can again find something in earthly conditions that can evoke a similar impression. This, again, is somewhat difficult, because this time we have to consider the plants, and we cannot reach the whole plant world of our earth. But it will suffice—comparatively speaking—if we fix our occult gaze upon a certain number of forms—plant forms—and gain the occult impression of what works and lives in plants. If we allow that to work upon our vision, it recalls the impression we received from the inner development of the fixed star.

The differences certainly become greater and greater. The resemblance of a human corpse after death to the totality of the moons is really very striking as regards the occult impression. This resemblance is also pronounced in the impressions made by the planetary world and the fixed star upon the human being. The resemblance is clearly present, but it is no longer so great as that between the discarded physical human body and the totality of the moons. However, the resemblance becomes infinitely greater if we now demand from occult vision something special; namely, when we have gained an impression of a number of plant forms, we must look away from these plants we have observed with occult vision, look away from the physical plant bodies and make use of those means the practical occultist uses when observing the etheric bodies of the plants. Thereby we make an additional observation. We noted the impression we gained from the fixed star; we then sought the similar though not yet satisfactory impression we gain from a number of plants. Now we go further—we abstract the external form of the plant and allow the etheric body within the plant to work upon us. The resemblance then increases and becomes almost as complete as that between the physical human corpse and the totality of the moons. Occult perception realizes then that, when we look up to the fixed star, what we perceive as working in the fixed star is the etheric body of the planetary system; for we actually gain the impression of an etheric body. We understand the impression the fixed star makes upon us when we observe the etheric body of the plants, where it works as yet unmixed with an astral body, where only the etheric body works in cooperation with the physical body. We then gain the knowledge that when we look at the fixed star, we actually see the etheric body of the planetary system raying down from it.

Now we can say: In the moons we have the corpse of the planetary system, in the totality of the planets we have its body, its physical body; and in the fixed star itself, raying out from it, we have the etheric body of the planetary system.

In fact, the possibility that occult vision will cling to the dead papier mâché ideas upon which all physical astronomy is based soon ceases; for this vision everywhere recognizes that the whole planetary system is permeated by life, and is a living organism. Indeed, a continual stream of etheric life flows from the fixed star to the outermost boundary of the system and back again. We have continually to consider life forces (as in living animal and plant bodies) which appear centered—I say this now by way of comparison—centered in the fixed star—as the life of the animal is centered—let us say—in the heart; or as plant life is centered in the various organs that regulate the rising and falling of the sap. In short, we have to do with a center of the planetary system, which we must seek in the fixed star.

After this, we can also direct our attention to the comets, to cometary life. Now I do not doubt that if the characteristics of the planetary system, just discussed, were heard in external science, this would be regarded as a very special folly, but that does not matter at all. Nevertheless, with regard to cometary life, things become particularly difficult because the opportunity to observe cometary life is such that a certain impartiality of occult vision is necessary in order to observe this peculiar life in the planetary system.

It must not for a moment be supposed that in the whole planetary system there is nothing except what we have now called corpse, physical body, and etheric body; for of course every part is permeated by the beings of the various hierarchies. Naturally there are spiritual-psychic forces everywhere and we need only grasp the fact that within the system are the spirits of the age, the archangels, and the luciferic beings—they all belong to it. We have now discovered in the planetary system the corpse, the physical body and the etheric body. From what we have now heard we can, of course, say that everywhere within the system there is also astral substance that is organized into beings; for there is astral substance even in the beings of the higher hierarchies.

If we describe humanity—the microcosm—as it passes before us, we say: Human beings consist of physical body, etheric body, astral body, and so on. If we describe a planetary system, we must only add something else to its lowest principle, and we must say: A planetary system consists of its moons (which are its corpse), its planets (which are its physical body), and of everything the fixed star directs (which is its etheric body). The astral body we can find there of itself; we learn to know of it by the fact that the beings dwell in it. As we humans dwell in our sheaths, so do the beings of the higher hierarchies dwell in the sheath of the corpse, in the physical sheath, and in the etheric sheath of the planetary system. We need not at first trouble about the astral body, for we already have that by means of esoteric-occult vision which is directed inward.

Now, even if you consider human life upon the earth, you will admit that by the agency of this human life—we know this from elementary spiritual science—there arise a number of astral beings, astral forms, that are actually harmful, hindering to life. From human beings themselves stream forth continually, erroneous, base, evil thoughts; these are, as we know, realities, which pass out into the astral world and continue to exist there, so that the astral sphere of a planet is filled not only with the normal substances of its psychic being, but also with this poured out astral substance. If we investigated all the harmful forces brought forth by the various luciferic spirits alone, we would find an enormous mass of harmful, astral substances in a planetary system. In a curious way occult vision, which has observed cometary life for a time, shows us that everything of a cometary or meteoric nature is forever striving to collect round itself all the harmful astral products, and to remove them out of the planetary system. We shall see furthermore in the course of these lectures how this particularly affects the harmful astral products of humanity. For example, we see that the comets carry away the noxious luciferic evils out of the planetary system. Before concluding this lecture, I should like to give you an idea of how this is done.

If I draw a planetary system with its sun, we can indicate a comet passing through it in such a way that its track crosses the system. Physical astronomy says that the comet comes from very, very far away.

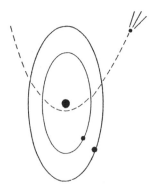

When the beginning of a thing cannot be traced, it is easy to say that it comes from very, very far away. So physical astronomy also says the comet comes from very far away and also returns to a very great distance. Now, because certain comets return periodically, physical astronomy cannot think otherwise than that these comets come from far away, pass through our system and again disappear. They are said to follow a very long path in cosmic space, and then come back again. Materialistic astronomy cannot imagine anything else. Occult vision, however, shows us as a matter of fact that, just about when the comet disappears from physical sight, it dissolves, and continues its way through a world not limited to the ordinary three dimensions of space—it no longer exists in the ordinary world. It actually disappears on the one side and appears again on the other. This is a conception of which, naturally, materialistic astronomy can make no use; it cannot conceive that a comet, when it again reappears, has not been in existence in the meantime. The anthroposophist should be able to understand something of such things. We know, for example, that the succession of physical bodies constituting human incarnations in certain respects form a complete whole, from the force aspect; and yet they are not connected physically. Thus, in short, with the exception of a few comets that really have long-drawn elliptical orbits, the comets for the most part are so formed that they come in at the one side and disappear at the other, and when they reappear they have formed themselves anew. Why? Because as a comet approaches, it exercises a power of attraction—it is, at first, merely a sort of spiritual force center; this center attracts all the harmful astral streams, develops them around itself and thus takes on form. We shall hear in the next lecture why it has a tail and a nucleus under the influence of this drawing-up of harmful astral matter. It attracts more and more of this around itself as it passes through the planetary system. In its journey toward the other side it draws this along with it until it arrives beyond the region of the planetary system—then it casts it out into cosmic space. Thereafter the center of force builds itself again at the other pole without needing three-dimensional space, takes up once more the harmful matter and throws it out on the other side. Thus we must regard cometary life as something that continually works as a thunderstorm in the planetary system, cleansing it. By the passage of a comet through the planetary system an effort is made to discharge from the system the injurious matters that have been called forth by the harmful astral radiations of beings. This is to say that we have something in cometary life of which we cannot, as in the physical and etheric bodies, find an analogy in the human being. The physical body of the planetary system is the totality of the planets. The etheric body is that which, raying out from the fixed star, streams through the system, but in the physical human being it is not the case that we carry our corpse about with us, as the planetary system does. On the other hand, the planetary has an arrangement for getting rid of the evil astral matter by means of its comets.

Now if we study what exists in the comet only as *maya*, yet which is active within it as force, it is extremely difficult to connect with it what we have learned in the course of these lectures. I have described to you, for example, how one may ascend to the thrones, and how this can only be done by studying the human will. If this study is undertaken with occult means, one can raise oneself up to the thrones. But in the comets there is nothing at all to be found, either of the spirits of wisdom or of the thrones. We find nothing in the comets that would be attainable by any other than those occult methods I mentioned in former lectures. These are methods that proceed from the fact that we study an individual who is not merely a thinking, feeling, and willing human being, but one who can give us a special impression. We described how this impression can be obtained by allowing ourselves to be influenced by someone who has behind them decades of rich experience of life; someone whose wisdom, as an extract of all this experience makes an impression upon us and does more than can be done by arguments of a logical or more rational sort. The actual power of conviction of the wisdom derived from human experience is so impressive that, developed by occult vision, one can actually see the spiritual through it, giving our occult vision a first idea of the cherubim. If we further school this occult vision on the direct, convincing effect of the unspoken wisdom and strength of such an individual, whereby what he or she has gained through life experience is displayed in his or her eyes, we then gain an understanding of the impression we need for the sphere of the seraphim. But the impression we can thus obtain does not yet lead us to the observation of the spiritual behind the comets. All this is of no avail for an occult study of the comets. Only the two methods leading to the cherubim and seraphim themselves can give us an elucidation of the comets. The sphere of the comets extends to the sphere of the cherubim. In order to understand the substance and movement of the comets, we must first know what is the nature of the cherubim and seraphim.

The evolution of the comets is dependent upon the beings of the higher hierarchies down to the cherubim; the evolution of the fixed star is dependent on the beings of the higher hierarchies down to the spirits of wisdom; the evolution of the planet itself, apart from the human beings who dwell upon it, is dependent upon the forces proceeding from the higher hierarchies down to the spirits of form; and what works on the moon is dependent on the forces that proceed from the higher hierarchies down to the arch-angels. Thus we have described the life of the planetary system from various sides, and can build further upon this foundation in subsequent lectures. To be sure, we must note particularly that we can never grasp these matters by means of merely mechanical definitions. How often has it been said that every microcosm corresponds to a macro-cosm! We may call the human being a microcosm, a solar system in miniature, but if we wish to point out the corre-spondence, we must not stop at these abstract assertions, but must proceed so far with the concrete connection that one realizes such mechanical descriptions have but an approximate value in the world. If we begin by describing the microcosmic human being from the physical body upward, as the being standing immediately before us, we must in the planetary system begin by describing the corpse, and must also find in the physical system the sub-stances of the cometary bodies, which are the external expression for the purifying astral thunderstorms in the planetary system.

LECTURE EIGHT

I T WILL BE WELL at the very beginning of today's lecture to speak of how far the physical world system, the physical cosmos, that we considered yesterday in relation to its parts, at least in reference to some of its parts, is of significance to our human outlook, to our perception and knowledge. We spoke yesterday of the life of the comet; of the life of the fixed star, solar life; of the life of the moon, lunar life; and of planetary life. In speaking of these heavenly bodies from the standpoint of ordinary consciousness, we naturally refer to the heavenly bodies visible to our eyes. In the course of our lectures we have, however, substituted something else for this system of heavenly bodies—we have substituted the study of the corresponding spiritual beings whom we have recognized as members of the various hierarchies. Perhaps what has actually been said will be made clearer if we state the following. We found the category of beings standing immediately above humanity to be the *angeloi*, or angelic beings. We also showed how, if we really wish to obtain a view of the spiritual supersensible world, we must, in a sense, organize ourselves up to these next beings above us—we must, as it were, learn to see the world with the kind of perception possessed by the angels. We can now raise the question: If such a being of the next higher category in the ranks of the hierarchies acquires consciousness of the cosmos by perception—which we call manifestation—how does the cosmos appear to it? If this question is answered, what I intended to convey will be clearer to us. Such an angelic being would really not see anything at all of what we see outside in the cosmos—all that we see is, as we know, *maya,* an illusion called up only by our human view. An angelic being would see nothing of all that we see; we must be quite clear about this. Instead of what we see, an angelic being would see and perceive in its own way, in the manner described, the various cooperative activities between the beings of the hierarchies. Instead of saying, "Over there is Mars," the being would say: "Over there cooperate (in the way we have described) certain beings of the higher hierarchies." This means that to those beings, to the angels or *angeloi,* the whole cosmic system directly appears as a sum of spiritual activities. How then would the planets and other bodies visible to our eyes appear to such a being? We may venture to speak of these matters, for indeed we could not speak at all of the whole supersensible world that lies behind the planetary system, the heavens or cosmos, if we were not able, by occult schooling, to translate ourselves to some extent into the consciousness of such a being. For clairvoyance simply means calling forth within us the possibility of seeing the world the way such beings see it. Thus to clairvoyant consciousness those forms, those light forms visible to ordinary sight as the heavenly bodies, actually disappear; they are no longer there. On the other hand, clairvoyant consciousness gains, as does the consciousness of an angelic being, an impression of what corresponds to the physical heavenly body. Clairvoyant consciousness cannot perceive the moon or Mars as these appear physically to a dweller upon earth. However clairvoyant consciousness is nevertheless able to know what exists there. I should now like to call up within you an idea of the kind of knowledge clairvoyant consciousness has of such a heavenly body.

You can gain an idea of this, at first theoretically—for only occult training can provide the practical knowledge—if you call up in your mind a memory picture, a recollection or picture concept of what you experienced yesterday or the day before. This picture concept in your soul differs from the picture concept of an object that is immediately before your eyes. You look at it only with the intensity that is necessary. If you remember this rose tomorrow, you will have a memory picture of it. If you realize clearly how the mere memory picture in your mind—in your soul—differs from what arises as a perception picture by direct impression, then it will be possible for you to understand how clairvoyant consciousness perceives the heavenly bodies. It transports itself clairvoyantly into the cosmos, and if, for instance, it transports itself to Mars, it does not know directly what would appear to sight if one were to observe the heavenly body physically, but by transporting itself thus it has something within it that cannot be described other than as a memory picture, a thought picture. And so it is with everything our ordinary, normal consciousness encounters as physical heavenly bodies in the cosmos. To clairvoyant consciousness everything appears in such a way that we have a direct knowledge that whatever we see there is actually something past, something that has had its life completely in the past. As it appears in the present, it is not really in its original, living form. It is—so to speak—like a snail shell from which the snail has gone. The whole physical system of heavenly bodies is a testimony of past times, telling only of past occurrences. Whereas we, on our earth, are contemporary with the things that appear before our physical eyes, what we see in the starry heavens is actually *maya*—for it does not represent an existing condition, but had its full significance in the past, and has remained behind. The physical world of heavenly bodies represents the remains of the past activities of the corresponding beings of the hierarchies, the aftereffects of which still enter into the present.

Let us examine the matter still more closely with a concrete example. When we observe our own earthly moon with clairvoyant consciousness—that has withdrawn from everything else and fixed itself, so to speak, only upon the moon—we get the remarkable impression that the external, physical moon disappears, and in its place something appears which gives the impression of being like a memory picture. One has the impression that what otherwise appears to the physical eye (and which, of course, is there physically, though everything physical is *maya*) gives the impression of telling of a past, just like a memory picture. And if we allow this impression that begins to tell us past things to work upon us, it says: "If what actually appears now to our occult vision were to be active, if its activity were not paralyzed by other things, our earth in its present form could not have endured the proximity of what we see there." The moon tells our occult consciousness of something that, if earthly life is to be possible at all, would not take place as it reveals itself there. Because of what the moon tells us about itself, if what is represented to us there now were not paralyzed, so to speak, by other things, we could not possibly live our present life. On the other hand, neither present day animal life on the earth, nor plant life, nor activity in the mineral world would be substantially influenced. Certain beings of the animal and plant kingdoms would certainly have to be quite different in form— we know this directly from the forces that work upon us from the moon with such vehemence. Fundamentally, however, though animal, plant, and mineral life upon the earth would be possible, human life would not. Thus the moon as we see it tells of a condition that, if it were active, would exclude human life from the earth.

I am trying to describe these things seen by occult vision as concretely as possible. I do not wish to speak in abstractions, which would enable me to relate all sorts of things; I only wish to relate things as they appear to occult vision. The impression one receives can only be compared with the following. If, let us say, all the ideas a person of thirty had when they were fifteen were suddenly to arise within their soul, and all the concepts that had been worked into their soul since their fifteenth year were to cease, the inner soul life of their fifteenth year would then be represented to their own consciousness, as it were, objectively. Then that person would be obliged to say: "If I now had within me only what was contained in my soul at that time, I could not think all I now think. The condition of soul in which I am now would not be possible." Such a person would be forced back to their fifteenth year and would see clearly that, although what was then experienced as the content of their soul could not bring about their present-day self, yet it has to do with what that person has become. In this way we can, in a certain sense, describe the impression we receive from the moon. We can say: "Before us is something that really points not to the present, but speaks of a past. Just as if I, in my thirtieth year—if I thought away everything that has developed within me since my fifteenth year—could perceive only the contents of my soul at that time, so must I now think away the possibility that there really is an earth. For the earth as it is now, comprising the requirements of human life, is not possible if what is represented by the moon were to be realized. As soon as this impression appears to clairvoyant vision, it is possible then to school this vision so that we can gain an idea, a conception, of what existed before an earth could have existed. For what we there see was possible only before the earth became possible after the condition thus perceived had disappeared.

You see, I have now described what the clairvoyant must do to travel back in the akashic records to an earlier condition of our planetary system; for by fixing occult vision upon the moon, we have recalled an earlier condition of our planetary system. If we try now to describe what we see, we can speak of the condition of our planetary system before our present earth existed. And because we must proceed in this way, we can only learn about conditions before the origin of our present earth by fixing our attention on what has remained upon the moon as a sort of memory—we have also become accustomed to call the preceding condition of our earth a moon condition. We can, however, only gain a complete elucidation of all the circumstances if we leave the clairvoyant state that we have developed for the purpose of obtaining a sort of memory picture of the planetary condition and, passing from this into the ordinary condition of consciousness, try to make clear to ourselves where the difference lies. The difference is ascertained by trying to bring the two impressions into a sort of harmony, and this bringing into harmony is only possible by first looking away from the moon—for the ordinary external vision of normal consciousness does not tell us much about the moon. You know, indeed, that external astronomy tries to tell us all sorts of things about the moon, but external observation in general does not tell us much. Rather for the sake of comparison we must make use of a certain clairvoyant observation of our own earth as it is at present, as a heavenly body upon which we ourselves walk. If we shut off everything physical which appears before our eyes in the various kingdoms of nature and observe our earth clairvoyantly, we see that this earth beneath our feet and around us, as a physical planet, reveals itself as a further development of what existed as the moon. When we compare the two impressions, we may ask: How has the one condition grown out of the other? And then, so to speak, there arises before clairvoyant vision the work that has been accomplished in order that the old condition of our earth might pass over into our present earth condition. We then have the impression that this transition has been brought about by one or several of those spiritual beings whom, in the ranks of the hierarchies, we have called the spirits of form. By this we gain a possibility of penetrating into the growth of the planet, into its earlier conditions. The question now is: Can we look back still further?

We must go into these considerations so that we shall understand in the right sense the spiritual beings who participate in the work on these heavenly bodies.

As a second attempt in occult observation we must once more look away from our earth—and also from our moon, from all that is of lunar nature in the whole planetary system—and, as far as we can, transfer ourselves into the conditions of one or several of the other planets, and compare their conditions one with another. I am referring now to actual facts which can be apparent to our clairvoyant consciousness. Clairvoyant vision can be directed to other planets of our planetary system—even if perhaps not simultaneously, which circumstances often do not permit—and can become aware of the impressions given by other planets of our system. If we thus observe a planet, or several together, we do not yet gain much, for we do not yet gain a clear conception of them; but we at once gain this if we proceed in a certain way with these clairvoyant impressions. I will once more give a comparison that will make clear what I actually mean.

Suppose you were to remember something you experienced in your eighteenth year, and were to say to yourself: "In my eighteenth year I took up a standpoint with regard to this experience for which I was ripe at that time. I shall perhaps be clearer about the matter if I call to mind another experience. In my twenty-fifth year I experienced something else connected with the same fact—I will now compare the two impressions one with another." Try to make clear to yourself what you can gain in life by comparing things that belong together but are apart from one another in time, and you then gain a general impression in which the one will always throw light on the other. By means of such a comparison you will actually call up and create a sort of arithmetical method, a quite new concept from the cooperation of your two memory pictures. That is what clairvoyants must do after succeeding in allowing their vision to be impressed—let us say—by Mars, Mercury, Venus, or Jupiter. They must now consider these separate impressions, not individually but in relation and connection with each other. They must let them work upon one another, bring them into relation with each other. If they undertake this work they will gain the feeling that through the comparison of these impressions they again have something like a memory concept of the planet system. This again is not a condition possible at that present time, but one that must have been possible in the past; for it expressed itself as something that, as I described for the moon condition, was the cause of what now exists in the planetary system. The impression obtained in this way has really infinite peculiarities.

What must thus be related in what must seem to be very dry concepts is really one of the most wonderful impressions one can possibly have, but here again, if we wish to describe the characteristics of this impression, we can only do so by means of a comparison. I must admit that I could not well endeavor to describe this impression in any other way. I do not know whether you ever had the following experience in ordinary physical life. No doubt there are times when you have been moved to weeping and sadness, in pity and sympathy for the beings around you in physical life. One may have yet another impression. Certainly many among you know the impression that comes occasionally on reading an overwhelmingly arresting description in some work of art—or, for example, when you read a scene that you well know, if you would only consider a little, contains no reality, yet your tears flow abundantly. You do not stop to consider whether it is true or not, but you take what is described into your thought and your perception so that it works like a reality, and draws forth a flood of tears. Anyone who has had this experience has a faint conception of what is meant when it is said: "One is inspired by something spiritual, concerning which one has no opportunity of asking whether it is based on a physical reality; one is inspired to an impression about which one wants to know nothing, but which grieves one and throws one back upon oneself. It fills one inwardly, one is filled as by some normal act of perception of one's normal consciousness." We must speak of such an impression if we are to describe the condition that overcomes us when we compare the impressions clairvoyant consciousness receives from the individual planets. Everything we thus experience works through our inner being alone, like a soul impression; we gain a quite definite idea of what an inspiration really is when we know things for which the impulse of knowledge can only come from within. For instance, none of us really understands the content of the Gospels unless we can compare the impressions they made on us with such an impression as has just been described. For the Gospels were written from inspiration, only one must go back to their original text. Even greater and more powerful is the impression received in the manner described through a comparison of the impressions made by the individual planets. This is the first thing I should like to say about this impression. The second thing is that we cannot gain this impression undisturbed and unchecked unless we are capable, at least for a few moments—in our present cycle of time scarcely anyone is capable of this for longer—of wholeheartedly feeling nothing but sympathy and love, of driving egotism utterly and completely out of the soul; for the smallest degree of egotism united with this impression immediately works deadeningly, and in place of what I have described, we immediately reach a kind of stupefaction, a deadening of the consciousness. Our consciousness is then immediately darkened. It is therefore one of the most blessed experiences to have such an impression.

If we are fortunate enough to have it, something very peculiar occurs. The sun, as such, no longer exists for our consciousness, no matter what we may do. Just as surely as the sun exists in our other conditions of consciousness, so it no longer exists in this. The sun ceases to be something apart from ourselves, but when we begin to find our way about, we gain the impression: "We have before us a condition in which a separate sun no longer has any meaning." For again we can only have the whole which appears before our occult vision if we look away from our present-day planetary system, and focus our occult gaze only upon our present-day sun—that is, when we extinguish the physical impression of the sun. We can best do this if we try to have the occult impression of the sun, not by day, but by night. Naturally the fact that at night the physical earth stands before the sun is no reason for the occult vision to have no impression of it, for though the physical earth is impenetrable by physical eyes, it is not so for occult sight. On the contrary, if we try in clear daylight to direct our occult vision to the sun, the disturbances are so great that we can scarcely succeed, without physical harm, in gaining a good occult impression of it. Hence in the ancient Mysteries it was never attempted to allow the scholars to gain an occult impression of the sun by day; they were taught that they might learn to know the sun in its peculiar nature when it is least visible to physical eyes, namely, at midnight. The pupils were taught to direct their occult vision to the sun, through the physical earth, precisely at midnight. Hence among the many descriptions of the ancient Mysteries, you find things—which for the most part are no longer understood today—like the sentence in the Egyptian Mysteries, for instance: "The pupil must see the sun at midnight."

What has not been brought forward by dilettantism to explain by all sorts of nice, neat symbols what is meant by "seeing the sun at midnight"? People as a rule have no idea that the things imparted in occult writings are correctly understood if no attempt is made to explain them symbolically, but they are taken as literally as possible. Modern people, as a rule, only feel themselves drawn to symbolic interpretations because the consciousness of today is no longer rightly organized for the understanding of these old facts. To those who reflect more closely, it should be clear that in ancient writings it was the custom to speak accurately. I should like (parenthetically as it were) to draw your attention to one thing that might have been added to the public lecture given yesterday, with reference to Kriemhilde.[1] It was stated that after Siegfried was dead, she took

---

1. Public lecture given on April 9, 1912. "The Nature of National Epics, with Special Reference to the *Kalevala*." See Appendix II.

for herself the treasure of the Nibelung and did a great deal of good with it; but Hagen took it from her and threw it into the Rhine. When later on, in the kingdom of King Etzel, she demanded it again of Hagen, he did not disclose to her the place where it lay. You see, this passage is given circumstantially in the Nibelung saga in order to throw light on certain things. In the symbolical explanations of the saga I have found intellectual and very brilliant interpretations that are supposed to elucidate what it all signifies. The treasure of the Nibelungs has a quite different meaning in them all. I admit that the intellectual labor brought to bear on such explanations is sometimes overwhelming—the treasure of the Nibelungs is generally explained as being the symbol for something spiritual. But, in the first place, it is very difficult to heal the sick with mere symbols. In the second place, one cannot conceal a symbol from anyone, even from Kriemhilde, by throwing it into the Rhine; at least I cannot very well imagine a symbol of the sort many expounders allege this to be, being sunk in the Rhine. Altogether it is very difficult for me to imagine how a thing that is only to be symbolically explained could be taken away from someone externally. Everyone who understands these things knows it was a question of something very special, something we should now call a talisman—an entirely physical talisman, compounded in such a way that it was entirely composed of gold. This gold was, however, only to be extracted from alluvial deposits left by the water in an estuary, and the whole power of this alluvial gold was compressed into the form—and now comes the symbol—into the form of this talisman. The effect of it on Kriemhilde was that it produced in her the forces by which she could heal the sick, and so on. Hagen could actually conceal this talisman from her, and later refuse to reveal the hiding place. Thus one has really to do with a physical thing—with a quite real thing in which occult powers existed only through the special nature of its composition. I have given this as an example, to show you how one must often understand things in the old writings.

So we must take the expression "seeing the sun at midnight" quite literally. Thus we can best acquire an occult impression of the sun if we are not disturbed by physical impressions; that is, if we see nothing of the sunlight at all but observe the sun at night. We then gain an impression of the present-day sun, which to a very great extent resembles what is obtained by the impression previously described. Through all that I have described to you there results an impression of a still earlier condition of our planetary system to which our earth also belongs, a condition when the sun was not yet separated, but when the whole planetary system was, in a sense, Sun, and contained within it the substance of our earth. This condition, which at the same time was that of our earth, is therefore designated as the Sun-condition. So that we say: Before our earth became earth it was in a Moon-condition; before it was Moon it was in a Sun-condition.

An approximate impression of a yet earlier condition of our earth planet can be obtained if we try to gain an occult impression of that category of heavenly bodies of which we spoke at the end of our last lecture—the comets. To describe this more accurately would absorb too much of our time, but in method it is very like what has been already described. If we now compare what we gain by the occult perception of cometary life with our concept of it—it is now a question of having to form a certain concept, for we cannot very well compare the memory concept thus obtained with anything at the present time—we receive an immediate impression (beyond this one cannot go) of having reached a condition lying still further back than the Sun condition, which for certain reasons is called the Saturn condition. Thus you see that the inner experiences we may have about the planetary system are decisive to occultists for the concepts they form concerning it.

We will now leave the planetary system for a little while. Everything I have till now brought forward has been mentioned with the aim and object of culminating in a general description of the modes of action of the spiritual beings in the heavenly bodies. Since, the heavenly bodies are, as it were, built up from the kingdoms of nature, we must also create, at least approximately, an idea—from the standpoint of the occultist—of the immediate facts revealed to occult vision when we allow the separate kingdoms of nature to work upon us. Let us proceed to the consideration of the kingdoms of nature, beginning with the human being.

You know that when we observe human beings we find that they consist of physical body, etheric body, astral body, and what we call I-ness, the "I" itself. Where is this four-membered human being to be found, according to anthroposophical observation? Well, this four-membered human being is in the physical world, for everything that has now been related of the human being takes place in the physical world. We will now pass over to the animal world. If we consider the animal, it is quite certain that we find the physical body of the animal in our ordinary sense world, as we do that of the human being. Of that there can be no doubt. We must, however, also ascribe an astral and an etheric body to the animal; for we ascribe an etheric body to humans in the physical world because it would not be possible for our physical body to exist alone in the physical world. This is evident as soon as someone passes through the gates of death. The physical body is then left alone in the physical world and falls to pieces; it is given over to its own forces. As long as a person lives, there must be a combatant present to carry on a perpetual battle against the crumbling away of the physical body, and this combatant is the etheric body, which is really only visible to occult consciousness. The same circumstances also prevail in the animal, so that we must ascribe to it an etheric body in the physical world.

	HUMAN	ANIMAL	PLANT	MINERAL
Higher Devachanic World				I
Devachanic World			I	Astral Body
Astral World		I	Astral Body	Etheric Body
Physical World	I Astral Body Etheric Body Physical Body	Astral Body Etheric Body Physical Body	Etheric Body Physical Body	Physical Body

Now because it is clear to us that facts and things not only affect people but mirror themselves in us, calling up something we may call an inner reflection, we therefore ascribe to the human being an astral body, which is visible to occult vision. It is exactly the same in the case of the animal. Whereas the plant does not utter any cry when an external impression is made on it, the animal expresses itself in a cry; that is, an external impression produces an inner experience. Occult vision teaches us that this inner experience is only possible when an astral body is present. Yet to speak of an I in the animal as a phenomenon of the physical world has no meaning except to certain modern natural philosophers, who live entirely according to analogy. If one judged merely from analogy one could maintain all sorts of things. There are even certain theosophists today who were filled with respect when a certain well-known student of nature, Raoul France, ascribed a soul to plants, and did not differentiate between what we call a soul in the animal and in plants. For instance he considered, and this is quite correct, that there are certain plants which, when a little insect comes near them, fold their leaves together so that they draw it in and devour it. This external observer then reflects: "Wherever facts appear in nature externally, analogous to the taking in of nourishment and consuming it, there must be something resembling the beings which, from something of an inner soul nature, take in such things and consume them." Now I know something that also attracts little creatures, but to this the modern natural philosopher would certainly not ascribe a soul; I mean a mousetrap, baited with bacon. This also attracts little creatures, and if we proceed according to the methods of these nature philosophers, then just as they attribute a soul to the plant called Venus's-fly trap, so must we attribute a soul to the mousetrap, for it attracts mice when well baited with bacon. All these investigators, who do not merely judge by the external, ought not to lose the longing that exists in many spiritually minded people, and be content if very little is said of the spirit.

In this connection, in German literature—as many say—much of beauty has been brought to light, but, as the occultist would say, "A great deal of nonsense has been talked." Just as little as one can speak of a soul nature resembling the animal soul dwelling in the Venus's-fly trap or any other plant, can one with unbiased vision say of any animal that it has an I. The animal has no I in what meets us on the physical plane. Only occult investigation could lead us to the I of the animal; for this is not to be found in the same region as the I of the human being. The animal I is only to be found apart from the physical body, so that we actually become acquainted with a completely different world when with occult vision we ascend to the animal I. If we do not care to make all kinds of diagrammatical divisions, we begin to say: The world consists of physical plane, astral plane, mental plane, etc. But since there is not much to be gained by such verbal designations, we must then proceed in other ways. I have found even in theosophical books a great deal said about the expression "Logos," but I have not found any clear concept called forth of what the Logos really is. As a rule I found that the writers of these books only knew that this word Logos consists of five letters, but as soon as one tried to arrive at real definite concepts on which one could fix one's mind, the concepts disappeared in smoke. For by relating all sorts of things, such as that the Logos "spins," and so forth, a consciousness desiring to be concrete does not know what to make of it. Whatever the Logos may be, a spider it certainly is not; neither can its activity be described as a web.

Thus, it is not good to begin with abstractions to call up concepts in speaking of things extending beyond the physical sphere of humanity. It is somewhat different when occult vision seeks in the animal for what in humans reveals itself in the physical world in all human actions and proceedings—namely, the I. If we seek the I for the animal, we will not find it in the world where the physical, etheric, and astral bodies of the animal dwell, but in a supersensible world that appears nearest to the sense world as soon as one draws aside the veil of the ordinary world. So we can say: We can find the I of the animals in a world of a supersensible nature. There it appears as a reality, but in the physical world this animal I does not appear to us as an individuality; we can only understand it here if we direct our attention to a group of animals—a group of wolves or of lambs, and so on. Just as a single soul belongs to our two hands, our ten fingers, and our feet—a soul that has within it its own I—so does a group of animals of one species possess such an I but we do not find it in our physical world; it only reveals and manifests itself in the physical world. The ordinary abstract materialist of the day says: That alone is a reality in the animal which we see with physical eyes—and if we form a concept of a wolf or of a lamb, these are just ideas and nothing more. For the occultist that is not so; these are not mere ideas that live within us, they are reflected pictures of something real which is not, however, on the physical plane, but in a supersensible world. With a little reflection, it is evident that even on the physical plane, beyond what can be perceived by the senses there still exists something that cannot be perceived in the physical world, but yet has a meaning for the inner relations of the forces of animals. I should like those people who, for instance, take the concept of wolf as an idea that does not correspond to any reality, to attend to the following experiment. Suppose we take a number of lambs—the wolf is known to feed upon lamb—and feed a wolf with them long enough for the whole physical matter to be transformed, according to what natural science has ascertained—so that the wolf, during the time in which his physical corporeality is being replaced, has been fed only upon lamb, that the wolf has nothing but lamb within it. All you then see as physical matter in the wolf proceeds from nothing but lamb; now try to find out whether the wolf has become a lamb. If it has not, you have no right to say that the concept that you have of the wolf is limited to what can be perceived physically, for there is something supersensible in it. This cannot be met with until we enter the supersensible world; there it becomes evident that just as our ten fingers belong to the one soul, so do all wolves belong to a group I. The world in which we find the group I's of the animals we designate concretely as the astral world.

Now as regards the plants, a similar observation shows that in the physical world we find nothing of the plant but its physical and etheric bodies. Just because the plants have only their physical and etheric bodies in the physical world they do not cry out when we injure them. We must therefore say: Only the physical and etheric bodies of the plant exist in the physical world. If with occult vision we investigate, which we do by simply transplanting ourselves into that world in which is the group I of the animals, we find something very characteristic with regard to the plant kingdom: we find that there is pain even in the plant world. This is certainly felt when we tear plants out of the ground by the roots. The collective earth-organism feels pain resembling that which we feel when a hair is pulled out of our body. Other life also, conscious life, is connected with the growth of plants. Try to imagine the sprouting forth—I have already touched upon this question during these lectures—the pushing forth of the shoots of the plants from the earth in spring; this springing forth corresponds to a feeling in certain spiritual beings—beings belonging to the earth and participating in its spiritual atmosphere.

To describe this feeling we may compare it with the perception one has at the moment of passing at night from the waking condition to that of sleep. Just as consciousness gradually dies down then, so do certain spirits of the earth feel when the plants spring forth in spring. Again, in the gradual fading and dying of the plant world, certain spiritual beings connected with the spiritual atmosphere of the earth have the same feeling as people have when they awaken in the morning. Thus we can say: There are certain beings connected with the organism of our earth who have the same feelings that our own astral body has in falling asleep and waking. Only one must not compare these abstractly. It would, of course, seem much more actual to compare the springing forth of nature in the spring with waking—and the dying-down of the plant world in autumn with falling asleep, but the reverse is correct: namely, the beings we are now considering feel a sort of awakening in autumn, but a sort of falling asleep at the springing forth of the plants in the spring. Now these beings are none other than the astral bodies of the plants, and we find them in the same region as the group souls of the animals. The astral bodies of the plants are to be found on the so-called astral plane.

Now we must also speak of an I of the plants when we observe them occultly. We find this I of the plants again in like manner as a group I, as something belonging to a whole group or species of plants, just like the group I's of the animals; but in vain should we look for the group-I's of the plants in the same sphere as the astral bodies of the plants and the group I's of the animals. We must pass into a still higher supersensible world; we must raise ourselves from the astral plane into a world that we perceive as still higher. Only in such a world can we find the group I's of the plants. In investigating this world we may again give it a name. To us it is first of all characterized by the fact that the group I's of the plants are there, although there is much in it besides these. We designate it—though names have nothing to do with the matter—as the *devachanic* world.

It is easy to see in the physical world that we have only the physical body of the minerals. Hence the mineral appears to us as inorganic, devoid of life; on the other hand, we have its etheric body in the same world in which are the group I's of the animals and the astral bodies of the plants. But even here we can find nothing of the mineral nature that reveals sensation. Yet even the mineral reveals itself as living. We learn to know the long-enduring life of the mineral, its growth and the self-development, so to speak, of the ores and the like—in short, on the astral plane we become acquainted with the various forms of mineral life on our planet. When we come across an individual mineral, we learn to recognize that it is not very different from our own mineral-like bones which yet are connected with our life. Thus everything mineral is also connected with a living being, but that living being is only to be found on the astral plane. The etheric body of the mineral, there-fore, is to be found on the astral plane. Now if we halt occultly, as it were, in that world in which are the group I's of the plants, we observe that the mineral kingdom is also connected with something in which feeling is possible, something astral. When stones are broken in a quarry, no perception of this is noticed on the astral plane, but on the devachanic plane it is immediately evident that when stones are pulverized and the parts fly asunder something like a feeling of well-being, a sort of enjoyment actually appears. That is also a feeling, but it is in contradiction to the feeling that animals and human beings would have in such a case. Were they to be smashed to pieces, they would suffer pain; with the mineral the reverse is the case. When it is crushed it is conscious of a feeling of well-being. If we dissolve cooking salt in a glass of water, and follow with vision directed to the devachanic world how the salt forms into crystals, we see that this causes pain: we feel that there is pain at the point of union. This is everywhere the case in mineral life when fluids, through crystallization, form into solids. This in fact is what happened to our earth, which was at one time in a softer, more liquid condition. Solid matter has gradually been formed out of the fluid, and we now walk about on solid ground and drive our ploughs into it. In so doing we do not give the earth pain; it feels it to be good. But it did not please the beings connected with the earth—and that as astral kingdom belong to the planet—to be compactly welded together in order that human life might become possible on the planet. The beings that as astral bodies stand behind the rocks had to endure pain upon pain. In the mineral kingdom the beings, the creation, suffer as the earth progresses. It gives one a very strange feeling when, after recognizing this from occult investigation, one turns again to the celebrated passage, written by an initiate: "All creation groaneth and travaileth in pain together, waiting for the Redemption; waiting for the adoption of the state of childhood." Such passages as this in writings based on occult vision are as a rule read carelessly, but when one reads them with occult vision, then, for the first time, one knows that though they yield a great deal to even the simplest mind, they give still more to those who can perceive all, or at least a great deal, of what is contained in them. The sighing and groaning of the mineral kingdom has to be, because the process of the civilization of our earth needs solid ground under its feet; that is what St. Paul represents when he speaks of the sighing of creation.

All this takes place in those beings that lie behind the mineral kingdom as its astral body which we find in the devachanic world. The actual I, the real group I of the mineral kingdom is to be sought in a higher world, which we will call the higher devachanic world. Here only do we find the group I's of the mineral kingdom. You must emancipate yourselves entirely from the conception of identifying what we call the astral body of a being with the astral world. With regard to the minerals, their astral body is to be sought for in devachan; on the other hand, their etheric body is in the astral world. The group I's of the animals are on the astral plane, and the astral body of the animals on the physical plane. We must say of the world, as we know it: We must not identify what we recognize as the individual principles of beings with the corresponding worlds, but must accustom ourselves to presuppose differentiations among the various beings. A more accurate occult discernment makes this quite clear. Thus provisionally we have to find only the group souls of the minerals in a higher devachanic region.

We have now spoken of the different beings of the various kingdoms of nature in their relation to the higher worlds, and this alone can give us a foundation for seeking the relations of these various kingdoms of nature to the creative beings of the hierarchies who are active and working in the world, as we have now learned to know them.

LECTURE NINE

·····································

I N OUR LAST LECTURE, we pointed to the relation between
the spiritual forces at work in the beings of the kingdoms of
nature on earth and what we see externally. Today, let us
recapitulate briefly how that has been worked out; for it is
necessary to examine more closely the things that form an
essential part of our theme, as they will lead us to what is to
be the culminating point of our lectures: a comprehension
of the living cooperation of the beings of the various hierarchies and their offspring in the heavenly bodies and in the
kingdoms of nature. We said that human beings have the
four principles of their being active on the physical plane:
the physical body, etheric body, astral body, and I. Then we
drew attention to the fact that, in the animal, three principles are active on the physical plane—the physical, etheric,
and astral bodies—while the group I is on the astral plane.
We saw also in the case of plants that only their physical
and etheric bodies are active on the physical plane—their
astral bodies work on the astral plane, and the group I on
the devachanic plane. Regarding the mineral, we found
only its physical body on the physical plane. Its etheric
body we found on the astral plane, its astral body on the
devachanic plane, and we found that in the region we designate as the higher devachanic plane dwell the group I's of
the minerals.

We will now go on to show more in detail what all this really means. Till now I have only been able to say that occult vision which raises itself to the first of the supersensible worlds lying above us does not—in relation to the animal—find in the physical world what it finds there in relation to the human being, namely, the I; for what in the human being we call the I can be found in the case of the animal on the astral plane only in the supersensible world; it is only there that it has the center of its activity. Occult science cannot ascribe an I to the animal in the physical world. It does not deny an I to the animal, but states that what can be designated as the I of an animal is only to be found in the astral world. One may easily raise objections to the fact that an I is denied to animals, even to higher animals, on the physical plane, for it might be said—and indeed often is said—that with regard to their actions animals display an extraordinary intelligence, a quite wonderful comprehension, so that much that animals do on the physical plane can be likened to what human beings do. Now, those who express themselves thus have not grasped the fundamental principles of this matter. It would not occur to anyone who penetrates into these matters to deny what we call human soul forces to animals on the physical plane.

There is no question of that. In this sphere lies the foundation of manifold mistakes and misunderstandings. Thus, misunderstanding would at once arise if a certain materialistic Darwinism were to say in our time: "Indeed you anthroposophists look at the matter as though humanity were definitely to be sought on a higher stage of spirituality than the animal, whereas we see that the animal develops intelligence, so much intelligence. So much even of a certain instinctive morality exists in the animal kingdom that what human beings have in their soul forces may well be but a sort of higher stage of what we meet with in the animal kingdom." The point of view involved here is quite false. No unprejudiced study would deny intelligence, even reason, to the animal kingdom. We need only consider such facts as that human beings arrived at the discovery of paper comparatively late in their evolution. The discovery of paper by human intelligence is represented in our historical descriptions as a very great acquisition, and in a certain respect it certainly is a sign of human progress. Yet wasps knew this art millions of years ago, for the material of which the wasps build their nests is really paper. We can therefore say: "What the human intellect as such accomplishes, the animal kingdom already possesses far, far down in its ranks." It would not occur to an unprejudiced observer to deny human soul forces, as such, to the animal. Indeed, in the realm of occultism we are even convinced that sagacity and intelligence in animals is much surer, more precise, and much more free from error than in humans. The essential point is that in humans all these soul forces relate to an I in the physical world, an I that is developing itself individually in a physical world, going through an individual development and education. Now as regards animals belonging to any one group, we know that the circle of their development depends simply on the species, the genus, to which they belong. The case of human beings who develop themselves as individuals is quite different. If we direct our gaze to the animal kingdom, we find in the animal world the most varied forms, which differ far more from each other than do the human races. Certainly we find great differences in the human races all over the earth, but if we compare these with the great differences among animals from the imperfect up to the more perfect species, we notice how powerful is the differentiation in the animal kingdom; quite different from that in humanity. On what then does this depend? We can best obtain an approximate answer if we first of all ask: What causes the variety of groups in the animal kingdom, the different species, which we find characteristically spread over the globe?

Occult vision shows us that the cause of the varieties of the animal species simply does not originate on the earth; rather the animal species receive its forms from cosmic space. Indeed the forces that produce one species come from a different part of cosmic space than those forces that produce another. The forces that construct the various animal forms stream down upon our earthly planet from the other planets of our planetary system. We may actually divide the whole animal kingdom into six or seven principal groups, and these chief groups have the highest group I's. They have the impulse for their activity in the six or seven principal planets belonging to our system, so that the forces that form the principal groups of animals work down spiritually from the planets. In saying this we have at the same time given the concrete explanation of what is actually meant when we speak of the group I's of animals. It means that in the animal dwell spiritual forces belonging to beings not to be looked for upon the earth itself, but outside the earth in cosmic space, and indeed primarily in the planetary world. The regents, as it were, of the principal group forms of animals live on our planets; they had to withdraw onto these planets in order to work down with their forces at the right distance from the earth and from the right direction. For what builds up the principal animal forms in the right way can only come from these directions in space. If the planets were to allow only these forces to stream down upon our earth, we would not actually have the multiplicity in the animal kingdom we now have, we would only have seven principal forms. Once upon a time, in far distant ages, there were only the seven principal animal forms; but these seven forms were very mobile and determinable, so soft and plastic in their formation that they could easily be transformed—one special form into another and again other forms into others. This actually occurred at a later period of time. The seven principal forms date far, far back; but then other forms appeared in addition to these and worked, as it were, either to strengthen or hinder the forces of the planets.

I shall now explain how these other forces came into being. If we direct our ordinary vision to the heavenly spaces we may easily believe that everything is actually of like form, but this is not the case. If we direct our gaze to a certain direction in space, occult vision perceives something quite different in one direction from what it sees in another. Space is by no means a homogeneous affair. It is not alike on all sides, for different forces work from the different directions of space. The whole of cosmic space is filled with spiritual beings of the different hierarchies working in different ways from various directions onto the earth. In those past ages when people had a certain original, primitive clairvoyance the following was clear to them: "If at a particular hour of the day I direct my gaze to one part of the heavens I encounter certain forces, while in another direction I encounter certain other forces." And people were also aware that from certain points precise and definite forces worked down from cosmic space that were of quite particular importance to the earth. These are all arranged in the stellar circle of cosmic space that has been called the zodiac since ancient times. People did not speak then without reason of the zodiac or animal circle; they knew why it was so called. In the heavenly spaces it is the case that forces that worked down from the planet Mars, for instance, and brought about in the still-plastic animal substance one of the seven principal forms, worked in a different way according to whether Mars stood before one sign of the zodiac or before another. The zodiac was divided into twelve signs, which represent the constellations, and according to whether the Martian forces that affect one animal form stood before Aries or Taurus, or any other constellation, their influence varied. In this way the seven different forms were modified. A number of different animal forms were thus made possible. If you consider that to this must also be added the fact that Mars, for instance, can work qualifyingly when it stands before Leo so that it supplants the Lion in relation to the Earth, or that from the other side it works qualifyingly when the Earth is between the sun and Mars, you see that there are a very great number of possibilities.

All these forces have worked together to differentiate the seven original groups of the animal kingdom so that the whole multiplicity of our animal forms on the earth arose from the fact that the forces of the planets are actually the abode of the group souls, the group I's of animals, and that these beings fulfill their tasks from these centers, for only from there can they do so. Only because that particular group soul of an animal form which was to work down from Mars selected that position in the heavens can it exercise the corresponding result upon the earth below. Here lie the forces that brought about the multiplicity of our animals. When we use the expression, "The animal group I is to be found on the astral plane," that really means that when occult vision wishes to seek the group I of any animal form, it must seek for it not on the earth, but on one of the planets. What is to be found on the earth with regard to the human being, can only be discovered by occult vision for the animal outside in cosmic space, among the planets. Just as, for instance, someone who has to accomplish something upon the earth that necessitates various standpoints must adapt himself or herself to these, so must the group I that dwells on a planet pass through cosmic space in front of the zodiac in order to differentiate its forces from there. If we bring the facts just stated into connection with the fact that the impulse for the animal forms is continually sought today in some principle of the earth itself—in the struggle for existence or in natural selection or the like— then the facts that have come into being through the efforts of Darwin, for example, are magnificent insofar as he did not go beyond the facts. Unconsciously, Darwinism has described the mobility of the original animal forms and how they were actually created from the basic forms. But, according to the whole predisposition of our time, humanity has looked away from the fact that the forces which create those forms work down from cosmic space, and that therefore the creators of the animal forms are to be sought in the world of the planets which belong to our planetary system, but are outside our earth.

If we now inquire how this matter stands in relation to human beings, we can only receive an answer by first answering that other question: Of what nature are the spirits which we have now described as the group souls of animals and which have their dwelling place upon the various planets? It is then seen that these group I's of animals are the offspring of that category of spiritual beings to which I have referred in this course of lectures as the spirits of motion. Thus we must look upon the group souls of animals as the offspring of the spirits of motion. The spirits of motion actually gave the astral body to humanity out of their own substance during the ancient Moon-condition. In order to complete the matter we may therefore say: This earth was preceded by the Moon-condition during which humans received their astral body from the spirits of motion. In other words, when the earth was Moon—the old

Moon, not the present one, for the present moon is only a detached portion of the earth itself, while the ancient Moon was an earlier incarnation of our earth—while the earth was in this ancient Moon condition, the spirits of motion hovered, as it were, over this old Moon and allowed their own substance to trickle in, to stream in to what humanity had brought over from previous conditions. So that what people acquired as astral body—which was new to them, for at that time they had only the physical and etheric bodies—was derived from the spirits of motion. The ancient Moon had disappeared; the earth had been formed; the spirits of motion had developed offspring, besides carrying on their own evolution. These are the beings we designate as the group I's of animals. They have not taken up their abode upon the earth but upon the other planets, in order to work upon the earth from there and bring forth the animal forms in the manner we have described. This is the special point in what I have stated: We can, in a certain sense, describe the group I's as offspring of the beings of the second hierarchy.

We must now put the following question: Since these offspring of the spirits of motion work down from the planets upon the animals, do similar spiritual beings work upon us, upon the human race spread over the earth? We cannot answer this regarding those spiritual beings we have cited as the normal members of the several hierarchies, but we have mentioned a special category of spirits which we have called the luciferic spirits, and we have described the relation of these to the normal spirits. In our present cycle of time there are luciferic spirits in every category of the hierarchies. Whereas the animal group souls are the normal and proper offspring of the spirits of motion, the luciferic spirits corresponding to the spirits of motion are those who resisted the normal path and have remained in opposition to the normal spirits of motion. These luciferic spirits of motion are grouped on the various planets in relation with the earth, just as are the normal offspring of the spirits of motion. They, too, have their parts assigned to them, so to speak, and have their abode apportioned to them on the various planets. Just as the group souls of animals dwell on the various planets, so also do certain luciferic spirits of motion. They have set themselves the task that really belongs to the spirits of motion—that of working formatively from the planets so that groups of corresponding beings arise upon the earth. Just as seven principal animal groups were formed, that have only been specified according to the relations described, so did the luciferic beings of motion work from the planets onto the earth to differentiate the human race, that was actually, in a certain sense, designed according to a single plan. While in the whole cosmic plan it was intended that a single human form was to arise throughout the earth, these luciferic spirits of motion worked down from the various planets and differentiated the human form all over the earth in such a way that the forms of the chief individual human races were able to come about. More details are to be found in my Christiania lectures as to the special way in which the luciferic spirits of motion work to form the different races.

Thus we have to distinguish between the offspring of the spirits of motion and the luciferic spirits of motion. But there is something else besides this! Naturally, we shall now have to ask the question: "Where are the normal spirits of motion now, who gave humanity its astral body during the ancient Moon period?" Where are those beings who attained the goal of their evolution at the time of the transition from the Moon to that of the earth? Those completely mature spirits of motion, where are they now? The peculiarity of these beings is that they too have their actual dwelling place, or rather, their field of operation upon the planets of our system; so that they do not, for instance, work directly as spirits of motion from the sun, in which they have their headquarters, so to speak, but first send out their rays to the planets and from these work back upon the earth. Insofar as we have to do with the true spirits of motion, their activity comes directly from the planets of our system—but of course everything that works from the planets from those spiritual beings belongs to the supersensible, invisible world as such. Only the effects themselves are externalized upon the earth; the results appear on the earth. What do these spirits do now for human beings who at one time, upon the ancient Moon, gave humans their astral body from their own substance? This astral body was preserved as a germ in earthly existence, and after the old Moon had disappeared and an interval had gone by, and the earth had been formed anew, this astral body once more developed from the germ. But the spirits of motion themselves have developed further, to a higher activity. Regarding their offspring, we know that they have become the group souls of animals; those that rebelled against them took part, as we know, in the differentiation of the human races. Where do the progressed, genuine, normally-developed spirits of motion now reveal themselves? An example will make this evident.

We know that each individual human being is guided by what we call his or her angel; we know that nations are spiritually led by their nation spirit or archangel (nations are quite different from races); we know that the successive periods of civilization are led by the spirits of the age, or *archai*; and, finally, we know that above the *archai* stand the category of hierarchies that we call the spirits of form; while above them are the spirits of motion. We will think of them as they are upon the earth—with the time behind them when they gave humanity the human astral body and having themselves made their proper progress. In human evolution there is something that goes beyond the character of the mere spirits of the age—something more full of significance, more important for collective humanity than the sphere of the individual spirits of the age. The spirits of the age work upon the earth for a definite period of time, but there are spiritual developments in the evolution of humanity as a whole that embrace wider spheres than that of the spirits of the age. These great epochs of humanity that extend beyond the influence of the spirits of the age have as their regent the normally developed spirits of motion who reveal themselves by their activity in the process of the growth of humanity so that they stimulate the great impulses of civilization. If we now survey human history, the history of human civilization, we see that individuals are guided by the angels or *angeloi*; nations and peoples by the archangels or *archangeloi*; certain periods of civilization are guided by the spirits of the age; and also certain spheres (as we shall see) by the spirits of form.

Then, however, we have the collective course of the different civilizations in human evolution, so that for certain long periods of time, much longer than those ruled by a spirit of the age, the spirits of motion are inspiringly active in great spheres—one spirit of motion working down from one planet at one time, another working down at another time from another planet. Thus these normally developed spirits of motion so work down from the planets that they succeed one another in the process of human evolution and reveal themselves in the great civilizational impulses in the evolution of the earth that reach out beyond the sphere of the spirits of the age. Thus, for example, from that spirit of motion who worked down from the planet that present-day astronomy calls Venus—and which ancient astronomy called Mercury (for these two names have been exchanged)—from that spirit of motion came originally that impulse of civilization which was expressed in Buddhism. Other impulses of civilization coming from beyond the mere spirits of the age came from the spirits of motion on the other planets. Thus, while from the offspring of the spirits of motion come the group souls of animals and from the luciferic spirits of motion the racial forms of humanity, these great impulses of civilization come from the spirits of motion who have attained their normal evolution. Many other impulses also come from this direction, but it is presently important to bear in mind the impulses of civilization from this point of view. Now, here you have in this development of our whole planetary system something you find mentioned among the great truths which, as every experienced student knows, are to be found in the *Secret Doctrine* of H. P. Blavatsky. Those who know find indications of this there. On one page is written "Buddha = Mercury"—that is, Buddha equals Mercury. That means the individuality who was the leader of Buddhism was traced back in occultism to the spirits of motion who work down from that planet. He is the inspirer; from him comes the influence expressed in that stream of civilization. It is indeed the case that this remarkable book, *The Secret Doctrine*, by H. P. Blavatsky brings great truths, but they must be recognized in the right way. We must not simply accept this as a book of dogmas; we must trace each single thing in it. Only then shall we recognize the greatness of this book. Of all the great truths taught by true occultists, significant intimations are to be found in the *Secret Doctrine* of H. P. Blavatsky. And when, through its inspirer, there was inscribed in the *Secret Doctrine*:—"Buddha is equivalent to Mercury"—that hinted at the great truth of which the inspirer of H. P. Blavatsky was well aware: that the individual who in his twenty-ninth year became the Buddha was able to begin to be inspired—at the time symbolically indicated as the "sitting under the Bodhi Tree"—by the spirit of motion enthroned in Mercury. This individual, from being a Boddhisattva became the Buddha. That means that his spirit was filled and inspired, not by what comes from the earth sphere, but from universal space, from the cosmos. He was thus withdrawn from the earth sphere to nirvana, that is, to a sphere in which the earth sphere no longer plays a part. H. P. Blavatsky, in her ordinary consciousness, knew nothing of many of these things, but her inspirer knew them. These things must be drawn forth from the depths of occultism, and in these subtle and great truths things must not be confused one with another. It is not my intention to assert that as soon as a Boddhisattva is raised to a Buddha, a spirit of motion alone works inspiringly upon that being; for the beings of the higher hierarchies work through a Buddha also. The essential point is that from that time onward the spirits of the lower hierarchies fell away, so that a Buddha could come directly in contact, so to speak, with those beings designated as the normally developed spirits of motion.

Now, before we consider the process of human civilization from another aspect, let us pass to the plant kingdom. In that kingdom we see that the astral body is to be found on the astral plane, where the group I's of animals also are. This leads back to the fact revealed to occult vision regarding plants—that, not only in their group I's but already in the astral body of the plant, forces are actively working down from the planetary system, from the stars. Thus, whereas in the animal the spirits of motion are only active in the group forces—in the forces that create the group forms—what belongs to the sphere of the spirits of motion works in the plant on the astral body. The offspring of the

spirits of motion belong also to this category, only they differ from the offspring of other beings because they were
formed at a somewhat different time. As offspring of the
spirits of motion they work not merely upon the I, but
upon the astral body of the plants.

We may say, therefore, that forces of the spirits of motion
or their offspring work down upon the astral bodies of
plants from the planets of our planetary system. In every
being the astral body is that which gives the impulse to
motion. Plants have only their physical and etheric bodies
on the physical plane. If any forces whatever were to work
upon plants from the sphere of the spirits of motion, these
forces would—as the astral body is not in plants, but
around them—bring about movement in the plants, though
not movements like those of men and animals, but such as
to draw forth the plants from the earth when they first
appear. When you see the forces developing in a spiral in a
plant from stipule to stipule, you then have the activity of
those forces that work down from the planets. And according to the way that the forces of the offspring of the spirits
of motion work down from one or another planet does this
peculiar line that puts forth the leaves vary. This gives a certain means of studying the actual orbits of the individual
planets through their reflection, and, when external science
has once recognized this fact, it will have to correct a great
deal of the former astronomical systems. Certain plants are
allotted to the forces of the spirits of motion who work from
Mars, others to those who are on Venus, others to those on
Mercury. According to the way they work in from one or
the other planet, they impart to the plant the movement
expressed in their spiral coil of leaves; it is the same movement the corresponding planet makes—the absolute movement it makes in the heavens. If you take an ordinary
convolvulus, in which the stalk itself is twisted, you have in

the spiral movement of the stalk an imitation of the planetary movements that proceed from the spirit of motion.
When the stalk is fixed, you have in the stipules images of
those forces that proceed from the spirits of motion of the
planets. These forces work upon the plants in cooperation
with the actual group I's, and these group I's work in such a
way that we can discover the direction of their forces simply by connecting the sun with the center point of the earth.
That is to say, together with the forces that come from the
spirits of motion, other forces work that go in the direction
of the stalk of the plant, which is always striving toward the
center point of the earth.

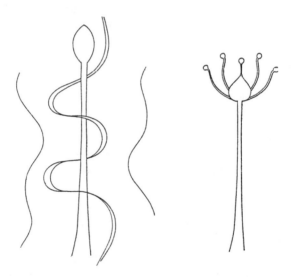

Thus we have to compose the whole plant out of what
grows toward the sun or toward the center of the earth and
what winds itself around and copies the movements of the
planets in the stipules. This corresponds, however, with the
fact that we have to seek the direct impulse of activity for
the group I's of plants in the direction from earth to sun.

That is, if we do not direct our occult vision to the planet but to the sun, we shall find the different group I's of plants. These group I's of plants are the offspring of the spirits of wisdom, just as the group I's of animals are the offspring of the spirits of motion. Thus in the group I's of plants we have to recognize the offspring of the spirits of wisdom.

In the course of these lectures I have stated that in the nature spirits we see the offspring of the third hierarchy, and that in the group I's we see the offspring of the second hierarchy. Now we come, in addition, to the spirits of the cycles of time—the rulers or regulators of the epochs. We have now reached a position in which we can allude to the functions of a certain category of such spirits of the cycles of time. At this point we can state that certain spirits of the cycles of time unite the forces of movement coming down from the planets to the plants that work spirally with the forces coming down from the sun. Both these forces are brought together at a definite time by the spirits of the cycles of time, and indeed it is at that time of the year when the plant is progressing toward its fructification that the spiral principle of movement is united with the principle that works in the stalk.

Hence, in the stamens we have the principle that works spirally, and in the ovary—in the center of the plant—we have the principle that is the continuation of the stalk. When the course of the plant is completed, that is, when the spirits of the cycles of time appointed to the plants unite their activity—the activity of the planetary spirits—with the activity of the sun-spirit, then, in the now completed plant, those organs that, till then, followed the planets spirally, are arranged in a neat circle like the stamens, while the stalk itself elongates and terminates in the ovary. These two are then united; the growth of the plant is complete when to the two spiritual activities of the offspring of the spirits of wisdom and of motion is added the activity of the spirits of the cycles of time, uniting the two spiritual beings in a sort of marriage. Thus, by means of the plant kingdom, we have had an opportunity of becoming acquainted with the offspring of the spirits of wisdom. Further, as you may read in my *Occult Science* or in the akashic record, we must assume that these offspring of the spirits of wisdom have been formed since the time when these spirits of wisdom themselves gave the etheric body to humanity from their own substance. That occurred when the earth was in the old Sun condition; the etheric body of the human being was then derived from the spirits of wisdom. But now, since that time, the Sun-condition has progressed to the Moon-condition, and this again has progressed to the earthly-condition. During the Moon-condition the spirits of wisdom who had, during the Sun period, been able to give humanity its etheric body out of their own substance, had already progressed so far that they no longer needed to develop the capacity of giving anything to humanity. On the earth they had progressed to still higher activities. Now it is not exclusively characteristic of the offspring of the spirits of wisdom—whom we discovered as the group I's of the plant kingdom—to give a direct impulse from the sun, so that it seems to come not only from the planets but from the sun; it is also peculiar to the actual spirits of wisdom that they reveal themselves as coming directly down from the sun to the earth. How are the impulses revealed that come down from these spirits of wisdom who have gone through their normal evolution?

We have seen that in such a personality as the Buddha, there is a normally developed spirit of motion working down from a planet and inspiring him. We now reach the point of seeking for the normal spirits of wisdom. According to the whole spirit of our considerations we must seek them upon the sun. We must seek them there in the same sense that we have to seek for the normal spirits of motion as working from the planets, though they, too, have their real habitation upon the sun. We have to seek the impulse of the normally developed spirits of wisdom as coming directly from the sun. Now, however, we come to something peculiar. Certainly, with regard to the plants, if we really investigate occultly, we can distinguish a differentiation because we are concerned with the offspring of the spirits of wisdom. But if we consider the plants on earth in relation to the spirits of wisdom on the sun, their movements all appear more or less as a vertical union of the sun with the center point of the earth. In the plant form we can distinguish what proceeds from the spirits who have their dwelling place in the planets, but what we perceive as proceeding from the spirits of wisdom flows together in a vertical line. In a similar manner—and everyone who is acquainted with the occult facts in this sphere would give precisely the same information—it is the case that, in the region we enter when we direct our gaze to the sun, where we must seek the normal spirits of wisdom, we can no longer distinguish any differentiations. There we perceive unity. What proceeds from the normal spirits flows together in a unity. When we come to the question, Where is that revealed which proceeds from the unity of the spirits of wisdom who have their dwelling place directly upon the sun?—where is that revealed in the activity of the earth?—we come to a still wider sphere.

The sphere of such a spirit as the one who inspired the Buddha—the spirit of motion on Mercury—is insignificant in comparison with the wider, more comprehensive sphere that, in the process of the development of humanity, is directed by the spiritual beings of wisdom perceived as unity, and that is to be sought upon the sun. If we go back to the civilization of ancient India, we find that the seven holy Rishis spoke of what each one of them had to give to humanity from their occult foundations. They were conscious of having preserved what, through seven long periods of civilization, had been directed by the spirits of motion. It was just as though seven successive periods of time were all at once to unite in the evolution of the earth, and were to work so that they represented a college of great individualities. So it came about that these seven successive activities of the spirits of the planets came to light in what the seven holy Rishis had to say to humanity—each one speaking what he himself knew. They did not assert that what they had to give was the direct outflow of a spirit of motion, but they said that it was like a recollection in the soul of each of them of what had been given earlier by the spirits of motion. For the exalted wisdom that the holy Rishis gave to humanity was the great recollection of the ancient Atlantean civilizations, only in a new form. At the same time, these seven holy Rishis said: "Above what we have to give as the civilizations of the seven successive periods of time lies something else that exists beyond our sphere." That which lay above their sphere the holy Rishis called Vishvakarma. Thus they alluded to something that lay beyond their sphere, and that comprised a greater earthly sphere than that of the separate spirits of motion. As it was with the spheres of the spirits of the age, so did the holy Rishis point to epochs of civilization that lie beyond the sphere of the individual spirits of motion.

Then came the civilization of Zarathustra; and Zarathustra again pointed to the same being whom the holy Rishis had called Vishvakarma, only he alluded to that being in his own way as Ahura Mazda. The holy Rishis knew, as also did Zarathustra, that what is meant by Vishvakarma represents the spirit of wisdom who streams down upon the earth and encompasses wider spheres than do the individual spirits of motion. Zarathustra also knew that Ahura Mazda has wider spheres than the spirits of motion.

Then came the Egyptian civilization, and for certain reasons it became necessary to say: The present time—that is, the Egyptian present—is not able to direct its vision to that sun-spirit of wisdom whom Zarathustra divined in his own way. Hence the Egyptian civilization clothed its concept of the nature of this spirit in the legend that when this spirit attempted to come down to the earth it was immediately dismembered. Osiris dismembered by his brother is a reference to what the holy Rishis pointed to in their Vishvakarma. During the fourth post-Atlantean period of civilization it was pointed out that what every epoch of civilization had alluded to was to be attained, by reason of certain special circumstances, in direct vision in this fourth period of civilization; that is, through special events of the fourth post-Atlantean period, it was made possible for a human being to be inspired. The seven holy Rishis had alluded to the fact that this sun-spirit of wisdom existed. Zarathustra said that with occult vision directed to the sun it was possible to see this being. Egyptian civilization stated that this being was still so far from the earth that humans could only meet him after death. The fourth post-Atlantean civilization was able to point out that conditions had arisen in our earth evolution which made it possible for a human being to be directly inspired by this spirit of wisdom for a period of three years. Hence it was possible to recognize as a fact that the sphere of this sun-spirit of wisdom is much more comprehensive than the sphere of the spirits of motion, for it now embraces the whole collective process of civilization on earth. What was designated in the language of the holy Rishis as Vishvakarma, in that of Zarathustra as Ahura Mazda, in the Egyptian—if one really understands what stands behind the name—as Osiris, and what we in the fourth period of civilization designate by the word "Christ," is what has shone down through the portal of the sun-spirit of wisdom. I have never said that only the spirit of motion shone through the Buddha, nor do I now say that the sun-spirit of wisdom alone shone through the Christ. He was the portal through which occult vision could be directed into infinite spheres to the spirits of the higher hierarchies, but the portal was the spirit of wisdom—the sun-spirit of wisdom. As the sun is related to the planets, so is the sun-spirit of wisdom related to the spirits of motion who, on their part, express themselves in such spirits as the one who inspired Buddha. H. P. Blavatsky intended to express this in her theory; it would never have occurred to her to identify any of the planetary spirits of motion with the Christ.

It would be a gross defection from the original spirit of the theosophical movement—in which there is so much that is great and true and important and in which so many occult truths have prevailed—if we were to confuse what we have been able to learn through occultism with regard to spirits that reached their height in such a name as Buddha, of whom H. P. Blavatsky so plainly points out in her simple allegation that he corresponds to the spirit of Mercury. It would be a breach with all the original starting points of the theosophical revelation—with that teaching which in its time was rightly understood and in which the spirit of Buddha was never mistaken for the Christ spirit—if today we were to confuse these different beings. It would be a breach if we did not know through our basic teaching how to distinguish between those spirits who guide the growth of humanity in the course of successive periods of time, reaching the summit in spirits such as Buddha, and that spirit to whom all the rest, even Buddha himself, have alluded, and who is the unitary spirit of the whole earth evolution—just as the sun is the unitary body of the whole planetary system. This unitary spirit must be designated, in the sense of the fourth post-Atlantean period of civilization, as the Christ. In the solar system we cannot speak, in the ordinary sense, of two suns and say that the sun which at one time covers the Ram is not the same sun which covers the Goat at another time; we must be quite clear that it is the same sun which passes through all the signs of the zodiac, but that there are different planets which pass through the zodiac. We must also be clear on the following point. When we speak of the Christ who passes through the spheres of the different civilizations of the whole evolution of humanity on the earth and who has always been recognized by all religions when they attain their climax, we must distinguish this Christ spirit from the spirits of the different spheres which reached their summit, as it were, in their great individualities—even as Buddhism reached its climax in Buddha. This shows how the objective must first be sought in these matters.

When the Western occultist has to allude to this fact he or she ought not to be reproached with wishing to bring forward something that would be seen as a lack of tolerance toward other religions—while Theosophy has the task of allowing every religion its right place. When such a reproach is made, we should not forget that what was demanded of the Western occultists has already been accomplished. Did the Christ Impulse arise in the West? Has any Western nation brought forth the Christ impulse from its own people, its own races? No, the Christ impulse as an impulse given to the whole of humanity has been accepted by the West, though this Christ impulse in relation to its external presentation was foreign to the peoples of the West. Western civilization first showed that it had a comprehension of the necessary renunciation of personal possession. When the West declined the spirit of motion on Mars as a direct inspirer, when it exchanged that inspirer for the Christ spirit—the inspirer corresponding to the sun-spirit of wisdom—it accomplished an historical and important fact. It is unfair that the West should be blamed by other religions for intolerance in respect of this matter. The great leaders of the other religions always show that they recognize the spirits of wisdom as being more exalted than the spirits of motion. Just those who wish to make their own spirit of motion a sort of leading spirit under another name and do not themselves wish to take the step of ascending from their own spirit to the sun spirit might say that intolerance is shown by those who have already practiced tolerance. Let them first exercise tolerance in other spheres, the tolerance that the West has already exercised in exchanging its spirit of motion for a spirit of wisdom.

Thus a theosophical act was accomplished before theosophy existed by seeing that the individual religions have their rights, inasmuch as no single impulse belonging to any one single group of humanity is claimed for the Christ, but only that to which theosophy also lays claim, namely, to seek the impulse that is an impulse of humanity as distinct from the special religions as the sun-impulse is from all the planets. It is from the depths of occultism, my dear friends, that these facts are represented objectively, and if it were ever to be said that this representation of the Christ impulse arises from any special national or racial interest, or from Western interests, such a remark could be made only through ignorance of the relation of facts, or through a misrepresentation of them. In all things we must boldly and sincerely face objective facts, and we can only do this if we look into the depths of the world's becoming. All occult truths show us finally how cosmic evolution comes about, but we must have the courage as well as the necessary impartiality to come face-to-face with this cosmic evolution. Regarding names, it does not concern us whether they are borrowed from the East or from the West, or whether they are borne by this or that personal spirit. What does concern us, what we must recognize, is what is at work in the world. Spiritual science teaches us to see and perceive what works in the world. In fact, in the field of spiritual science, we have developed the instinct—I might say—for finding the right. We must not always long for new sensations, but try to understand a little of what lies in the first impulses of the theosophical movement. When H. P. Blavatsky identified the Buddha with Mercury, a great truth was expressed, which will be so much the more recognized the more the relation of the Buddha to Christ is recognized in occult spheres, just as we learn to know cosmic relationships better when we recognize the relation of the planet Mercury to the fixed star—the sun. These things cannot be shaken from their foundations through human prejudices, but they only work aright in the process of civilization if we impartially look them in the face.

This had to be added to what was stated today regarding the spirits active in the planets and in the sun; for these spirits extend their activity to the earth, and the world has no idea how deeply much of what must be taught in popular lectures is rooted in occult foundations. How deeply grounded is that relation which has just been given of the successive spheres of civilization of which the one culminated in Buddha, the other in—call it what you will—what the fourth epoch of civilization called *Christ*. How far the one differs from the other can only be learned from the depths of occultism. But occultism also convinces us how, rightly looked at, the cosmos everywhere offers us signs for what is so deeply instilled within our hearts. So we must say: "If we learn the writing spread forth in the cosmos, in the stars, in their ordering and motions, we shall find that from the cosmos everywhere there speaks what permeates our hearts with truth, love, and that piety which carries forward the evolution of humanity from epoch to epoch."

LECTURE TEN

FOLLOWING THE STATEMENTS we were able to make yesterday on the cooperation of the spirits of the various hierarchies in the kingdoms of nature, there still remains the mineral kingdom to be considered. We call to mind that we described the mineral kingdom by saying that only its physical part exists in the physical world, while we have to seek what corresponds to the etheric body of the mineral in the so-called astral world, the astral body in the lower devachanic world, and the actual group I of the mineral kingdom on the higher devachanic plane. Thus the mineral kingdom presents a remarkable contrast to humanity. While we must say of human beings that all four principles of our being are active on the physical plane—the physical as well as the etheric body, the astral body, and the I—in the case of the mineral we must distribute, as it were, all that we humans have on the one plane and say: as far as the mineral is concerned the mineral we must seek what corresponds to the human etheric body on the astral plane, we must seek the astral body on the devachanic plane, and the group I of the mineral on the higher devachanic plane. Thus, what in the human being is concentrated on the physical plane is in the case of the mineral divided in its activity among the various worlds. Again, when we trace what is really in question with occult vision, we arrive at the following result. In the occult sense we must seek, in the first place, only that part of the mineral kingdom on the physical plane that is perceptible to the external senses. We must be quite clear as to the fact that only what we call the forms—the shapes of the mineral kingdom—are perceptible. We know—this can only be touched upon here—that the mineral world, at any rate in part, encounters us formed, organized in such a manner that we perceive this formation as suitable to the mineral nature. If we look at a certain body of cubic form and at another of a different form, we know that these forms are not accidental but are connected in a certain way with the nature of the mineral. Occult investigation teaches us that the forms in the mineral, which we call crystal forms, can be traced back to the action of the spirits of form. Because occultism always starts from reality and seeks to find the origin of this or that, names are so given in occultism that the name points to something characteristic. The name "spirits of form" was chosen for the reason that in the kingdom that we on earth describe as the mineral kingdom, the spirits of form display their activity, and further that the offspring of the spirits of form—in the sense that we have spoken of offspring of the higher hierarchies in the course of these lectures—are, above all, active there. To understand the nature of the minerals we must be quite clear that to physical perception, generally speaking, only the forms of the minerals exist. To be sure, certain forces are evident in the mineral kingdom—such as the forces of electricity and magnetism—that cause the minerals to appear in certain colors, but we must be quite clear that in general only the form of the mineral kingdom is to be observed on the physical plane. Without taking the other qualities into account, let us consider the forms we encounter at any rate in most of the mineral kingdom, and let us be quite clear that this pure form proceeds from the mode of operation of the spirits of form or their offspring.

Next we come to the so-called etheric body, which we must describe as the second principle of a being of the mineral kingdom. Occult investigators cannot find what they describe as the etheric body of the mineral in the mineral world, but they find it in the same realm in which they seek when, for instance, they wish to find the astral body of the plant, or the group I of the animal. As we saw yesterday, they need make no other preparation regarding their soul than that necessary for finding the group I of the animal. With the same condition of consciousness with which they perceive the group I of the animal, occult investigators also perceive the astral body of the plant, and what lies behind the mineral kingdom as its etheric body. Now we have seen that we must extend our observations into the region of the planets of a planetary system—in our own planetary system to those planets existing outside the earth. And we have shown that the corresponding forces that externalize themselves in the group I's of animals and the astral bodies of plants work directly from the planetary centers. There we must also go if we wish to seek what works etherically in the mineral. How a mineral is laved by life powers can first be seen if we penetrate to the universal life that is common to all—from the earth to the rest of the planets of our planetary system. Thus the principle by which the mineral is animated, the life of the mineral, is not to be found in the physical world or in the realm of what our earth directly offers us, but in the life streams pouring down from the planets which are stimulated constantly, to be sure, by the sun, but still streaming down directly from the planets and permeating our earth planet in a living way in order to permeate all that is form with their offspring—the etheric nature spirits, of which we have spoken. Thus form has inner being. In other words, the form of the mineral which proceeds solely from the physical plane is not permeable but offers resistance. Were nothing active in the mineral but what is active on the physical plane, then the mineral would only make itself perceptible as form; but this form is filled with inner being. For the mineral has also inner being; it has the inner being of the various mineral substances. It not only has form, it has matter, it has substance. When we directly perceive this substance in the physical world, it appears to us as a dead, lifeless substance. To cosmic space it is not dead, to planetary space, at least, it is something that is part of its own life, that is precipitated from the life of the planetary system. Just as the human or animal organism separates off hard products—the nails, for instance—so is the mineral substance put forth; but the active forces that put it forth are not to be looked for upon the earth itself; hence it appears on the earth as if it were dead. These streams of life, these life forces, this etheric body must be sought as streaming down from the several planets. Just as in considering the group I's of animals we could say: In reality only the general forms are created by the group I's of animals, and these are then further developed, so must we say: The streams of life sent down by the individual planets that permeate the earth from all sides do not create forms for the minerals, for those are created by the spirits of form; but through these streams the minerals are permeated with inner being. This occurs in such a way that this inner being is given certain main types, main substances: and each substance is thereby connected with a stream proceeding from one of the planets.

Because the minerals immediately acquired solid forms, mobile types are not created from the planets by means of these planetary streams, but types of one kind only. And then through the various positions of the planets, as I have already described with regard to the group souls of animals—besides the main types and substances—other types, subordinate substances are created, which again depend on the constellation of the individual planets. But what the planets create, each through its own original nature, is expressed in the principal substances of the earth's organism. Thus we have certain main mineral substances of the earth's organism of which we can say: Here is a substance that is what it is because it is permeated by an etheric stream from one of the planets; another is permeated by a stream from another planet. Thus we have to trace back the nature of mineral substances to activities in the planetary system that externalize as etheric streams in the organism of the earth. Therefore the occult schools that have investigated such matters have also connected the principal substances of our earthly organism to the planets in such a way that they have designated those substances that have been produced quite directly—not through the constellation but through the principal activity of the planet—by the same or similar names as the planets; and indeed in such a way that occult observation has been strictly adhered to. If we observe the planet Saturn in our system we find that the life stream that permeates the earth directly from Saturn is connected with the substance that is inwardly animated by Saturn. From Jupiter we get tin as main substance; from Mars, iron; and from Venus, in its occult sense, copper. With regard to Mercury we must take into consideration that it was later confused with Venus. The life activity (in the sense of true occult nomenclature) produced creatively by Mercury, on account of its greater proximity when it penetrated the earth organism, bears a still greater resemblance to the planet itself, for Mercury stands nearer to the Earth than the other planets. Therefore this substance has been given the same name as the cosmic body itself, namely mercury or quicksilver. These are the principal substances that are connected in their etheric body with the corresponding planets of our system. If we recollect how we had to speak of all that works from the planetary system regarding the group souls of animals and the astral bodies of plants, we find it is always a question of the beings in connection with the spirits of motion, either with themselves or their offspring, who work in their totality on the earth from the planets of the system. Thus we must also reckon as belonging to the sphere of the spirits of motion what permeates the mineral substances.

Now if we wish to consider what belongs to the mineral kingdom as astral body, we have to ascend, as it were, to a still higher world. In the whole sense of our past considerations it will be clear that in the same way that we had to ascend from the astral body of the plant to the group I, from the planets to the sun—to the fixed star; so, too, regarding the mineral kingdom, if we pass from the etheric body to the astral body we must again ascend to the fixed star. That is, we can understand, and occult vision tells us, that the astral nature of the mineral works from those beings in the ranks of the hierarchies through whom comes from the sun what is directly perceptible—from the beings we call the spirits of wisdom, or from that which is connected with their sphere. Thus even the offspring of the spirits of wisdom come into consideration. What thus works in the mineral is seen by occult investigation as quite separate, outside the mineral; but it is so seen that the life just described as existing in the mineral, as the etheric body of the mineral, is pressed in from outside. Whereas the astral body in the human being or animal holds together the etheric body from within, the etheric body of the mineral is, as it were, pushed toward it from outside, not concentrated and held together inside as in the human being and the animal. If we consider the relation of the human

astral body to the human etheric body, we see that what
works as etheric body is held together by the power of
attraction. In the mineral the etheric body is compressed
together by forces from outside; thus, in the mineral the
content, the inner nature expressed in the etheric stream, is
compressed by means of active astral forces into the form.
The mineral is held together astrally from outside because
it is determined through the different positions of the sun
to the earth in relation to this astral pressure. One might
say that the etheric substance is driven into the mineral
from the point from which the sun shines upon the earth.

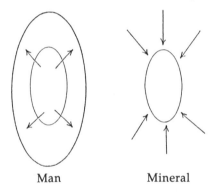

Man   Mineral

Thus while this etheric substance is itself directed by the
planet, it is driven into and held within the mineral or crystal by the sun, by the forces belonging to the sphere of the
spirits of wisdom. But now something very remarkable is
seen. If we investigate occultly the activity exercised by the
astral forces from the sun upon the mineral, we recognize
very clearly at this point a very important fact. We learn
that while all the etheric forces proceeding from the planets
work upon the mineral and actually form its basic substances, other etheric streams also pass down from the sun
as such to the earth. Thus, while generally for the normal
formation of the mineral the etheric substance passes down

from the planets, and is only compressed from outside by the forces proceeding from the sun, yet we cannot say that no etheric streams come down from the sun, for it is a fact that such an etheric stream does come down. What is the reason for this? Why does there come down from the sun an etheric stream that can, as it were, inwardly animate the mineral? Why does this take place? It is brought about by the activity of what I have designated as the luciferic principle. The spirits in the ranks of the higher hierarchies that work astrally upon the mineral are—as we have just said—the spirits of wisdom; while the spirits of motion work etherically.

There are spirits of wisdom active on the sun who have gone through their full normal process of evolution; they work, as has been described, astrally upon the mineral. But certain of the spirits of wisdom have become luciferic. We have designated this "becoming luciferic" of certain spiritual beings of a hierarchy as a sort of rebellion in the cosmos. This rebellion comes about because certain spirits, having reached a given stage in their hierarchy, resist their brethren and work against them—work in an opposite direction. This opposition comes about simply because they do not wish to go through the evolution that the others have gone through; so they simply remain behind at an earlier stage, just as we know in our own souls that we wish to progress, yet the ideas and habits we have acquired will not allow us to do so, because they wish to remain as something permanent. Our habits often rebel against what we have acquired in a new epoch of life. In like manner the spiritual beings who remain behind at an earlier stage are rebels in the cosmos. The luciferic spirits—the spirits of wisdom of the second hierarchy who have not gone through their development with the rest—instead of sending astral streams from the sun to the mineral, send etheric streams to the earth. This resulted in a certain basic substance being formed that received its inner being not from the planets, but directly from the sun. This mineral is gold. Gold is that luciferic mineral that in regard to its inner being is not influenced etherically by the planets, but by the sun. Hence the occultist has allotted gold to the sun. In a certain sense, therefore, this mineral is somewhat different from other metals.

You can now easily grasp that because etheric streams come from the sun, and work something into the earth which is actually a rebel principle, the equilibrium of the earth is thereby disturbed. The equilibrium of the earth in relation to the mineral kingdom would be maintained if all the etheric influences came from the planets and none but astral influences came to the minerals from the sun, but there are also direct etheric forces coming from the sun and they disturb the equilibrium. This equilibrium had to be reestablished by the wise leaders of the world, for the earth could not carry out her evolution under such conditions. The hierarchies had to work in cooperation so that the equilibrium might be reestablished. The stronger luciferic forces had to be opposed by other forces which, in a certain sense, paralyzed them and arrested their effects. This could only come about through the etheric stream that came from the sun being opposed by another, which counteracted, and in a certain sense balanced, its effects. Thus while certain spirits of wisdom proved themselves luciferic and sent down etheric currents from the sun into the mineral kingdom on the earth, other spirits took care that these were opposed by other currents. These opposing currents which readjusted the equilibrium were created by a part of the disturbed equilibrium substance being detached from the earth and circling around the earth as the moon. Thus the etheric streams coming from the sun came into opposition to the etheric stream which flowed from the moon to the earth from quite a different quarter, and in this way the balance was reestablished. Thus, because luciferic spirits of wisdom on the sun had attained the possibility of sending forth etheric streams, other spirits of wisdom renounced their claim to working from the sun and consented to apply their forces to restoring the equilibrium. That is, a cosmic colony, a planetary colony was founded on the moon, from which there now streamed etheric currents to the earth, so that a substance was created which had to be in the earth so that the direct power of gold might be weakened. This came about as a result of the moon being separated from the earth. From the spirits of wisdom who separated from the moon—and who, in a sense, became the opposers of the luciferic spirits of wisdom from the sun—stream down to the earth those etheric forces that have produced the substance silver. Thus you see that in the universe—in the cosmos—certain things work in such a way that one might explain it by means of a certain diagram; but the peculiar thing is that the diagram would everywhere be broken through. If anyone were to prove by means of a diagram that all the etheric forces for the minerals come from the planets, that person would be in error; for in reality two etheric streams come from two different sides, the one from the sun, the other from the moon; hence two basic substances are formed in a different way.

If we wish to make what I have just described objective, perceptible to our senses, and to find an external expression for it, we can achieve it in the following way—but we must first of all be clear as to what it really is that we see when we look at the sun. We pointed out previously that only the spirits of the higher hierarchies down to the spirits of wisdom go through their own evolution on the fixed star; what we see when we look at the fixed star is the actual content-substance of the spirits of wisdom. That is the true content of the fixed star. Indeed, we human beings can only gain a concept of what is the substance of the spirits of wisdom by contemplating what exists in us as, at any rate, an image of this substance. What is that in us, in humanity, in the human soul, that is a symbol of the substance of the spirits of wisdom? Our thoughts! But we do not see our thoughts with physical eyes—that is the point. Neither can the fixed stars, insofar as they are the fields of activity for the genuine spirits of wisdom, be seen with physical eyes. We have now reached a point where we can point again to the enormous significance of what we find in the religious documents that are based on occultism. You know that the Bible, in Genesis, states that human beings were created in a very peculiar way. We are told that Lucifer appeared to Eve and told her that if she would do as he wished her eyes would be opened. Anyone who knows the original text will not readily be put off with a merely symbolical explanation, for what the Bible means by good and evil does not refer to moral good and evil—that belongs to quite a different part of the development of civilization. What is meant here as good and evil is what is seen externally, not as something spiritually psychic, but something seen with the physical eyes: "Your eyes shall be opened." Till then they were not open. This must be taken quite literally. Human beings could perceive before Lucifer approached them. They saw the fixed stars with the primitive clairvoyance that had been given to humanity, but their vision was such that they saw the substance of the fixed stars as the substance of the spirits of wisdom; they saw them spiritually. They only began to see the fixed stars physically—that is, light first streamed toward them that was able to be perceived by their physical eyes—when they themselves, the human beings, had yielded to the luciferic temptation. That means that the fixed stars as directed by the spirits of wisdom are not physically visible, they do not shed physical light. Physical light can only be shed if there is something underlying it that serves as a bearer to the light when light is, as it were, held captive through a bearer. For a fixed star to become visible, something more is necessary than the mere presence of spiritual beings of wisdom at work there. It is necessary that luciferic beings should work in this fixed star who resist the mere substance of wisdom and permeate it with their own principle. Thus within the fixed star is mingled what is only visible spiritually and resists this merely spiritual visibility: the luciferic element in the fixed star that carries forth the light into physical phenomena.

The fixed star would not be visible if it had not within it, in addition to the spirits of wisdom who have progressed normally, those who have not attained their goal, who remained at a lower stage, either at the stage of the spirits of motion or that of the spirits of form. Thus we have to recognize the backward spirits of wisdom who have not attained their goal as light bearers in the lightless spiritual substance of the fixed star. Now, if we are clear as to the fact that from the fixed stars, from our own sun, physical light only reaches us because the normal spirits of wisdom have as companions those who have remained behind and who have become light bearers—Light—Lucifer—Phosphoros—we must also be clear that the same cause which makes the sun visible, which sends light to us from the fixed star, is also that which sends the etheric life stream to the earth and produces gold. It was necessary therefore that other forces should work from the moon (which occult vision perceives as etheric currents), forces which produce silver. Since they are spirits of wisdom who oppose the moon to the sun in order to bring about an adjustment, we must say: "These spirits of wisdom upon the moon cannot shine"; for the spirits of wisdom do not shine. Hence, if occult vision searches for these spirits on the moon, it does not discover them as luminous; for these spirits of wisdom who founded a colony on the moon were obliged to exclude the luciferic spirits from the moon, otherwise the balance would not have been maintained. That is to say, the moon cannot ray out any light of its own, only what is reflected as sunlight. Quite normal spirits of wisdom made a sacrifice and took up their position on the moon in order to supply the earth with the necessary currents for keeping the equilibrium, in opposition to the luciferic currents which stream from the sun. Hence the moon is excluded from having light of its own, and it is not difficult in this external fact that we encounter in the physical world to see the symbol of a deep occult connection. The sun has its own light which appears to us, but the moon has not; and the reflected light that rays to us from the moon, and of which lucifer is the bearer: Lucifer-Phosphoros, tells us that the moon has no light of its own. Therefore what is Lucifer can only appear to us symbolically, in a *maya*, shining down from the moon, because the sunlight is reflected. When, for instance, the crescent moon reflects the sunlight, there are then no luciferic spirits of wisdom on the moon itself, but what is poured forth from the sun by the luciferic spirits of wisdom is reflected as light.

Now, when we turn our occult vision to the moon, what the physical eyes perceive—the shining crescent moon—disappears, for that exists only for physical vision; but in its place occult vision sees the real being behind all visible light in the cosmos, sees the form of Lucifer, though certainly as a reflection. Thus, if we think of the image of Lucifer as seen by occult vision in the place of the crescent moon, we must say: The moon owes its origin to the circumstances that certain normal spirits of wisdom renounced their dwelling

200 SPIRITUAL BEINGS IN THE HEAVENLY BODIES

place on the sun and have taken up their abode in this colony to restrain what streams forth from the luciferic spirits. Hence, to occult vision the spirit of wisdom does not reveal itself here, above the crescent of the moon, but is to be seen restraining the luciferic principle. The occult fact is thus presented symbolically to the imagination as a normal spirit of wisdom holding the luciferic principle in subjection. The occultists therefore represent a form, usually taken to be a chief messenger of the higher spirits of wisdom, for the one who curbs Lucifer; and they represent Lucifer chained, curbed in the place of the crescent moon. This is an occult picture. Among our occult pictures there is this one representing the chief messenger curbing Lucifer. This is an allusion to profound occult mysteries. What is thus shown externally in *maya* is in reality to be ascribed to the cooperation of the spirits of the hierarchies. When we see with physical eyes the crescent moon shining silver bright, there is often to be seen a sort of shadow above in the dark part; then to occult vision the crescent moon is transformed into a living being, with the restraining spirit above it, maintaining the balance from its place on the moon. Thus you see that even to produce a phenomenon such as our earthly moon many preparations had to be made in the cosmos. The cooperative activities of the various hierarchies in the cosmos is a very complicated matter and even in a much longer course of lectures we could still give only indications of it; we can make clear only the principle of how these spiritual hierarchies cooperate.

Please remember the thought just mentioned in connection with the astral body of the minerals. We have, indeed, still to consider the group I of minerals; that has to be sought in a still higher supersensible world—in a world not found in the regions where the group I's of animals or plants are to be found. Therefore we cannot find it upon the sun. Where then does the group I of minerals reveal itself to occult vision? The peculiar thing about the group I of minerals is that, strictly speaking, it does not end anywhere when we search in cosmic space; it is in the whole widths of cosmic space and it works from there. We are therefore driven to seek for the group I of minerals actually outside the planetary system; we must look upon it as something that works into the planetary system from outside. Thus far this coincides with what we know from the akashic records, that the next higher class of beings above the spirits of wisdom are the thrones, or spirits of will. These spirits of will belong to the first hierarchy and though their offspring are not so far advanced that they can be reckoned within it, these spirits of will or their offspring give forth what becomes the group I of minerals, and what, in fact, works into the planetary system. This also coincides with the fact that simultaneously with the outpouring of the substance of the spirits of will begins the formation of the planetary system on ancient Saturn that was brought about by the spirits of will. They still work in the same way at the present time as when the first embodiment of our earth was built up out of the universe by these beings. We can really only see these spirits of will when, having become luciferic, they reveal themselves in a sense in certain phenomena that we find as minerals in the sphere of the earth and that come, as it were, from cosmic space. The cosmic origin, the super-earthly origin, of what we are now considering is revealed by the fact that these spirits of will combine very, very easily with that which works into the planetary system as the cometary and meteoric beings—as cometary or meteoric life.

We have pointed out what meaning this life has in the planetary system. I should like at least to indicate that in reality a comet is something that comes in from outside, but it makes certain combinations. Inasmuch as the comet travels through the planetary system it combines with the mineral kingdom that also arises through the spirits of will. And the result may be that as the comet rushes through the planetary system it attaches mineral substance to itself, which is then attracted by the earth and falls down upon it. This of course is not the comet, but rather does it announce its approach to the earth by a fall of meteors taking place. These things are absolutely harmonious, and if certain things appear to contradict what was represented earlier, we must always understand that these contradictions will solve themselves if everything is taken into consideration and studied. This was only an example to show that in the planetary system we really have to do with influences working in from the cosmos. These group souls of minerals work in the form of rays from without inward. And since various modes of operation come from the various aspects of space—for space is not homogeneous—these group souls of minerals, belonging to the sphere of the spirits of will, ray toward us from different sides in the most varied manner. Now through the cooperation of what comes to the minerals from the planets, what comes from the sun, and what streams in from the universe from the various directions arises the possibility that not only have those basic types already mentioned come into existence in the mineral kingdom, but all sorts of other forms, all sorts of differently modified substances of the mineral kingdom have been formed. The kind of substance a mineral exhibits simply depends on the way the forces that come from the planets are again influenced by other forces either streaming astrally to the earth from the sun or from various directions of cosmic space. The variety and multiplicity of the mineral kingdom can be understood in this way.

If we observe our present-day Saturn, it presents itself in the first place to occult vision as the outermost planet of our system. Why? Because actually Saturn as planet, as well as ancient Saturn—the first of the successive incarnations of our earth known to us—was produced by the furthest currents coming from cosmic space. Had we been able to observe Saturn at a very early condition of our earth evolution, we should have seen that in its orbit it had a sort of nucleus and a sort of comet's tail, which passed out into cosmic space. In the distant past Saturn would have revealed itself definitely with a nucleus and a comet's tail extending into cosmic space. That is, in the primeval periods of our earth, Saturn would have been seen circling around its orbit with its tail pointing outward. Saturn was earlier like this (see below). The facts of the akashic records show it thus:

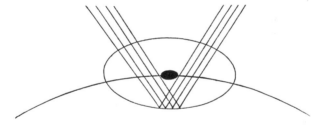

The tail of ancient Saturn took the most varied directions out into space, corresponding to the currents that came in from the cosmos directed by the spirits of will, who are the group souls of the minerals. At a later period, when the planetary system was enclosed by the spiritual beings of other hierarchies, what had formerly gone out into cosmic space was drawn together so that the tail became an enclosed ring; through the power of attraction of the planetary system the ring was formed. To occult vision the ring of Saturn is absolutely the same phenomenon as the comet's tail. If you were to take the ring of Saturn as it circles around Saturn and open it out, you would have a comet's tail (See diagram).

In this way it is possible to look back to the streaming-in of the group souls of the minerals into our planetary system; and again the signs of the zodiac in general give us their individual positions. It is to be noted that the two outermost planets now reckoned as belonging to our system by physical astronomy—Uranus and Neptune—did not originally belong to our solar system; they came much later into the sphere of attraction of our system. They then joined company and remained within it. They cannot therefore be reckoned in the same sense as the other planets as belonging to our system from Saturn onward, for they, so to speak, belonged to it from the beginning. Thus, when we consider Saturn, especially in its ancient form, we see in it a planet that, by sending forth etheric currents from its own center to our earth, creates—we can even say—the substance of lead. At the same time we see how these group souls of the minerals stream in, we see how they are affected when a power of attraction is exercised on them from the sun, from which the astral body of the mineral streams out. From the sun, the astral body of the mineral streams out into space; from outside in cosmic space, the I of the mineral streams in. When these currents are united something takes place which, in a modified way, expresses itself, as it were, in a fructification of the group I by the astral body, and by this means alone does the mineral come to its perfection. Now if we go back to the comet, here, too, we have something which, in fact, streams in from cosmic space—a similar stream of beings to the group souls of the minerals. The group souls of the minerals belong to the sphere of the spirits of will; but above them lie the beings who essentially form the basis of cometary life. But as everywhere there are luciferic beings, so also within the comet there are such as

stand at the stage of the thrones, not of the cherubim and
seraphim. That is why the comet acquires a mineral
nature—appears as a mineral intervention in the planetary
system. In other words, we have to look upon comets as
cosmic bodies that fly in from the cosmos after the planetary system is already formed and thus do not come as far
as the bodies composing the system itself, but remain
behind at a considerably earlier stage. It would certainly be
very fascinating to trace the stages of cosmic growth; how
worlds are formed by the cooperative activities of the spirits of the hierarchies in a fixed-star system; how those same
spirits themselves appear when we direct our gaze back to
cosmic mists and far-distant fixed stars. Whenever we
direct our occult vision to a fixed star, we first of all encounter the normal spirits of wisdom. The whole heavens would
be invisible to physical sight and only visible to clairvoyant
consciousness if none but these normal spirits of wisdom
were active; but everywhere luciferic spirits are mingled
with the normal spirits of wisdom and bring physical light
of their own into the world of the fixed star. When at night
the starry heaven is illuminated, phosphorus actually
works down upon us from countless points; and everywhere in the universe we find the possibility of formation
only by the cooperation of the opposing forces, by the combined working of the normal spirits of the hierarchies with
those who are rebels—that is, those who have remained
behind. The starry world of the normal spirits of wisdom is
unillumined to physical eyes but visible to spiritual sight. It
became luminous to physical eyes—and it is revealed in
maya—through Lucifer or the luciferic spirits who are, and
must be, active everywhere.

Thus, we have seen something very remarkable in the
mineral kingdom also. Today we have, so to speak, grasped
the moon as a field of action from which a spirit of wisdom

works and restrains Lucifer, because a place had to be created where the luciferic activity would be opposed and balance restored. Now what significance did this have for humanity? We have seen that in humanity everything is compressed onto the physical plane which for the mineral is, as it were, distributed over the worlds. We have found group souls for the minerals, plants, and animals. Is there also a sort of group soul for the human being? Oh, yes, there is. The group souls of the minerals are to be found in the sphere of the thrones, those of the plants in the sphere of the spirits of wisdom, and the animals in the sphere of the spirits of motion; but humans have so received their group soul that with the inflowing of their I, a group soul was originally given them as an emanation from the spirits of form. This human group soul was originally allotted by the spirits of form to be a unitary soul for the whole of humanity. What differentiated this group soul into such variety that differences of race, differences of tribe arose? This was brought about through the action of other spirits. Humanity was created to be one all the world over; in this unity the primeval human I was to assert itself as a group soul dwelling in all human beings, a group soul that had descended to the physical plane. Just as only the external form of the minerals can be brought into being by the spirits of form, so by these same spirits of form was the group I created for humanity, which was then differentiated by the activity of other beings of the various hierarchies. Now the balance brought about for the mineral kingdom by the formation of the moon was also brought about for humanity; and indeed in such a way that while for the mineral realm on the moon there is a physical readjustment, in exactly the same way a moon principle exists for humanity that works against the luciferic influence in human nature, just as in the mineral kingdom the dark moon principle works against the Lucifer principle. Just as in the mineral kingdom something is active on the moon that keeps the balance with regard to the luciferic forces streaming down from the sun, so does a spiritual moon principle work from the moon against the temptation of Lucifer that humanity has encountered in the course of the earth evolution. As we have seen, all the planets, all the heavenly bodies stand in connection with beings of the higher hierarchies, and so, too, is it with the moon. The spirits of wisdom established a colony upon the moon in order to preserve the equilibrium; and so from the direction of the moon compensating spirits work in upon humanity against Lucifer—who approached humanity as a tempter. Just as the tempter disseminated light so, too, did his spiritual principle sink down into the human soul. So we can also point to the moon as the bearer of the opponent of Lucifer, as the dwelling place of dark spirits who yet must be there to maintain the balance regarding the light-bearers who are pressing forward and who, at the same time, are the tempting spirits of humanity. In fact, the secret of the moon and its spiritual principle was first revealed to humanity in the old Hebrew records, and what we have found physically in the moon is, in its spiritual aspect, what Hebrew antiquity designated as the Jehovah principle.

According to this the moon, so to speak, is designated as the starting point of the forces working upon humanity as the opponents of Lucifer. Jahve, or Jehovah, is the opponent of Lucifer. The secret doctrine of the ancient Hebrews looked up to the sun, saying: In the sun work the invisible spirits of wisdom who are only visible to spiritual, not to physical, sight. The latter sees the principle of Lucifer raying down. What is to be seen externally as the sun principle is Lucifer; but therein works secretly, invisible to physical vision, everything attainable through the spirits of wisdom who form the gateway to it. One of these spirits of wisdom separated and sacrificed itself, and has taken up its abode upon the moon in order through its activity there to curb the light and also to counteract the spiritual work of Lucifer. Hebrew antiquity saw in Jehovah an ambassador of those truly exalted spirits to whom vision is opened through the spirits of wisdom if the sun is looked upon with spiritual sight. Hebrew antiquity justly concluded that Jehovah must continue to work from the moon until humanity has become inwardly mature enough to perceive and feel at least a little of what gradually in the course of evolution will be both seen and understood—that from the same sun proceeds not only the physical part of Lucifer, but also the dissemination of what the spirits of wisdom are the portal. Thus to the ancient Hebrew there appeared in Jehovah what is similar to the spirits of wisdom in the sun, and we can say: Just as the sunlight is reflected from the moon in space, so to the ancient Hebrew who really knew, Jehovah was the reflection of that spiritual being who—when humanity has become sufficiently mature—will ray down from the sun, and whose appearance was foretold by the holy Rishis, Zarathustra, and the worshippers of Osiris. Just as in space sunlight is reflected from the moon, so Jehovah is revealed as a reflection of the principle of the great sun-spirit whom you may designate by whatever name you will—Vishvakarma, as the ancient Indians called him; Ahura Mazda, as he was called by Zarathustra; Osiris by the ancient Egyptians; or as the Christ, as he was known to the fourth post-Atlantean period of civilization—that is the esoteric comprehension of Jehovah. He is Christ reflected by the moon principle, and because he was reflected in time, Christ could be announced prophetically. Hence in St. John's Gospel we come across a passage that otherwise can never be understood, in which it is said that Moses spoke of Christ. Actually, he spoke of Jehovah, but it is Christ, prophetically announced. This passage in which Jehovah is mentioned is referred to because the bearer of the Christ wishes to point out that in antiquity Jehovah is but Christ foretold.

Thus we see that these things are harmonious, and that what we have heard today is connected with what was said in the last lecture. In what we call the external light and its bearer we must recognize something that is in opposition to the spiritual principle that is at the normal point of its evolution, and that appears to us as the spiritual center of our planetary system. It is not a question of names, but of recognizing the whole significance of this principle. We must recognize that in the realm of the spiritual we speak of Christ just as in that of the physical we speak of the sun; that in the realm of the spiritual we speak of the planetary spirits and of the planets just as in the development of earthly civilization we speak, perhaps, of the principle of Buddha. Here again is a point where you find one of the important revelations in H. P. Blavatsky. What great revelations there are in the *Secret Doctrine* you can see by the way H. P. Blavatsky treats the concept of Jehovah. We need not recoil at this, or think things are not correct because she shows a certain antipathy toward Christ and Jehovah. The truth nevertheless presses through, and the description of Jehovah as a moon divinity and the presentation of Lucifer as his opponent that is given by H. P. Blavatsky is—one might say—the broken expression of a truth. The presentation given from inspiration by Blavatsky is only given a subjective coloring by her because she had a feeling that Lucifer was really a good divinity—she felt him as such. She preferred him, in a certain sense, to the moon-god because to her Lucifer was a sun-god. That is correct—he is that, but we had to represent the true connection in order that the expression used in former times: "Christ is the true Lucifer," "Christus verus

Luciferus," may be understood. It does not sound quite right to us today, but at that time people knew from the old secret doctrine that the light-bearer manifests in the external physical light, and that if we penetrate through the physical light to the spirits of wisdom, to the spiritual light, then we reach the light-bearer of that light.

"Christus verus Luciferus"—I think, in spite of the incompleteness that was inevitable in our rendering of this comprehensive theme, what we always wish to attain in the sphere of spiritual science has come before your souls: that the treatment of every theme leads us to look up from the physical to the spiritual. With regard to the heavenly bodies that as the expression of the wonders of the universe shine forth from space this is, in many respects, very difficult because in the heavenly bodies there is a complicated cooperation of the beings of the various hierarchies and because everything that takes place in cosmic space can only be comprehended if behind all matter, even behind the substance of light itself, we find the spirit or spirits. Behind all this spiritual life lies the universal, divine Fatherhood, an omnipresent and ever-working, all-divine life that before it comes to expression in the physical is differentiated into countless worlds of spiritual hierarchies. We look up to these worlds, however, and see within them what works down into our kingdoms of nature and is the foundation of all the wonders of the heavens. For even in our kingdoms of nature either the hierarchies themselves or their offspring are revealed. When we thus look out into the spaces of heaven we can, through such reflections, also gain a moral impression that must, if we allow the mighty operations of the hierarchies in cosmic space to gain a little influence over us, result in our being drawn away from the passions, desires, impulses, and concepts that our physical earth life brings to maturity. These are, in essence, what flings down into the development of the earth and divides humanity into factions, what makes people all over the world opponents or partisans in the most varied directions. In a higher moral sense we attain a sense of freedom, if but for a brief time we free ourselves from the consideration of earthly things and contemplate the worlds of spirit in cosmic space. Then do we become free from what otherwise plays in our egotistical impulses that are the original cause of all the smallnesses and quarreling upon earth. Hence the most certain means of attaining the high ideals of our anthroposophical life is to direct our gaze from time to time to the starry worlds and their spiritual guides and leaders—the hierarchies. If we investigate the different civilizations, as we have tried to do, and the significance of the inspiring spirits of the various religions and of the bearers of wisdom to humanity, we shall cease to strive on earth as followers of individual systems. We shall not depend on names, nor on the creeds of the several groups of humanity on the earth. When people seek their knowledge where the vision of all the humanity of the earth can be directed, and where the knowledge common to all can be obtained— knowledge that unites and does not separate—when people actually reach that heavenly language which expresses the significance of the various religious founders and inspirers of humanity, then will the anthroposophical ideal of a tolerant and unbiased consideration of all religions and cosmic conceptions be really able to appear. People will no longer quarrel when they no longer claim for their own group a particular bearer of religion or stream of civilization, but seek for the origin of these bearers outside in cosmic space. In this sense such a contemplation may acquire great moral importance if peace and harmony are established in much that formerly brought divisions and disharmonies upon earth. Only we must learn to read the mighty writing given us in the forms and movements of the heavenly bodies—learn to read how, in reality, not different but the same spirits work for each single individual on earth—that they belong to all people. This might be explained by means of a physical picture. As long as we remain on the earth a group of people may dwell in the North or in the South, East, or West. But when we look upon the movement of the earth we observe how it turns its face to the stars when it changes its position, whether in short periods of time or in millions of years; how the southern half turns to the northern and the stars of our northern heavens become visible; and then how the northern part of our earth turns to the south and perceives the stars of the southern heavens. Just as the earth in the course of time turns its countenance, so to speak, to all the stars that shine to us from cosmic space, so may humanity learn through the ideals of anthroposophy to look in an unbiased manner upon all that speaks spiritually from cosmic space. Through such a positive consideration of facts this ideal will best be reached—not through a sentimental emphasis of love and peace. In a real way shall we attain love and peace and harmony if we direct our vision away from the concerns of earth that divide humanity into races, nations, religions—to the starry heavens, where spirits speak the same language to us through all time, even through all eternity—the same language for every human soul, for every human heart, if only we understand it rightly.

In this sense I should like now, at the end of our course of lectures, to point to the moral effects of such considerations, if we take the trouble to learn to know the facts of occultism. If we learn to know them in the true occult sense, what has been learned will so stream into our hearts that it becomes a life force within us, a living hope. Above all it will become moral energy, and really make us what we may call citizens of the heavenly worlds. Then through our spiritual life we carry heaven into the concerns of earth, and thus in the course of the processes of civilization bring about what, in the highest sense, we can designate as harmony, as peace. Then will we become more and more conscious that at the very beginning as well as at the end of the evolution of civilization an undivided spirit really governs, a spirit of form who works uniformly throughout humanity. This spirit is stimulated by the other spirits of form who serve it in order to work consistently through the whole of humanity. Thus through true heavenly science something uniform is brought to human beings, and this will promote the intellectual and moral understanding of humanity on the earth. Thus we do not wish to consider merely the abstract and theoretical, but every such consideration ought at the same time to become in us a source of power, above all, a source of moral power. Then will all our teachings, even those that appear drawn from afar, serve to forward the direct aims and ideals of spiritual science.

With these closing words, my dear friends, which should gather up the whole spirit and character of these lectures into a certain nuance of feeling, I should like to bid you all farewell.

APPENDIX I

.1.

Address to the Russian participants in the lecture course:
*The Spiritual Beings in the heavenly bodies
and in the kingdoms of nature*

HELSINKI • APRIL 11, 1912

Our involvement with the life and knowledge of Theosophy is constantly deepening; but as it does so, from the depth of our hearts, one question keeps arising: why do we wish to bring Theosophy into the spiritual life of our times? But whenever the question arises, one word emerges in our soul, almost effortlessly, a word that will clarify, and more than clarify, our feelings in the matter: the word *responsibility*.

Responsibility! This single word should be enough to banish immediately from our souls and hearts any notion that our involvement with Theosophy is primarily aimed at satisfying some personal longing. If we then try to understand what this word *responsibility* signifies for us, consciously or not, in relation to the spiritual life of Theosophy, we shall see more and more clearly that our concern with Theosophy is something we owe to contemporary humankind as well as to the best in ourselves. We can not study Theosophy for the pure pleasure it gives us or to appease any private longing; on the contrary, we must feel that today's humanity *needs* Theosophy, if the whole process of human evolution is to go forward. We must indeed recognize that without Theosophy—or whatever you like

to call it—without the (particular) spiritual life that we
have in mind, human life on earth will face a truly desolate
future.

The reason for this is that all the spiritual impulses of the
past are exhausted, everything that has been given to
humanity by way of spiritual impulses is gradually dying
away, and it cannot sow any seeds for human development
in the future. If nothing but the old impulses were to oper-
ate, the only future in sight would be one in which technol-
ogy would not only dominate the whole of our external life
but would overpower and paralyze us, driving out from
the human soul anything of a religious, scientific, philo-
sophical and artistic, and even of an ethical nature in the
higher sense. Without fresh spiritual impulses, humans will
turn into something like living automatons. Thus, when we
think of Theosophy, we must feel that we are the ones led
by karma to some knowledge of the fact that humanity
needs new spiritual impulses.

At this point we may ask: what can each one of us, with
his or her individual qualities and attributes, do regarding
this responsibility? In answering this deeply felt question it
will be instructive to consider how Theosophy came into
the modern world and how it has developed through the
last decades up to the present.

We must never forget that the way in which the word
Theosophy has come into the world in the recent past
amounts to something of a cultural miracle. This extraordinary phenomenon is connected with a certain personality who stands very near to you, since she had her
spiritual roots among your people. I mean, of course, Helena Petrovna Blavatsky. And no one in Western Europe
would possibly maintain that the body in which the individuality known in this incarnation as Helena Petrovna
Blavatsky was contained could have emerged anywhere

but in Eastern Europe, in Russia; for she had all the Russian qualities. But as the result of a peculiar chain of circumstances, she was taken out of your midst, and the particular karmic conditions of the present time led her over to the West. Let us see then what sort of strange cultural wonder this really was.

Take first her actual personality. Fundamentally she remained throughout her life a child, in many respects a genuine child; she never really learned to think logically; never learned how to hold in check her passions and impulses and desires, which in any case tended always to extremes; she really had very little scientific education. Through this personality—through the medium of this personality, one must say—there was revealed a comprehensive body of great external wisdom pertaining to humankind, but revealed as a confused, chaotic medley. Those familiar with such matters will find in Helena Petrovna Blavatsky's works examples of wisdom, truth, and knowledge, which the person Helena Petrovna Blavatsky's intellect and soul could never have come near to understanding. To anyone looking at the facts without prejudice, it must be obvious that her ordinary soul and intellect were merely a channel, a medium whereby great and significant powers were able to communicate with humanity. It is equally clear that, if things had gone as they were expected to go at the beginning of the last third of the nineteenth century, the desired impression could not have been made on anyone in Western Europe. It took the quite peculiar nature of Helena Petrovna Blavatsky—a nature almost literally selfless, devoid of self, on the one hand, and on the other thoroughly self-centered and egotistic—in order to bring about what in fact was brought about by higher spiritual powers. The selfless side was necessary because any Western European mind would have transformed all that was revealed to it into its own thought patterns, its own intellection. The self-centered, egotistic side was necessary because, given the crudely materialistic way of life in Western Europe at that time, only an extreme temperament such as hers could as it were put an iron glove on the fragile hands whose task it was to nurture and cultivate occultism of the modern age. It is indeed a remarkable phenomenon. But Helena Petrovna Blavatsky made her way to the West, to the civilization which in its whole style and structure and configuration was the most thoroughly materialistic civilization of our modern age—America excepted—one which was completely materialistic in its language, feelings, and ways of thinking. It would take us too long to explain which power it was that led Helena Petrovna Blavatsky precisely to England. Nevertheless, the Summa of occultism which came so remarkably to expression through a medium—I do not mean this in a spiritualistic sense—was guided first of all to Western Europe.

Within this European West, the destiny of occultism was sealed, for with the foundation of the Theosophical Movement in the materialistic environment of Western Europe, an important strand of karma came to fulfillment. The European West bears a weighty karmic debt, and can never penetrate the secrets of existence without in some way activating this karmic obligation. Wherever occultism comes into the picture, that karma is immediately deepened, forces are brought to the surface which would otherwise have remained hidden. What I now have to say is not said critically, but merely to describe what happened: While carrying out an historically necessary task, Western Europe perpetrated countless injustices against the bearers of an old spiritual culture and its occult secrets. As a result, this old spiritual life is now truly frozen, no longer available for the present time, although it lives on in the depths of human souls. This is truly what has happened in India, in South Asia. At the moment when occult impulses came to Western Europe, a reaction immediately set in against the spiritual forces active in the depths of Indian culture, and it became impossible—impossible even in the days of Helena Petrovna Blavatsky—to hold fast what certain spiritual powers had intended to be the spiritual movement fitted for our time.

The intention had been to give human beings a body of occult teachings that would be suitable for all human beings, for all hearts, one in which anyone and everyone could partake. But when, due to various necessities, the new impulse was transplanted into Western Europe, an egotistic reaction set in. The spiritual powers whose wish it had been to bestow a new impulse on the whole of humanity without any differentiation were thrust into the background; and India, which had suffered from the suppression of its own occultism, took the first opportunity for karmic revenge. The moment occultism appeared in the West, India brought in its own form of self-centered national occultism. This was happening in the time of Helena Petrovna Blavatsky, even while she was gathering the great truths and wisdom of her *Secret Doctrine*. Her first work, *Isis Unveiled*, brings out the chaotic, illogical, passionate, confusion of her nature, but it also shows throughout that behind her were guardian Powers who wished to lead her towards the universally human. *The Secret Doctrine* was written, we find, side by side with the genuinely great, a special human bias emanating from certain occult centers representative of a parochial, particularistic interest, not the interests of humanity at large. Today the Tibetan, Indian, and even the Egyptian initiations do not have an impartial human interest at heart; they merely want to take revenge on the West for the suppression of Eastern occultism, and

for the conquest of the East by the materialistic resources of
the Western world. The West did indeed conquer the East
by materialistic means; but it "conquered" also insofar as
Christianity was accepted into the true, progressive stream
of human evolution. Christianity did not pass over from
Asia to the East, nor did it go from Asia to the South; it trav-
elled from the East to the West.

Now, my dear theosophical friends, you may well say: so
all's well after all. The West accepted Christianity, and since
Christianity is a stage in the progress of humanity, it is only
natural that on this account the West should have tri-
umphed over the East. If only that were so!   Then it would
be easy to understand—but it is not like that at all. The
Christianity which finally came into the world, after hun-
dreds and thousands of years of preparation, has still not
won the victory anywhere on earth. Anyone who could
believe today that in any true and genuine sense he or she
represents the Christ Principle and the Christ Impulse
would have fallen prey to indescribable arrogance. What,
then, has really happened? Simply that the peoples of Western Europe have taken over some of the most external
aspects of Christianity, and in the name of Christ have
clothed their old warlike cultures in the trappings of modern industrialism. No member of any occult movement
would ever grant that Christ has reigned at any time in our
so-called Christian Europe. On the contrary, he would say:
"You talk of 'Christ', but you still really mean what the old
peoples of Central Europe meant when they spoke of the
god, Saxnot." The symbol of the crucifix stands over the
peoples of Europe, but in a certain way the traditions of the
god Saxnot still prevail. His symbol was the old Saxon short
sword, signifying the expansion of material interests alone,
for that was the vocation of the old Middle-European tribes.
And this vocation produced the finest flower of materialistic

culture: the institution of Knighthood. In no other culture will you find anything like Western Knighthood. One shouldn't even dream of comparing the heroes of the Trojan War with the medieval knights. So Christ still lives very little among human beings; they merely speak of Him. Hence, while the Westerners speak of the Christ, the Eastern peoples feel that they themselves are far ahead in spiritual understanding of the world and in knowledge of the secrets of existence. The Eastern peoples know that with certainty.

Some quite ordinary things will show you that the Eastern peoples rightly value their superiority in spiritual matters. How do most Western people respond when secrets of existence are to be disclosed? Well, we hold very small gatherings where, let us say, we are to speak about the prevailing spiritual Powers and the secrets which surround us everywhere, as we were yesterday evening. For ordinary Western Europeans look on that sort of thing as folly or madness; they are still unable to understand Paul's saying, "God's wisdom is often folly to humanity, and what is folly to humanity is wisdom to God." No one in the East, unless infected by Westerners there, would dream of quibbling about the deep truths concerning the spiritual secrets of the cosmos, as we try to reveal them here, for to those who live within the spiritual life of the East things like the ones we were discussing yesterday, for example, are self-evident. So it is not surprising that when these Eastern people were assailed by Europeans, they often felt rather as people feel when attacked by a herd of wild beasts: they defend themselves, but without resentment, for they look on the assailants as an inferior species. For the reasons I have given— whether or not these are still justified today is irrelevant here—we Westerners are regarded by all adherents of Brahmanism, and in accordance with Eastern traditions, as obviously inferior beings.

Let us now turn from Brahmanism and consider the cultures of Central Asia, the Tibetan, or Chinese culture. In the quite near future these cultures will acquire for the world a significance of which people today have no notion, although it will not be long before this comes about. If we look at all this, and realize that the souls of many pupils of Zarathustra are even now incarnated in those cultures, we shall have to take these things very seriously. We shall also see how, into Helena Petrovna Blavatsky's communications, Indian, Tibetan, and Egyptian occultists have been able to introduce their own heritage of wisdom, although by nature it belongs to a past stage of human development. We must recognize this outdated element in the Blavatsky teachings. And we must not look away from the fact that, if Chinese culture were to break its chains and run over the Western world, it would bring with it a spirituality which in many respects is the still unaltered successor of the old Atlantean culture. It would be as though something that had been under pressure were to fly asunder and scatter throughout the world—on a small scale this is what the old culture of India has done at the very first opportunity. As a result of this, the Theosophical Movement has acquired a distinctive character which no longer makes it a suitable instrument for the further evolution of European culture. Any occultist is familiar with the saying that no special interest of any kind must be allowed to override the general interest of humanity, either on the part of the leading powers of occultism or on the part of anybody active in occult dealings. It is impossible to be effective in the occult realm if a special interest comes to prevail over the general interest of humanity. The moment a parochial interest takes the place of universal human interests the field is open for substantial errors. That is why, since that time, every possible error has crept into the Theosophical Movement. England's karmic connections with India made it possible for those sublime Powers who presided over the birth of the Theosophical Movement to be falsely impersonated. It is quite ordinary in occultism for Powers bent on pursuing their own special interest to assume the guise of those from whom the true impulse had originally come. So from a certain point in time it became impossible to accept without demur all that was contained in the Theosophical Movement, and that karma saw to it that this became less and less possible as time went on. Hence when the call came for us to join forces with the Theosophical Movement, we could do nothing else than go back to the original sources— those sources which stood for humanity as a whole, as against any special interest. And so you may have seen that, in Central Europe, we tried to go back to the original sources in such a way that you will not encounter anything connected with any special interest. If you compare whatever special interests can be found in Central Europe, and in Theosophy as we pursue it here, you will find them entirely incompatible. You can take this Theosophy and— apart from the fact that my books are written in German, since they must after all be written in some language—you will find nothing distinctively German in it, nothing connected with the external traditions of Central Europe. And wherever the temptation arises to connect Theosophy with any special interest, you immediately reach an impasse.

It has been the particular task of Central Europe to free Theosophy from the special characteristics it has acquired in Western Europe. Our mission was to purify Theosophy by removing any trace of special interests from it. And the further you delve into these matters, the more clearly will you see that to a certain extent I personally was well placed to detach my contribution to Theosophy from any particular interest. If I may put it symbolically, I needed only to allow myself to be guided by an impulse which sprang directly from my present incarnation. Please don't misunderstand what I am saying here, I am merely stating facts. The people who were the physical bearers of the blood from which I am descended all came from the German districts of Austria, but I myself could not be born there. I was born in a Slavonic region which was entirely alien to the whole character of the environment from which my forefathers came. So from the very start of my present incarnation, it was impressed upon me—again in a symbolic sense—that our task in Central Europe is that of freeing Theosophy from any kind of special interest, so that Theosophy might stand before us as a goddess, untouched by any human bias, and as relevant to people living in one place as to those living in another.

This is our ideal, and we must it keep before us always; for, simple as it may sound, it is much, much easier to talk about than to achieve. It must stand for us as our ideal of truth and integrity, truth unsullied and divine. If we strive for this—not for our own sake, but so as to endow Theosophy with that impersonal character which Central Europe has to develop for Europe as a whole—then perhaps we may find the way by which this divine Theosophy can be transmitted to the East. And if I now go on to describe further how Theosophy, having found a place in the West, should pass through Europe to the East, I would like once more to emphasize most strongly the word I mentioned earlier—responsibility, a sense of responsibility. The cultures of the world evolve as though within a spiritual sheath that develops one culture by way of another. One culture becomes linked with another. Because Theosophy in Central Europe had to be so impersonal, it has acquired a particular kind of spirituality, one that remains neutral in relation to all special interests. On this account it has a certain dryness about it: the dryness that comes from being untouched by such interests. As a result, it will not appeal to people who are unable to open their hearts to anything which does not serve a particular interest of some kind.

But the spirituality which belongs to this Theosophy can be found by souls who long and thirst for it. And here I must tell you that I became acquainted with a soul out of the spiritual world, a soul with a great longing for the spirit that expresses itself through Theosophy. It was in the purely spiritual world that I came to know this soul. When we go up through the ranks of the hierarchies and come to the individual Folk spirits, and then speak of the Folk souls within the Folk spirits, among the Folk souls who are, so to speak, still young and have to evolve further, as every being must, we find the Russian Folk soul. I know that this Russian Folk soul *longs*—longs with all its strength—for the spirit that finds expression in Theosophy. I have spoken here of the sense of responsibility because you, my dear theosophical friends, are children of this Russian Folk soul. It reigns and works within you, and you have a responsibility toward it. You must learn this responsibility! Do not take it amiss when I say that this Russian Folk soul was able to tell me many things. Most tragic of all was what it could show me in the year 1900 or thereabouts—because it was possible then to see something which I was not able to interpret correctly until much later—how little the Russian Folk soul is understood today. We have learned much, very much, from Russia, and much of it has made a great impression on us. We have come to know the powerful impulses of Tolstoy, the psychology of Dostoevsky which set its mark so deeply on Western Europe, and finally we have learned to know such a man as Solovyov, a man who makes us feel, if we let him work upon us, that as he wrote, so he was. And we see his writings in their true light only if we feel that behind him stands the Russian Folk soul. And this Russian Folk soul has far more to say than Solovyov himself could say, for with him we still always feel that much—much too much—derives from Western Europe.

Think of this word—responsibility—and remember that your task is to make yourselves worthy of the Russian Folk soul and to recognize its longing for impersonal Theosophy. Then, having learned to know the innermost impulse of this Theosophy, you will find yourselves asking all sorts of questions which can be put to the spirit of Theosophy only by a Russian soul.

I have experienced so much fine and noble and beautiful feeling coming to meet me from Eastern Europe, so much true human love and goodness and overflowing sympathy, that one can attribute it only to an unusually delicate and intimate observation of all that the world has to give, and to a close personal connection with the powers of existence. And out of these noble and beautiful feelings many, many questions have been put to me by our Russian members— questions which must be put, because unless they are answered humanity will not be able to live in the future. The questions that can come only from Eastern Europe were formerly put to me only by the Russian Folk soul on the higher planes. I was often led to think that the children of this Folk soul still have a means of understanding the true longing of their Folk soul, and yet how far they are still separated from it. Do not in this account shrink from finding the way to your Folk soul, for you can find it if you really want to. You will learn from your Folk soul the questions that must be answered if humanity is to have a future. Do not be afraid of leaving behind you all personal interests, and be mindful of the great responsibility you have towards the Russian Folk soul, for in the future the Folk souls will need their human children in order to reach their goals. And do not forget one thing. The same power that can carry a person to the heights, the most beautiful light-filled heights of the world, that same power will most of all lay him open to the danger of falling into errors. *Your task is to permeate the spiritual with the necessary element of soul.* This is something you can do, because the Russian Folk soul has immeasurable depths and potentialities for the future. At the same time you must recognize that the soul element, which can raise itself to the spiritual and permeate it, exposes you to a great danger of losing yourselves in the personal and of remaining stuck there. For the personal is particularly strong when nourished from the element of soul.

You will not come up against the many obstacles that keep arising in Central and Western Europe. You are less inclined toward skepticism; it cannot touch you except by infection from Western Europe. You will have a certain feeling for learning to distinguish truth from untruth and dishonesty in the realm of occultism, where truth and charlatanry are such close neighbors. Neither skepticism nor cynicism will be a danger for you.

Your danger will be that the strength of soul in your personalities can surround you with astral clouds, which would then block your way to the objectively spiritual. Your fire and warmth could spread around you a cloudy aura through which the spiritual would be unable to penetrate. Your very enthusiasm for the spiritual could hinder the spirit from finding its way to you.

But you have one great advantage—in a spiritual sense, I mean—for whereas in Central Europe Theosophy has to be taken as a divine power, raised above all human concerns, it is your destiny—which means the destiny of your Folk soul—to receive Theosophy in the special interests of the Russian people, and to cultivate and cherish it as your very own, which is something no other people can do. You have been equipped by your destiny to breathe into the spirit the element of soul. That has often been said in our circles, but now it is up to you to take the first possible opportunity not merely to cultivate your feelings and your will, but above all to develop energy and persistence. If I may speak in practical terms, you should learn to talk less about what Theosophy has to be in the West, and in Russia, and what is good in the one case or in the other, and so forth, and resolve to unite yourselves heart and soul with Theosophy. The rest will then follow; it will certainly follow.

That is something of what I wanted to say to you, my dear friends, because whenever I have to speak directly to people as human beings, there must stand before us that feeling of responsibility which we, as human beings of the present day, owe to Theosophy. In the West people should feel that if they could receive something of Theosophy and decide to reject it, they are sinning against humanity— nothing less. That may be hard to grasp, for one must have an almost transcendental feeling of obligation if this responsibility towards humanity is to be embraced. Your own Folk soul speaks to you of it, for your Folk soul has itself assumed this responsibility towards mankind. You have only to find the way to this Folk soul. You need only allow your thoughts, perceptions and impulses of will to speak, and then, if you have this feeling of responsibility towards your Folk soul, you will at the same time fulfill your obligation towards humankind. It is on this account that you are placed geographically between the European West, which must have Theosophy but cannot make it a personal concern to the same extent that you can, and the Asiatic East, which has possessed occultism and a spiritual culture since primeval times. In this difficult geographical situation you might not be able to accomplish your task for the spiritual culture of mankind if you had to think only of your obligation to humanity. You will be exposed to very great temptations, for active on one side of you is Western Europe, which has led many children of your Folk soul to be untrue, in a fundamental sense, to themselves. A great deal that has been written about Russia, and has been brought to us in the West, gives one the feeling that it has nothing to do with the Russian Folk soul but is a reflection of all kinds of things in the West. The second temptation will come from the East, when the power of that spiritual culture reaches you. It will then be for you to realize that however great may be this spiritual culture of the East, the task for modern people is not to preserve the past but to carry new impulses into the future; not simply to accept any kind of spiritual impulse that comes from the East, but to cherish that which the West can draw from its own spiritual sources.

If you fulfill your obligations to your Folk soul, the time will come, in Europe to begin with, when there will be a little understanding of what the Christ Impulse means in the whole evolution of humanity. Seek everything I have tried to say to you, and seek above all to find whatever in these words can become an impulse of your own—an impulse that will not merely enable you to feel and experience that Theosophy is something great and significant, but will lead you to take Theosophy into the reality and willing of your own souls, and to direct your lives and your actions in accordance with it.

.2.

Address to the Russian participants at the lecture-course
The Occult Foundations of the Bhagavad-Gita

HELSINKI • JUNE 5, 1913

When we were gathered here last year those of you who
were present with our Russian friends carried in their
hearts the buds, as it were, of something which has
unfolded over the past year, namely the awareness, which
should permeate our hearts more and more, that Theosophy—or *Anthroposophy*, as we call it—is not just some
knowledge or credo that people pick up; rather, it should
lay hold of the whole soul of each individual, and the soul
of all humankind in our epoch. This awareness will have to
develop gradually, and we must remain totally immune
from any illusion that its full significance and impact can be
easily attained. Only very slowly, and by degrees, can we
achieve—through a living experience of it—a full awareness of the real significance of the theosophical impulse.

This truth may seem quite commonplace, but this is one
area where precisely the things that seem most ordinary
must be treated with the utmost seriousness. Let us consider simply one thing, in the light of all that belongs to
such a consciousness. Let us consider that it is nearly 2,000
years since the Christ Impulse came down from on high
into earthly life; that the gospels are among the most
widely distributed books in the world; and that for centuries and centuries millions of human souls have believed

themselves to have a right relationship with the Christ. Now set against this the fact that any honest person, unless so immodest as to claim an understanding he or she does not possess, such a person must wrestle with the question, What really is the Christ Impulse? And that, in order to gain any genuine understanding of the Christ Impulse, such a soul would have to hope for new revelations from the spiritual world!

Other facts: last year, I attended with a few friends the Easter service at the Russian Orthodox church. Immediately afterward, I had tried to put into word my experience, believing it would be food for thought: what flowed forth from that Easter service was strictly a consciousness of the dead Christ. Yet the message needed for human salvation today and in the future must be one about the eternal life of Christ. And as a kind of background to that religious service, something else came to mind when I abstracted what was being performed by individuals who did not measure up to the cult they were celebrating. What I perceived behind the service was a kind of tableau of ancient sacred mysteries; those mysteries have evolved into the external forms of the religious service, and many people feel it in the depths of their hearts, but the very people who consider themselves the most qualified interpreters of those mysteries are least capable of understanding them.

Try to let one thought sink deeper and deeper into your soul, the thought that Theosophy proceeds from the heart of each individual, and that through Theosophy, or Anthroposophy, something entirely new must flow into human evolution. Try to impress into your hearts one truth: namely, that the signs of the time require us, at least in the intimacy of our own souls, to refuse any kind of compromise with the surrounding world. A plant cannot give rise to a new plant unless it dies and forms the new plant out of

one small point in itself, the seed. In the same way, my dear
friends, Theosophy is something that actually must
develop out of a small, totally new seed in our souls; and
from all that was part of the old plant of humanity only that
must remain which is universal, only that which we contemplate when we consider the mystery of Golgotha. The
leaves, the trunk, of age-old human culture will have to fall
away; the blooms, the mystery of Golgotha, will have to
remain like a reminder of the seed that must come to frui-
tion in Theosophy. And this seed, my dear friends, will
have to carry within itself the awareness that we must seek
to help those flowers unfold in ever renewed ways. Then
the Christ Impulse will live in many forms through human
evolution and yet remain the same, just as each new flower
bears in itself the force and the beauty of the old flowers.
But at the same time the impulse will be what it seeks to be
in its innermost essence—something that arises again and
again, an ever self-renewing understanding of the thing
that was given as a new beginning of human evolution,
when the blood flowed from the wounds of the One who
had taken human form in order to experience death within
humankind.

All the worlds we can pass through when we move from
our physical world into ever higher worlds have one thing
in common. It is in general correct that on entering a higher
world we always find much that is completely new, but
also something that belongs to the world directly below it.
But when we come to know the higher worlds, we learn
that one thing is not to be found there, for it can exist only
in the physical world. *The gods of the higher worlds can have
manifold experiences, but they cannot experience death.* For in
the supersensible world, there is no death. The beings of
those worlds transform themselves; they pass from one
form to another; but they cannot die. And among all the

gods and spirits there has been only one, the Christ, who, in order to make common cause with humanity, descended into the human world; and He united Himself with humankind not only through His life, but also through His death. And through His death, new forces of life streamed out. If they are to be new life-forces for humanity, the contemplation of Golgotha must be the starting place, for at this single point in human evolution is concentrated all that God wished to accomplish, for humans, through infinite sacrifice. If you try to take these thoughts and make them into a living meditation, you will see that they can become the source of the strongest life-forces for every human being. There is no more exalted picture than that of the cross raised on Golgotha.

My dear friends, an imagination such as that of the Cross on Golgotha can be endlessly fruitful for human beings. This symbol, which was at the same time a reality, was given to us nearly 2,000 years ago, and yet we must learn to understand it more and more deeply in the future, as human evolution continues. These are simple, primitive thoughts, but they are not meant to be turned into metaphysics, but to create feelings which will fit us to play a rightful part in human evolution.

You know that, in the course of evolution, humanity has become differentiated into separate nations and peoples. Each people has a distinctive character, due to the fact that each people is under the leadership of one of those spirits we include in the hierarchy of Archangels; these Archangels are the highest representatives of the separate peoples. A spiritual outlook on the world must result in each individual realizing a closer and closer link with the Archangel who is the leader of his or her people. And only if we understand what the Folk soul intends for us—only then shall we be fitted to cooperate in the spiritual evolution of mankind. And in this context we must draw a sharp distinction between the Western European Folk soul and the East European, Russian Folk soul.

I am not speaking now of the external culture of the Russian people, as we know it on the physical plane. I am speaking of the Russian Folk soul, who is present in the spiritual world, awaiting with confidence and hope its future task. Compared with the Western European Folk soul, we get the impression that the Russian Folk soul is still young and in the ascendant, while the others are old and worn. The culture of Central Europe stands as a go-between between East and West, and to equate it with the others would be a fundamental misunderstanding. In a very special way, the task of that Central European culture is to act as the herald of the past in later times. Just think how the whole European culture of the Western world came into being. The oriental peoples had advanced into ancient India, and had developed there an impressive culture, as we encounter it in the *Bhagavad Gita*. These peoples had pushed on as far as southern Asia. While they had such great wise teachers as the Rishis and Zarathustra, the wisdom of evolution had arranged that quite primitive people should be left behind all over the wide regions of Europe, and in your own country also.

While in Asia there flowered the far-reaching conceptions that we find in the Sankhya and Vedanta philosophies, the European peoples had simple, primitive forms of culture. Why? Because cultures can progress only in such a way that everything which is to emerge later as a new impulse must first be received by primitive peoples. The peoples of the East, who had risen to a certain height of intellectual development, would never have been able to understand, for example, the Christ Impulse; it would have been beyond the bounds of possibility for them.

The peoples of the culture of the West had not yet come to the stage of accepting the spiritual with their heads. The force which lives in the heart and rises to the head had not reached the head. In India everything was a culture of the head—but the European peoples were still imbued with the original strength of primitive feelings concentrated in their hearts. Only such peoples, because their soul-qualities were still centered in their hearts, could gradually absorb the Mystery of Golgotha into their feelings. Thus it was European Culture, because by remaining backward it had kept its primal forces fresh—and primal forces are more nearly related to the divine—which was ready to receive the Christ Impulse. So in the Western world two streams flowed together, and anyone who can perceive these things will know that the two streams must be sharply distinguished from each other. Otherwise one could not clearly distinguish the fundamental tone of Fichte, the Central European philosopher, from the fundamental tone of Spinoza, another European philosopher. It can happen in human evolution that something that belongs to the general culture of the time is carried on by the same individuality, and—as some of you may know—the individuality of Spinoza reappears in Fichte. But Fichte, as a separate personality of the 18th-19th century, was a man who could be penetrated by the full force of the Christ Impulse; while Spinoza, although the same individuality, belonged to the other stream, and the Christ Impulse was quite alien to him.

There is a great deal still lacking in European culture which must develop; those parts of it which have grown old must be brought to work together with those that are still young and fresh with hope. The Russian Folk soul, the Being which belongs to the order of Archangels, is young and hopeful. Its task is still to come. It will be for Russian Theosophists to find the bridge from individual souls to the

Folk soul—to learn what the Folk soul asks of them. Given certain preconditions, you will find it particularly easy with the aid of all that lives in your souls to bring the Christ Impulse to life in your hearts. But just because you are inwardly predisposed to find this easy, you will have great difficulties to face. You will learn that precisely to you a deep truth applies in the highest degree—the truth that you must take your stand on your own souls and bring Theosophy to life in your own hearts. For Theosophy, being essentially the message for our epoch, can make no compromise with other outlooks. To other outlooks, it speaks stern words—words that have been heard before in the course of evolution. Those who look for Theosophy in the old materialistic cultures—all contemporary cultures come under this heading, or at least nearly so—or those who seek a compromise with them, must hear spoken to them with all sternness the words of Christ Jesus: "Let the dead bury their dead. Follow me!" The "dead" are the cultures which verge on materialism; they are already well equipped to dig their own graves. "Let the dead bury their dead!" But the duty of human souls is to follow with understanding the spiritual power which goes through the world as the Christ Impulse. Therefore, if you look for an answer to your quest in the old traditions and practices, you will not find in them what has led you to Theosophy. It is good to discern how the divine enters into these old traditions, but those who come to Theosophy today will do so precisely because their soul is not marked with age but is a soul like yours—fresh and direct, coming to meet Theosophy uninfluenced by any traditions. The forces of life, not merely those of knowledge, are what the theosophical impulse requires from your souls.

My dear friends, many of you, perhaps most or even all of you, feel in yourselves—though you may put it differently—the pain of being separated from your Folk soul for the time being. Many of you, perhaps most or even all of you, feel you need a new stimulus for your energies and your will, though again you may not see it quite like that. Try to see—resolve to see!—the pain that comes from your lack of energy and will-power as indicating a virginal, untouched quality of will, waiting only to be stirred by the theosophical impulse. Turn this impulse into a force of will; transform your pain into strength, your weakness of will into theosophical activity. By this path you will enter into the heart of Theosophy. Try to refashion whatever in you is weak, or not fully present. Then you will be able to become the best representatives of Theosophy. Remember too, that the souls which now inhabit your bodies are not destined to be incarnated next time in Eastern Europe only. They are destined to be spread all over the earth. When in the course of your life between death and rebirth you are approaching a new incarnation, you will hear words spoken to you. To one it will be said: "You have fulfilled your task: you will be able to carry into the world what you acquired on earth, and could acquire only on the soil of Eastern Europe." To another it will be said: "You cannot do it!"

Think of the feeling you now have for Theosophy as an instinct for what I have just been saying—as a vague feeling for the task that is to be yours. Think of it in such a way that it will carry strength from your I into your thinking, feeling, and willing, and thence into your blood. Then you will interpret rightly this instinct which urges you toward Theosophy.

You have found it possible, despite the difficult conditions that prevail in your country, to assemble here unhindered. Make use of this opportunity to achieve the greatest possible inward relatedness among you, in order to build the bridge between each one of you and your Folk soul. It cannot be my task to speak in detail of the services you can render to your Folk soul. But I would like to say something else, and would ask you, though I speak in words, to allow the words to change within you into feelings. You are in a special situation, at the opposite pole as it were from a people, the people of North America, who are rising to a short period of brilliance. Reflect that these American people, your opposites, began to advance slowly westward just at the time when the epoch of materialism had begun in Europe, and they developed this materialism still further. Remember that materialism prevails in the very roots of American civilization. Remember that the people who colonized America took with them the ideas that were current in educated Europe only a few centuries ago. While they were making their way through primeval forests, clearing the land bit by bit and preparing it for agriculture—activities we generally associate with quite uncultured people— they were already imbued with a whole range of materialistic modern concepts. They thought in terms of parliaments, natural science, modern social organization. Everything they accomplished was done under the influence of materialism. Think of the man who is generally regarded as one of their most important writers, the man whom they elected as their President—Woodrow Wilson. In the context of the present day he really is a significant writer; he has produced some brilliant literary studies of social life. But if one looks at his concepts and ideas, at everything he stands for as a representative of the American people, what does it amount to? A house of cards. If the spiritual world were once to breathe upon it, this house of cards—and the whole culture it typifies—would collapse. This American civilization can be traced back in every detail to the history books and the cultural history of previous centuries. It all lies there openly; everything about it is man-made.

Ask yourselves whence your character as a people comes; whence comes your spiritual life and all the best qualities you can cherish in your souls. You will not find the origin of all this on earth; its roots are in the spiritual world. All this is living and organic, it is no house of cards. It should never be a source of pride, however, but of modesty and humility; we should derive from it a feeling of responsibility, not an arrogant self-consciousness.

Yesterday I spoke to you about freedom. A great deal of water will have to flow under the bridges of Europe before any considerable number of people come to understand fully what freedom in this sense means. What is freedom? Looking to the West, what does it mean for an American? Whatever gives him the most comfortable life. For him, freedom signifies a social order which gives every individual the best chance to get on in the world! Our idea of freedom, says Woodrow Wilson, is different from that of Europeans, because we think of it in practical terms. A knife is used to cut with and a fork to eat with, because they are practically useful for these purposes. Freedom for an American is a utility product; it is something that serves his convenience. For the Western European freedom has been something very different—a lofty ideal to which he looked up. One could almost apply the words of the poet and say that for a European freedom is "a high and glorious goddess"—while for the American, freedom is the useful cow which provides him with milk and butter. I am not the one putting it this way; it is the man who will be responsible for guiding the United States during the next few years. My task is not to advance opinions of my own, but to act as an interpreter of the living realities of the spiritual world. An outstanding American, Woodrow Wilson, has himself characterized freedom in this way. If now we take all that heroic spirits in Europe struggled to express in describing this divine freedom as a lofty, majestic goddess, we shall have to say: All our enthusiasm, our feelings and our thoughts go out towards the ideal of freedom as it hovered before these Europeans.

But now you must understand that for the adherents of a spiritual worldview, freedom has to become something quite different again. You would be badly mistaken if you failed to realize that everything has to be made anew. We are faced with the demand that freedom has to become quite different from the idea of it which the best human minds have cherished hitherto. For we know that, in the near future, we as human beings will be enabled to approach a divine source and drink from it the waters of the spirit; that these waters will live on in our souls, and that with their aid we shall have to learn how to enshrine freedom in our souls, just as we enshrine our souls in our bodies. In the eyes of some people, freedom is a practical convenience for external life; for others it is a lofty spiritual ideal; for us it must be something we enshrine in our souls and which is higher than the soul to the same degree that the soul is higher than the body. In order to accomplish this, we need to learn much, and then we shall go forward in the way intended by the eternal spiritual Powers who have caused Theosophy to flow into your souls.

My dear friends, such are the simplest words, spoken not to your intellects but to your hearts, that I wished to say to you on this occasion, now that you have found it possible to devote yourselves to Theosophy as an organized movement in your country. So let us take the opportunity at this moment to become clearly conscious of the lofty task assigned to us by a spiritual comprehension of the world. Then, if you live in this consciousness something will radiate out as a healing influence for the whole country from the quiet work in theosophical branches. We will only begin to understand spiritual life once we know that the spread of Theosophy is not accomplished only through external achievements, but that when we work together as well as we can to gain an understanding of Theosophy, the effects of our spiritual endeavors stream out invisibly. We know indeed that a town in which a theosophical lodge exists becomes after thirty years a quite different place—even though only a few Theosophists have worked there—from a town which has no theosophical lodge. So will your country become quite different if you receive with inner understanding what Theosophy has to give. I am not speaking to you as Western Europeans, or as members of this nation or that. I know that any such description would not apply to you. But just for this reason I may perhaps be allowed to say: Salvation can come to Russia, but it must not be sought along a false path. I am saying this not because I love Theosophy, but because the whole evolution of humanity can teach us to take it as the truth. There is a way of salvation for Russia, and its name is Theosophy. In other regions of the earth Theosophy will be an excellent means of progress for mankind. For Russia, Theosophy is the only way; the indispensable means of enabling the Russian people to unite themselves with their Folk soul, so that this Folk soul may not be called away to tasks other than those destined for it.

With these words I should like to inaugurate your newly-founded branches, for I know how your hearts respond to the sacred significance of these words. Then there will be established in your souls that connection which is necessary for the salvation of your country—the connection between the Mystery of Golgotha and the human understanding of that Mystery. Then in your hearts will reign the Spirit who must become the regenerator of your country; then from your gatherings there will radiate out that which

your part of the earth needs. With these thoughts in my
mind, and with my gaze directed in reverence and devotion to the guiding Powers of human evolution, I say that
my wish is to call down every blessing on your work; the
blessing of those Powers who are today causing the Mystery of Golgotha to find its way into human hearts, so that
this blessing may flow out from your souls and from your
work and radiate over your country. And I know that this
blessing is always present, if we are worthy of it. At this
time, as we stand at the outset of your work, may the vision
of a new impulse hover before our minds, the spiritual
impulse which must pour into human evolution, and may
the spiritual leaders of this impulse overshadow the work
which we resolve to carry through rightfully. Then from
this vision will arise the conviction that what we are doing
for a limited region must be done for the whole human
realm, and your duty will be clear. In this sense, may the
blessing of the wise leaders of the world and of humankind
prevail in your work and rise powerfully to illuminate your
souls. Then its light will stream out from you, and you will
be able to accomplish much that is essential for the healing,
progress, and true evolution of humanity.

APPENDIX II

The Essence of National Epics

with special reference to the *Kalevala*

Public lecture

HELSINKI • APRIL 9, 1912

To begin with, I would like to apologize for being unable to give this lecture in the language customary in this country. This lecture is being held in response to the wishes of friends of our Theosophical Society. Since I have been called here to hold a series of lectures for them lasting fourteen days, they thought that during this time it would be possible to hold the two announced public lectures. I must further ask your pardon if I, as one unfamiliar with the language, do not pronounce correctly some of the names and characterizations taken from the national epic of the Finns. Spiritual science itself will be introduced only in the lecture to be held next Friday. The observations presented in today's lecture will be much more concerned with a neighboring field that can be illuminated by spiritual science. We shall speak of a subject which, in the very deepest sense of the word, is one of the most interesting in the study of human history and reflection on that history.

National epics! We need only think of some of the well-known folk epics, for example, those of Homer which became the national epics of the Greeks; the middle-European Nibelungen legend; and finally the *Kalevala*, and we realize immediately that we are lead by these folk epics deeper into human souls and human striving than any historical research could bring us. Through them ancient times become alive for us as though they were placed directly in front of our souls in the present moment; we are touched by them in the same way we are touched by the destinies and lives of people immediately around. In terms of history, the ancient times of the Greek peoples reported to us by the Homeric epics are uncertain and vague. But when we let the content of the *Iliad* or the *Odyssey* work upon us, we can see right into the souls of those people, who are otherwise entirely beyond the reach of ordinary historical observation. It is no wonder that the study of national epics is full of riddles for those considering them from the point of view of science or literature. With respect to the ancient Greek epics we need only point out one fact, which a brilliant observer of the *Iliad* expressed repeatedly in a very beautiful book concerning Homer's *Iliad* that appeared just a few years ago. I am thinking of Herman Grimm, the nephew of Jacob Grimm, the great researcher of German language, myths, and legends. When Herman Grimm let the characters and facts of the *Iliad* work on him again and again he felt called upon to say: Oh! this Homer (we do not need today to go into the question of Homer's personality)—when he describes anything taken from handwork or art, he actually appears to be an expert in that craft. When describing a battle or a fight he appears to be fully acquainted with all the strategic and military principles that come into consideration in conducting war.

Herman Grimm quite properly points out that Napoleon, a strict judge of such things, was a great admirer of Homer's objective battle descriptions. Napoleon was a man no doubt entitled to judge whether or not, out of the spirit of Homer, military things are portrayed with immediacy, objectively and filled with life. We ourselves know, from the universal human point of view, to what extent Homer places characters before our souls as though they stood directly in front of our physical eyes.

How have such national epics continually proven themselves through the years? Truly, anyone observing the situation in an unprejudiced way will not conclude that humanity's artificial institutions, for example, educational institutions, are responsible for maintaining the centuries of interest, even into our age, in the *Iliad* and the *Odyssey*. This interest is a given; it is a universally human interest. But, in a certain sense, these folk epics give us a task. When we study them they immediately present us with a very specific, one would like to say, an interesting task. Namely, they want to be taken precisely with all their details. We notice immediately that something in the content of such folk epics becomes incomprehensible if we try to read them as we would any modern work of art, like a novel, for instance. From the first lines of the *Iliad* we can feel that Homer is speaking with precision. What does he describe to us? He tells us right at the beginning. From other portrayals of the story we know a number of things not contained in the *Iliad*, events from the past that lead up to the story told in the epic. Homer wants only to describe to us what he stated so exactly in the first lines: the anger of Achilles. And if we read through the entire *Iliad* looking at it carefully then we must say: In truth there is nothing within which cannot be characterized as a fact resulting from the anger of Achilles.

Something else also occurs right at the beginning of the *Iliad*: Homer does not begin simply with the facts; or with any personal opinion; he begins rather with something that the modern age would perhaps like to understand as a phrase. He begins by saying, "Sing to me, O Muse, of the anger of Achilles!" And the deeper we penetrate into this national epic the clearer it becomes that we cannot understand the meaning, spirit, and significance of this epic unless we take seriously these words at the beginning. Then we must ask ourselves: What exactly do they mean?

Now look at the description itself, at the way the events are brought before our souls! Not only experts and scientific students, but many people—even artistically complete spirits such as Herman Grimm—asked: What do these words mean: "Sing to me, O Muse, of the anger of Achilles!"? This question went to their heart. How do the deeds of spiritual, divine beings in the Nibelungen legend, the *Kalevala*, or to begin with, the deeds, intentions, and passions of the Olympic gods in Homer's writings, relate to the deeds, intentions, and passions of human beings? How do they relate to human beings like Achilles, who in a certain sense are distant from ordinary people; and how do they relate to the passions, intentions, and deeds of men like Odysseus and Agamemnon, who are closer to common humanity? When Achilles appears before our soul he seems to us to be lonely, in contrast to the people with whom he lives. As the story advances we quickly come to feel that in Achilles we have a personality who actually cannot speak to any of the other heroes about the deepest concerns of his soul. Homer also shows us how the things that really stir Achilles' heart he must discuss and arrange with divine-spiritual beings who do not belong to the human kingdom. He shows us how Achilles, all the way through the *Iliad*, stands lonely in the kingdom of human beings while standing close to supersensible, super-earthly powers. It is strange that when we gather up all the human feeling and thinking achieved through human culture and turn our attention to behold this Achilles, we must say because of the way he appears to us: How egotistical, how merely personal! A being with divine-spiritual impulses flowing into his soul is acting entirely out of personal considerations! For a long time this war, so important for the

Greeks—this Trojan war of legend—only progressed, that is, the particular episodes described in the *Iliad* only took place because Achilles was personally settling accounts with Agamemnon. And we constantly see supra-earthly powers getting involved. We see Zeus, Apollo, and Athena distributing impulses, so to speak, placing mortals in their places. Before the task came to me to approach these things from the point of view of spiritual science, I always found it strange how a very intelligent man, with whom I had the good fortune of often discussing these things, how Herman Grimm came to terms with these things. Not only in his writings but also in personal conversations—and there with even greater clarity—he often said: If we consider only the historical powers and impulses playing into the development of humanity then we cannot come to terms with what is living and working in the great national epics. Therefore, for Herman Grimm, the gifted observer of the *Iliad* and of folk epics altogether, there was something that exceeds ordinary human powers of consciousness, exceeds understanding, reason, and sense observation, exceeds normal human feeling, that became a real power, a power that is creative just like other historical impulses. Herman Grimm spoke of a genuinely creative fantasy that accompanies the development of humankind; he spoke of this fantasy the way one would speak of a being, of a reality, of something that held sway over human beings and, at the beginning of the times we can observe, had more of a say in the evolution of individual folk groups than what ordinary soul forces could say to human beings. Herman Grimm always spoke of this creative fantasy as of another world shining forth into the human world, which could not be completely contained in the usual human soul forces and which he therefore saw in the roll of a co-creative force in the process of human evolution.

Now it is peculiar, but when we consider this battlefield of the *Iliad*, this portrayal of the anger of Achilles with all the involvement of supersensible, divine-spiritual powers, we are not satisfied with a study such as Herman Grimm has produced. In his book on the *Iliad* we find many references to resignation that show us how today's usual literary or scientific point of view cannot adequately account for these things. What conclusions does Herman Grimm arrive at concerning the Nibelungen legend or the *Iliad*? He comes to the conclusion that there were dynasties or ruling families that preceded the historically known dynasties. That is how Herman Grimm thinks, one would like to say, literally. He thinks that Zeus with his entire entourage represents a kind of reigning family that preceded the reigning family of which Agamemnon was a member. He sees the human history having a uniformity; he thinks of the gods or heroes portrayed in the *Iliad* or the Nibelungen legend as ancient human beings. The people who came later only dared to represent them by dressing their deeds, their character in the clothing of superhuman myths. There is much that cannot be accounted for if one begins with such a supposition. Above all, the particular way the gods intervene in Homer's stories is hard to explain. I ask you to consider just this: How do Thetis, the mother of Achilles, Athena, and other gods intervene in the events of Troy? They intervene by assuming the form of mortal human beings, inspiring them, so to speak, and leading them to their deeds. The gods themselves do not appear; instead they permeate living human beings. Living people do not figure as the representatives of the gods but rather as the sheaths or garments permeated by invisible powers who cannot appear on the battlefield in their own form, in their own being. It certainly would have been strange to assume that ordinary people from the most ancient times should have been portrayed as needing representatives from the tribe of mortals to serve as their sheaths. That is just one indication among many that can prove to us all that we will not be able to explain the old national epics in this way.

It is just as difficult to understand the characters in the Nibelungen legend. I am thinking of Siegfried of Xanten on the lower Rhine who went to the court of Burgundy in Worms to court Kriemhilde, the sister of Gunther. Siegfried then courts Brunhilde for Gunther using special talents only he, Siegfried, possesses. How strangely are these figures such as Brunhilde of Issland or Siegfried described to us. Siegfried is described as having overcome the so-called race of the Nibelungen, as having acquired or conquered the treasure of the Nibelungen. By means of what he has acquired through victory over the Nibelungen he has been given special powers. These are expressed in the epic when it is said that he can make himself invisible and that, in a certain sense, he is invulnerable. Furthermore, he has powers that the ordinary Gunther does not have; for Gunther cannot win Brunhilde, who cannot be conquered by an ordinary mortal. Siegfried is victorious over Brunhilde because of the special powers he has as possessor of the Nibelungen treasure. Because he can then hide these powers again he is in a position to lead Brunhilde to Gunther, his brother-in-law. Then we find Kriemhilde and Brunhilde, two very different characters, present at the same time in the court of Burgundy. We experience them as having forces working into their souls that cannot be explained as powers ordinarily present in the human soul. Because of these powers they come into conflict and Hagen, the faithful servant, can be misled by Brunhilde to kill Siegfried. This points out a motif that is strangely characteristic of middle-European legends. Siegfried has higher, superhuman powers because he possesses the Nibelungen treasure. But in the final analysis they do not necessarily make him into a victorious character; rather into a character who stands tragically before us. The powers Siegfried has through the Nibelungen treasure are also a tragic fate for the human being. Things become even stranger when we consider further the related Nordic legend of Sigurd, the dragon killer. But it also helps to clarify our discussion. Sigurd, who is none other than Siegfried, immediately appears to us as the conqueror of the dragon and in this way has acquired the Nibelungen treasure from an old race of dwarfs. Brunhilde appears to us as a figure of superhuman greatness, as a Valkyrie.

We see then that there were two ways to represent these things in Europe. One way connects Brunhilde directly to the divine-supersensible world and also shows us that something is to be found in Brunhilde that belongs directly to the supersensible world. The other way humanizes the legend but, nevertheless, we can recognize that even here the divine is found "sounding through" everywhere.

Now let us turn from these legends, from these national epics, to another region, a region of which I am only allowed to speak as one who can see things from the outside, that is, as one who can recognize them while not speaking the language. I ask you to take into consideration that I can only speak about all that comes to meet a West European in the *Kalevala*, as one who considers the spiritual content, the great and mighty figures therein. Of course, the fine points of the epic, which are no doubt present and only come out when one really masters the language in which the epic is written, these external fine points must escape me. When we study the *Kalevala*, how strangely the trinity of figures appears to us. These three...well, one is really in a predicament when trying to find an appropriate name to

use for them. One cannot say gods, one cannot use the
word heroes for the three beings: Vainamoinen, Ilmarinen,
and Lemminkainen. These three figures speak a strange
language when we compare their characters. We can clearly
recognize through this language that the events related to
us go far beyond what the usual powers of the human soul
can achieve. When we observe these three figures only
externally they grow into frightful proportions. What is
strange is that even though they grow into frightful proportions and every single characteristic stands graphically
before our eyes, still we never have the feeling that the
frightful proportions become grotesque or paradoxical.
Everywhere throughout the story we have the feeling that
it is natural for what needs to be said to appear with superhuman greatness, with superhuman significance.

And then the contents contain such riddles! There is
something that spurs us on to think about the deepest contents of the human soul, yet seems to go beyond everything
that can be comprehended by the forces that ordinarily live
in our soul. Ilmarinen, who is often called the smith, the
artistic smith of everything, abetted by Vainamoinen,
forges the Sampo—a region where live what may be called
the older brothers of humanity, a region, at least, where a
more primitive people than the Finns live. And we see this
strange thing, that a lot of different events occur far from
the theater in which the main events take place. Time goes
by and we see Vainamoinen and Ilmarinen forced to
retrieve what was left in a foreign land: the Sampo. When
we allow this strange language of the spirit that speaks
through the forging of the Sampo, its separation at a distance and its retrieval, to work upon us, we gain the definite impression (as I said, I ask you to bear in mind that I
am speaking as a foreigner and therefore can only speak of
the impression a foreigner receives) that the most essential,

the most significant aspect of this grand composition is just
this: the forging, the separation at a distance, and the later
retrieval of the Sampo.

The conclusion of the *Kalevala* touches me in a very peculiar way. I have heard there are people who believe the conclusion to be, perhaps, a later addition. For my feeling just
this conclusion with Mariata and her son, this involvement
of a very strange Christianity—I say expressly, of a very
strange Christianity—belongs to the whole. The *Kalevala*
acquires through this conclusion a very special nuance, a
coloring that serves, so to speak, to make it entirely under-
standable. I would like to say that, for my feeling, there is
altogether no portrayal of Christianity to be found anywhere as delicate and wonderfully impersonal as that
found at the end of the *Kalevala*. The Christian principle is
freed from any geographic limitations. The approach of
Mariata to Herod, whom we meet in the *Kalevala* as Rotus,
is structured in such an impersonal fashion that we are
hardly reminded of any kind of location or personality in
Palestine. Indeed, we are, we could say, not even in the
least reminded of the historical Jesus Christ. At the end of
the *Kalevala* we find the penetration of the noblest cultural
pearl of humanity into the Finnish culture delicately hinted
at as the most intimate concern of the heart of humankind.
Connected with this is the tragic development that can
affect us so deeply in our souls. In the moment when Christianity enters in, when Mariata's son is baptized, Vainamoinen departs from his people in order to go to an
undetermined destination. He leaves his folk with only the
content and the power of what he, through his singing, had
been able to tell them concerning the ancient mysteries
included in the history of this people.

This withdrawal of Vainamoinen when the son of Mariata appears seems to me so significant because we can see,

in the moment when Christianity found entry into Finland, the living interplay of everything that held sway in the ground of the Finnish people, the Finnish Folk soul, that held sway since ancient times. The way this power holding sway since ancient times related itself to Christianity is such that we can feel with a wonderful intimacy all that was involved in the souls of the people. What I am saying is objective. I am not saying it to make anyone happy or to flatter. We West Europeans have in this national epic a wonderful example of how, in the immediate present, the members of a folk bodily stand before us with their entire soul so that through the *Kalevala* we in Western Europe can become well acquainted with the Finnish soul.

Why have I said all this to you? I have said it to characterize how something speaks in national epics that cannot be explained by the ordinary powers in the human soul, even when one speaks of fantasy as a genuine power. And even though much of what will be said may only sound like a hypothesis to many—nevertheless, perhaps I can now add what spiritual science has to say concerning the nature of national epics. I am, of course, aware that what I have to say touches something that today, in our time, very few people can give their assent to. It will be seen by many as a reverie or fantasy. Others will accept it at least as one hypothesis among others, one that can be suggested to explain the evolution of humankind. However, for those who penetrate into spiritual science I will not be speaking of a hypothesis. In the next lecture I will permit myself to describe spiritual science in such a way that I will speak rather of the results of genuine research that can be placed alongside the results of other scientific research. These things we must speak about sound strange because the present-day scientific establishment—which thinks it is standing firmly on the ground of real facts, of the only true and reachable reality—

limits itself to what can be perceived by the external senses, to what human understanding bound to the brain and to the senses can discover about things. Therefore, it is considered unscientific today to speak of a research method that reaches for other forces in the soul, forces that make it possible to see into the supersensible, to see the influx of the supersensible into the sensible.

We are lead by this research method, by spiritual science, not merely to the abstract fantasy to which Herman Grimm was lead when studying national epics, but we are lead rather to something going far beyond fantasy, something that portrays a condition of soul and consciousness entirely different from what human beings can have in the present moment of our development. Through spiritual science we are lead back to antiquity in an entirely different way than, let us say, through ordinary science.

When looking back at the evolution of humankind ordinary science customarily sees what we today call the human being as having gradually developed out of creatures similar to animals. Spiritual science does not confront this modern research prepared for battle. It rather fully acknowledges the great and mighty accomplishments of this science of the nineteenth century. It acknowledges the full significance of the idea that animal forms have been transformed from the least perfect to the perfect and that the external form of the human being can be connected to the most perfect animal form. But spiritual science cannot stop with such a study of human evolution, of the evolution of organisms altogether. It cannot stop with a study that would portray from the point of view of external senses only what has taken place in the course of the earth's history in the organic world up to the appearance of the human being. For spiritual science the human being today stands alongside the world of animals. In the world that surrounds us we see variously shaped animal forms. We see, spread out over the earth, the human race which is, in a certain sense, uniform. In spiritual science we also have an unprejudiced view of how, in external forms, everything speaks for the human being's relatedness to the other organisms on the earth. But when, in spiritual science, we pursue the evolution of humankind backward, we cannot go back to a time when, in the grey mists of antiquity, the stream of humankind flows back directly into the line of animal development. When we go back from the present into the past we find that there is no place where we can directly line up the present human form with any animal form that we know from the present.

When we go back in the evolution of humankind, we find the same soul forces, the same powers of understanding, feeling, and willing in human beings, but in primitive, ever less-developed, forms. Then we arrive back at the grey, dim ages of the past, concerning which the old documents tell us little. Even when we can go back as far as the Egyptians and other Near Eastern peoples we still find an ancient form of humanity with the same powers of feeling, thinking, and willing as our own. In a certain sense, though, those powers were grander as well as more primitive than ours. These powers have only attained their present forms in recent times; we see them as important impulses of humanity, as important historical impulses, to the extent that we can trace humankind backward and take into consideration its present soul configuration. Nowhere do we find it possible to establish a kinship between present-day animal forms and any form of the human race, even the race of men and women lying farthest in the past. This is what spiritual science must assert; and today there are even thoughtful natural scientists who acknowledge it. We can go back into the past and observe how the human soul has changed. We can compare how a human being thinks today, let us say scientifically or otherwise, how we use our intelligence and our powers of feeling, with how people thought in the past. We can follow this back into the past with relative precision and see how, at a certain time, modern thinking first flared up in humankind: It first appeared in the sixth or seventh century before Christ. The entire configuration of present-day feeling and thinking does not actually reach any further back into the past than into those times when the first Greek philosophers of nature are said to have lived.

Going back further with an unprejudiced view, we find, without even touching spiritual science, that all scientific thinking ceases, that the human soul is constituted in an entirely different way. The constitution of the human soul then was much less personal; its powers must be described as much more instinctive. We would not want to say that the people of that time acted out of the same kinds of instincts as the present-day animals, but the kind of guidance present today through reason and understanding was not present. In its place a certain instinctive, immediate certainty was present in human beings. Their actions proceeded from direct, elemental impulses; they did not control their actions through intellectual understanding tied to the brain. We find the forces still holding sway there that we modern people have separated into intellectual forces and the forces of fantasy. Today the forces of fantasy are carefully separated from those intellectual forces that lead us to science.

Fantasy, understanding, and reason worked all mixed up together in those ancient times. The further we go back into the past the less we are able to call what held sway in the soul of human beings—what worked as fantasy and understanding inseparably bound up together—the less we can characterize this mixture the same way we characterize the power in the soul called fantasy today. We are well aware that when we speak of fantasy today we are speaking of a power in the soul, the products of which we are not really allowed to use; we are not really allowed to ascribe reality to them. The modern human being is careful in these matters. We are careful not to mix the products of fantasy together with what the logic of reason tells us. If we look at what the human spirit produced in those prehistoric times before fantasy and intellect were separated from one another, then we can feel how an original, elemental, instinctive power held sway in human souls. We can find characteristics of present-day fantasy in this ancient power but we should remember that what fantasy gave the human soul in those days had something to do with a reality. Fantasy was not yet fantasy; it was still—I will not hesitate to use the term—a clairvoyant power. Fantasy was still a special ability in the soul; it was a gift of the soul through which the human being could see things that are hidden from people today, during an epoch when understanding and reason should be especially developed. Those forces that were not fantasy, but clairvoyant powers, penetrated deep into the hidden forms of existence and the hidden forces lying behind the sensible world. An unprejudiced consideration of the development of humankind backward through time must lead us to this conclusion: Truly, we must take the words "evolution" and "development" seriously.

The powers of understanding and reason that have brought humankind to its present "advanced" state are the result of an evolution. The present powers of the soul have developed from others. Our present soul forces are limited to what can be perceived of the external world by the senses. But originally humankind, which had to do without science in the modern sense, without the use of the intellect in the modern sense—humankind, with its primal powers of soul that existed in the depths of every individual folk, saw into the foundations of existence, into a region that lies supersensibly behind the sensible. Clairvoyant powers once belonged to the souls of all folk groups. Present-day powers of understanding and reason, our present way of thinking and feeling has evolved, has been formed from these clairvoyant powers. The soul forces that we can call in a certain sense clairvoyant powers were such that the human being felt at the same time: I, myself, am not the one who is thinking or feeling within me. With this entire body and soul human beings felt themselves devoted or given over to higher, supersensible powers working and living within them. In this way human beings felt themselves to be like vessels through which supersensible powers spoke. We see the meaning of humankind's continuing development in light of this. Human beings would have remained dependent beings able to feel themselves only as sheaths, as vessels for higher powers and beings, had they not advanced to the use of their own understanding and reason. Through use of their intellect human beings have become more independent, but at the same time cut off, in a certain way, from the spiritual world for a while during their development; they have been cut off from the supersensible background of existence.

In the future this will change again. The further back we go the deeper the human soul was able to see into the background of existence through the use of clairvoyant powers. Such a soul could see how, out of this background of existence, those powers came forth which were at work on the human being. The human soul could see back to that point in time when earthly conditions were entirely different from today's, when the forms of living beings were much more mobile, much more subject to a kind of metamorphosis. We must go back a long way from what is called the human cultural epoch of present-day humanity. We must pursue the evolution of the human being alongside the evolution of animals. Indeed, the separation of the animal form from the human lies much further in the past than is usually believed. At the time of separation the animal forms became rigid and less mobile while the human form, remaining completely soft and flexible, could be formed and imprinted by what it experienced inwardly in its soul. Here we arrive back at a time in the evolution of humanity to which our present-day consciousness cannot reach. But there was another consciousness then present in the soul, a consciousness connected to the clairvoyant powers just characterized and able to reach back to that time in the past. Such a consciousness was able to see into the past and see humanity evolving out of the past already completely separated from an animal life. It also saw how, in a living connection with supersensible powers constantly entering in, human forces held sway. It saw what was still present as a faint echo in the times when, for example, the Homeric epics arose, and it saw what had been present to a much greater degree in yet earlier times.

If we were to go back to the times before Homer we would then find that people had a clairvoyant consciousness able to remember human events from prehistory. Their memory could relate the details of what happened in human evolution. By Homer's time things had reached the point that people felt clairvoyant consciousness was present but disappearing. That was a time when human beings did not speak out of themselves as independent, egotistical beings; rather gods, supersensible, spiritual powers, spoke through them. We must, therefore, take it seriously when Homer says he is not speaking out of himself but says: "Sing to me, O Muse, of the anger of Achilles." Sing to me, higher being, being that speaks through me, that takes possession of me when I sing and speak. These first lines of Homer are a reality. We are not lead to ancient, reigning dynasties similar to our present-day humanity. We are lead by Homer himself to the fact that, in ancient times, there were people in whom the supersensible was living. Achilles is clearly a personality from the time of transition from the old clairvoyance to the modern way of seeing things. We find this modern way in Agamemnon, Nestor, and Odysseus; it has been lead even further to a higher way of seeing. We can only understand Achilles if we know that Homer wants, in him, to present a member of ancient humanity, one who lived during an era lying between the time when human beings could directly reach up to the old gods and the time, beginning approximately with Agamemnon, of present-day humanity.

In the same way we are directed to a prehistoric time of humanity in the Nibelungen legend. The entire portrayal of this epoch shows us this. We are dealing there with people of our time in a certain sense, but with a special kind of human being of our time, one who has preserved something from the time of ancient clairvoyance. All the characteristics listed as belonging to Siegfried, that he can make himself invisible, that he has powers enabling him to overcome Brunhilde, who could not be overcome by an ordinary mortal—all that, along with other things related about him, shows us that we have in him a human being who has carried over into present-day humanity, as if in an inner memory, the achievements of the old soul powers, which are connected to the old clairvoyance and to nature. What is the transition in which Siegfried finds himself? Brunhilde's relationship to Kriemhilde, Siegfried's wife, shows us the answer to that question. It is not possible here to go into greater detail concerning the significance of these two characters. We succeed in understanding all these legends if we see in the figures appearing in them pictorial representations of inner clairvoyant, or remembered clairvoyant, conditions. We can see, then, in Siegfried's relationship to

Kriemhilde, his relationship to the soul powers working within himself. In a sense, his is a soul in transition between two ages. With the Nibelungen treasure, that is, with the clairvoyant secrets of the ancient times, he brings over into the new age something that makes him at the same time unfit for his present age. People of ancient times could live with the Nibelungen treasure, that is, with ancient clairvoyant powers. Conditions then changed on the earth and as a result, Siegfried, who bears in his soul an echo of the old times, no longer fits into the present. He becomes a tragic figure. How does the present relate to what is still living in Siegfried? Something of the old clairvoyant powers is still alive for him because, when he is overcome, Kriemhilde is left behind. The Nibelungen treasure is brought to her and she can use it. Later we discover that the Nibelungen treasure is taken from her by Hagen. We can see that Brunhilde, too, in a certain sense, is in a position to work with the ancient clairvoyant powers. Therefore, she stands at odds with the people who do fit into that age—Gunther and his brothers—but above all Gunther, the one in whom Brunhilde has absolutely no interest whatsoever.

And why was that? Now, we know from the story that Brunhilde is a kind of Valkyrie figure, that is, again a picture in the human soul of something with which the human being could still unite through clairvoyant powers in ancient times. But now it has withdrawn, become unconscious, and because of the way human beings presently live in our age of intellect, only after death can they unite with it. That is the reason for the union with the Valkyries at the moment of death. The Valkyrie is the personification of a power living in the soul of human beings of the present age. It is the soul power that the old clairvoyant consciousness could reach, but that is now only experienced by human beings when they pass through the gate of death.

Only then are they united with this soul power represented by Brunhilde. Because Kriemhilde still knows something of the old clairvoyance and the powers the soul receives from the ancient clairvoyance, she becomes a figure whose anger is described like the anger of Achilles in the *Iliad*. It becomes abundantly clear to us that the people gifted with clairvoyant powers in ancient times did not exercise self-control with their intellect; instead, they acted directly out of their most intense elemental impulses. That is the origin of the personal element, the unmediated, egotistical element we find in Kriemhilde and Achilles.

The study of national epics becomes especially interesting when we add the *Kalevala* to those already considered. Because of time limitations, today we can only mention that spiritual science in our time can point out the existence of the ancient clairvoyant conditions of humankind because today it is again possible to call forth clairvoyant states of consciousness through spiritual training. Of course this clairvoyant condition, permeated by the intellect and not dreamlike, is a more elevated state of mind than in the past. Human beings of the present are gradually growing into an age when hidden powers from the depths of the soul will again lead us into the supersensible. Now, however, these powers will be led by reason, not left uncontrolled. In this way we will again come to know the regions from which the old national epics speak to us from the dim conscious-ness of ancient times. We find that it is possible to experi-ence a revelation of the world not only through the external senses, but through something supersensible, something upon which the external physical human body is based.

There are methods, which will be discussed in the next lecture, that enable us to make the spiritual, supersensible, inner part of our being, the part so often denied today, inde-pendent of the sensible, external body. Following these methods we are not in an unconscious state as we are when asleep, when we become independent of our bodies, but we are able rather to perceive the spiritual world around us. In this way modern clairvoyance shows us how it is possible to live and have knowledge in a higher supersensible body, a body that fills like a vessel the body of senses. In spiritual science this higher body is called the etheric body. It resides within the body of senses. When we separate the etheric body from the physical-senses body, we enter through it into that state of perception wherein we become aware of super-sensible facts. We become aware of two kinds of supersensi-ble facts. First of all, at the beginning of the clairvoyant state we become aware, we begin to know, that we are no longer seeing by means of our physical body; we are no longer thinking by means of the brain that is bound to the physical body. At first we know nothing at all of the external world. (I am telling you things that will be more thoroughly estab-lished only in the next lecture.) But just for this reason the first stage of clairvoyance leads us all the more to a vision of our own etheric body. We see the supersensible bodily nature of the human being upon which the physical nature is based, and which we must describe as something that works and creates like a kind of inner master builder or building contractor who permeates our physical body with life. We become aware that what we perceive within our-selves, what we ourselves perceive as the actual life of our etheric bodies, is modified through our physical bodies, that it is dressed as with clothing, so to speak, on the physical side. When the etheric body undresses, so to speak, the eyes and ears, undresses the physical brain, we belong, in a sense, to the earthly element. In this way we perceive how our etheric body becomes a special, individual, egotistical human being who is incorporated into the sheath of his or her physical body. On the other hand, we perceive how our etheric body leads us again into those regions where we stand impersonally over against a higher, supersensible element, something which is not us yet is fully present within us, and works through us as a spiritual, supersensible power and force. As seen by spiritual scientific observation, the life of the soul falls into three parts that are, so to speak, enclosed in three external sheaths of the body, that are filled out with these three parts. To begin with, we live with our soul life in such a way that we experience within it what our eyes see, our ears hear, altogether what our senses take in and our mind can grasp. We live with our soul in our physical body. Inasmuch as our soul lives in the physical body, spiritual science calls it the consciousness soul. This is because the human being has only been able to advance to an I-consciousness in the course of human evolution by living completely into the physical body.

The modern clairvoyant then comes to know the life of the soul in the etheric body. When the soul forces are working in the etheric body then, although it is true to say that we have the forces, we cannot say they are our own personal forces. They are universal forces of humankind, forces through which we stand close to all the hidden facts of nature. Inasmuch as the soul perceives these forces in an external sheath, that is, in the etheric body, we can speak of the intellectual or mind soul as a second member of the soul. Just as we find the consciousness soul enclosed in the sheath of the physical body, we find the intellectual or mind soul enclosed in the etheric body. We have further an even finer body, through which we extend up into the supersensible world. Everything we experience as our most private secrets, what at the same time is hidden today from consciousness, and what was experienced as the power of becoming in the age of the old clairvoyance, what was experienced as if one could look back into the events of the grey, mist-filled prehistoric times—all that, we ascribe to the sentient soul. The sentient soul is enclosed in the finest of the human bodies, in what we call—please do not take offense at the expression; take it as a technical term—the astral body. It is that part of the human being that connects what works into our inner life to the external, earthly world in an inspiring way. This is what we cannot perceive through the external senses; neither can we perceive it when we look into our own etheric body. It is something we perceive when we become independent of ourselves, independent of our etheric body, and are united with the forces of our origin.

We have then the sentient soul in the astral body, the intellectual soul in the etheric body, and the consciousness soul in the physical body. In times of ancient clairvoyance people were more or less conscious of these things, for they could see into themselves and saw this three-membered being of the soul. It is not that they intellectually analyzed the soul into its parts. But because of their clairvoyant consciousness the threefold human soul stood before them: the sentient soul in the astral, the intellectual soul in the etheric, and the consciousness soul in the physical body. When they looked back they saw how the external aspect of the human being, the external form, developed out of something that continued to evolve and has lead to the result we see today in the threefold power of the soul. They felt that the threefold membering of the soul was born out of creative, supersensible powers. They felt that the sentient soul was born out of supersensible, creative powers given to us by the astral body, the body we possess not only between birth and death like the etheric and physical bodies, but can take with us when we pass through the gate of death—the body we had before we entered existence at birth. The old clairvoyants saw the sentient soul united with the astral body. They saw what was working out of the spiritual world upon human

beings, creating and inspiring the astral body as the power
that creates the human being out of the entire universe.

They saw a second creative power in something that,
with time, has resulted in what we today know as the intellectual or mind soul. This second power has created the
etheric body in such a way that it can transform all the
external substances, all external matter, to the point where
those substances can permeate the human physical form in
a human, not in an animal, way. The old clairvoyants saw
the creative spirit for the etheric body—the creative spirit,
the results of whose work appear in our intellectual soul—
working as a superhuman cosmic power into the human
being just as, for example, magnetism works into physical
matter. They looked up into spiritual worlds and saw a
divine-spiritual power constructing, forging the etheric
body of the human being. This etheric body then becomes
the master builder that can transform external matter, pul-
verize it, so to speak, and mill it so that what is normally
present in matter is transformed—with the result that the
human being acquires human abilities. The old clairvoyants saw how this creative power transformed all matter in
an artistic way so that it could become human matter.

Then they looked at the third power, at the consciousness
soul, which actually makes the human being egotistical,
which is a transformation of the physical body. They
ascribed these forces that hold sway in the physical body
solely to the hereditary line, to what derives from father
and mother, from grandfather and great-grandfather, and
so forth—in short, to what is the result of human powers of
love, human powers of reproduction. They saw in this the
third creative power, the power of love working from generation to generation.

The old clairvoyants looked up to three powers. They
looked up to a creative being that eventually called forth

our sentient soul by shaping the human being's astral body, the astral body that can be inspired by supersensible powers because it is the body which the human being had before becoming a physical being through conception. It is the body the human being will have after passing through the gate of death. This structure of forces—we could better say, this heavenly structure in the human being that endures while the etheric and physical bodies pass away—is at the same time for the ancient clairvoyant that which has brought forth all human culture. Their direct experience told them this. For this reason, they saw in the bringer of the astral body that power which carries the divine and which, itself, consists of nothing but what endures, the power through which the eternal of the world sings and sounds forth into the world. And the ancient clairvoyants from whom the figures in the *Kalevala* arose, have given us in Vainamoinen the living, graphic expression of that power of creation which confronts us now as the sentient soul, which inspires the divine into the human. Vainamoinen is the creator of that part of the human being that endures beyond birth and death, bringing the heavenly into the earthly.

Let us consider the second figure in the *Kalevala*: Ilmarinen. When we go back to the ancient clairvoyant consciousness, we find that Ilmarinen creates out of the forces of the earth and out of what belongs to earth's deeper nonsensible forces, everything that is an image of the living form of the etheric body. We see in Ilmarinen the one who brings the power able to completely transform all matter. We see in him the one who forges the human form. And we see in the Sampo the human etheric body, forged by Ilmarinen out of the supersensible world so that sensible matter can be pulverized and then lead from generation to generation. The third divine-supersensible being gives the forces in which the human consciousness-soul continues working in the physical body from generation to generation through the powers of love. We see this third divine-supersensible power in Lemminkainen. In this way we see mysteries of humankind's origins in the smithies who forged the Sampo. We look back into human prehistory and see deep secrets coming forth from the ancient clairvoyant consciousness on the basis of the *Kalevala*. We can say: That was not the age when we could have analyzed natural phenomena with our intellect. Everything was primitive but within this primitive consciousness people perceived what stands behind the sensible appearances around us.

Now, when these bodies of human beings were forged, that is, when the etheric body of the human being, the Sampo, was forged, it first had to be worked on for a while; human beings did not immediately have the forces that were being prepared for them by supersensible powers. After the etheric body was forged it first had to become accustomed to the new conditions, just as when a machine is prepared for use it must be fully developed, completely ripened as it were, in order to be placed in position and put to use. In human evolution—this is true for all evolution—there must be a transition time between the creation of a specific member and its use. In this way human beings forged their etheric body in distant primal times. Then an episode came when this etheric body was sent down into human nature. Only later did it light up as the intellectual soul. Human beings learned to use their powers as external forces of nature; from their own nature they brought forth the Sampo which had remained hidden. In a wonderful way we see in a series of pictures this secret of human evolution in the forging of the Sampo: in its being hidden, in the ineffectiveness of the Sampo, in the episode that lies between its forging and rediscovery. We see how the Sampo is first sunk into human nature, and then pulled out to become a part of the cultural life, which only first appears as primitive forces of culture as described in the second part of the *Kalevala*.

Everything in this great national epic acquires deep significance when we see in it descriptions achieved through clairvoyance of ancient events in the evolution of humanity, in the coming-into-being of human nature through the addition of its various members. I can assure you that it was a wonderful surprise for me to find in this epic—which I truly only got to know long, long after the facts of the evolution of human nature had become clear to me—what I had presented more or less theoretically in my book *Theosophy* at a time when I had not yet read a single line of the *Kalevala*. So we see how secrets are presented to humanity by Vainamoinen, the creator of supersensible inspirations: the history of the forging of the etheric body. But there is yet another hidden mystery. You will remember that I do not understand Finnish and can speak only out of spiritual science. I would be able to explain what the word Sampo means only if I may speak in the following way: We see the etheric body become active in the animals as the master builder for the most varying forms, from the most perfect to the least perfect. Something was forged into the human etheric body that collects and embraces all these animal forms into a unity. But the following must also be said: The etheric body, that is, the Sampo, is forged over the entire earth according to climatic and other conditions, so that this etheric body has within its forces the special folk characteristics, the special idiosyncrasies of different peoples. One people is configured one way, another people differently. For each people the Sampo is what constitutes the particular form of the etheric body; it is what brings precisely this particular ethnic folk to life so that the members of this ethnic group all look the same because of what is

shining through their physical, living form. To the extent
that identical appearances in the human form are constructed by the etheric, to that extent the etheric forces of
the etheric body lie in the Sampo. We have then, in the
Sampo, the symbol of the cohesion of the Finnish people;
we have what constitutes their humanity in the depths,
which the Finnish people have brought to expression in its
own particular form.

This is the case with every national epic. National epics
can only arise where the culture is still enclosed in the
forces of the Sampo, in the forces of the etheric body. As
long as the culture is dependent upon the powers of the
Sampo, that is how long the people carry the stamp of this
Sampo. For this reason the etheric body maintains the characteristics of the nationality throughout the entire culture.
When could, in the course of the cultural process, a break
occur in this national, ethnic, or popular culture? It could
happen when something entered into the cultural process
of humanity that is intended not for a single person, for a
single tribe, or for a single folk, but for all humankind. This
something must be taken from depths of human nature so
intimate and profound that it applies to all human beings
without reference to nationality, race, or anything similar,
and then incorporated into the cultural process. This is just
what happened when certain powers spoke not to an ethnic
group, but to all humankind, powers that are hinted at in
an impersonal way, also in terms of the nationality, when at
the end of the *Kalevala*, Christ is born of Mariata. When the
child is baptized, Vainamoinen leaves the country. Something has happened that brings together this particular folk
with the universal human. Here at this point in one of the
greatest, most significant and meaningful national epics,
where the story leads into an entirely impersonal and—
please pardon the paradoxical expression—non-Palestinian

description of the Christ impulse, the *Kalevala* becomes especially significant. The *Kalevala* leads us to feel the happiness and beneficence manifested by the Sampo when it continues working through all human evolution, when it is experienced working together with the Christian idea, with the Christian impulse. This is the illimitably delicate moment at the end of the *Kalevala*. This is also what makes it clear that the events preceding this birth in the *Kalevala* belong to the time before Christ.

But as true as it is that the universally human can only continue to exist by preserving what is individual, just as true is it that the individual cultures of nations, which derive their being from the ancient clairvoyant states of their people, continue to live in the universal human. It is just as true that everything the *Kalevala* alludes to as Christian at its conclusion is perpetually uniting with the inspiration Vainamoinen represents. For what Vainamoinen represents works on without end and will retain its own special consequences. With Vainamoinen, something is intended that belongs to the part of our being that is above birth and death, something that goes with us through every stage of human evolution. In this way epics such as the *Kalevala* present us with something eternal that can be permeated by the Christian idea. This idea makes itself felt as something individual that will always prove that the universal human, like white sunlight split into many colors, will continue to live in the many folk cultures. And because this universal human permeates the individual element in the national epics, the individual element that shines into every individual human being, that speaks to every man or woman—for this reason the people live so very much in the being of their national epics. For this reason the people of ancient times stand so full of life before our eyes, the people who, in their clairvoyance, have beheld the essence of their own nationality as it is described to us in all national epics. We can learn about this essence when, as in the *Kalevala*, humanity with its intimate details of life is surrounded by the circumstances that live in the Finnish nationality, when this national temperament found in the depths of the soul is portrayed in such a way that it can be placed directly alongside what modern spiritual science reveals concerning human mysteries.

In this way, ladies and gentlemen, such national epics in their essence are at the same time a living protest against all materialism, against any theory that derives the human being out of forces, conditions, or beings that are merely material. Such national epics, especially the *Kalevala*, report to us that the human being originates in a spiritual-soul condition. Therefore a renewal, a reconception of ancient national epics can accomplish an immeasurably great service for a living, spiritual culture. For today, spiritual science would altogether like to bring about a renewal of human consciousness. It would like to remind us that humanity is rooted in the spirit, not in matter. An exact study of an epic such as the *Kalevala* shows us that the best the human being has, also the best that the human being is, originates in the realm of soul and spirit. In this sense I found it interesting that in one of the runes, the kantele protests directly against a materialistic interpretation of what appears in the *Kalevala*. That harp-like instrument of the ancient singers is indicated in a picture as if it were constructed out of materials taken from the physical world. But the old runes protested against this, protested in the spiritual-scientific sense, one would like to say, against the idea that the stringed instrument for Vainamoinen was put together from products of nature visible to the physical eye.

In truth, so said the old runes, the instrument came from the realm of soul and spirit—the instrument upon which human beings played the songs that came to them directly out of the spiritual world. In this sense the old rune is to be interpreted entirely in terms of spiritual science. It is a lively protest against the materialistic interpretation we are so capable of. It is a message to the effect that what human beings possess—what they *are*, in essence—and what can be expressed only symbolically in an instrument such as is ascribed to Vainamoinen, originates in the spirit; such an instrument originates in the spirit, as does indeed the whole human being. The following Finnish folk rune can act like a motto for the attitude of spiritual science. I would like to sum up the prevailing mood or nuance of what this lecture has attempted to explain concerning the essence of national epics with this rune.

> Certainly those speak falsely
> and find themselves in error
> who believe that Vainamoinen
> shaped the kantele
> our beautiful stringed instrument
> from the jawbone of a pike
> and that he spun the strings
> from the tail of Hiisi's horse.
> It was shaped from want,
> affliction bound its parts together,
> and its strings were woven
> by suffering and tears of longing.

And so all being is born, not out of matter, but rather out of the realm of soul and spirit. So, too, this old folk rune, and so spiritual science, which seeks to play a role in the living process of culture in our time.

[Translated by James H. Hindes]

Occultism and Initiation

Public lecture

HELSINKI • APRIL 12, 1912

Whoever speaks of occultism today should realize that much of what they have to say will be taken, not simply as a compilation of doubtful hypotheses, but even as dreams and fantasies. Regarding any disagreement aroused by what I will say tonight among hearers who are involved with contemporary culture or science, let me assure them that I, for one, fully understand their objections. First, then, let me indicate what I really mean by occultism, which is the subject of today's lecture, and by the methods of investigation leading to the results of occultism, which may be summed up by the word initiation.

Simply put, initiation is the sum total of what we must accomplish in order to arrive at the results of occultism. When I speak of occultism, I do not mean all those things which are now designated under this name and are spread about here and there. I mean the precise results of a kind of spiritual science subjected to scientific thinking and to the logical requirements of the present. By occultism I mean everything that under this name, and from the standpoint of science as mentioned above, seeks to take its place in modern life through the study of things inaccessible to ordinary science and ordinary knowledge. What is often published these days as occultism is more than calculated to arouse the opposition of many of our contemporaries, who say: What is this occultism, coming forward with insights concerning supersensible life and supersensible facts! What is it compared with the results achieved by modern science, based upon such strict and conscientious research!

The insights which are thus advanced, those which I am talking about, are primarily those which lead us beyond sense-perception and beyond the things which can be recognized by ordinary understanding, which is connected, as it were, with the instrument of the brain. These insights lead us beyond things which can be experienced between birth and death into regions we enter when we pass through the portal of death. The results obtained through spiritual science, or let us say, through this form of occultism, speak of the development of the true spiritual core of the human being, and they show us that when one passes through the portal of death, one's soul-spiritual core passes over into a supersensible, spiritual world. From the life led between birth and death in a physical body, one takes along certain forces and, by entering into relation with other purely supersensible forces and powers during an intermediate period between death and a new birth, one's soul-spiritual being can connect itself with the forces given by physical heredity, with what comes from father and mother and from the ancestors in general—in short, with what unites itself with these purely physical substances and forces—so that the whole human being comes into existence.

This will show you that the results of such a spiritual form of research must speak of the development of a person's soul-spiritual core, a course of development that goes through repeated earthly lives. Consequently it speaks of reincarnation, of repeated lives on earth. It also explains that the inner capacities that we unfold within our soul during one life, and even the blows of destiny which we experience, are in a certain way the results of what we have prepared for ourselves during an earlier life on earth. It explains moreover that everything we experience during this earthly life, all the capacities we acquire, pass through the portal of death—we elaborate them in a supersensible, purely spiritual world, and when these qualities have been elaborated to a sufficient degree in the spiritual world, we once more enter a new life on earth, as already described.

This perception in itself may strike some people as a rather daring assertion. To it must be added the things that explain, upon the basis of spiritual science, the supersensible part of human nature which belongs with the physical being. These things will explain that, in addition to the physical body that we perceive through our external senses, there is also a part of the human being which is the bearer of a supersensible essence. This part can be perceived with the aid of spiritual-scientific means, so that it can be recognized as a human being's soul-spiritual core, passing through repeated lives on earth and experiencing the destinies mentioned above.

The publications of this spiritual science even draw attention to earlier conditions of human life in remote epochs of earthly existence. From a spiritual-scientific standpoint, these publications also speak of cosmic conditions during a time when the earth did not as yet exist in its present planetary form, that is, they point to conditions which existed before human life on earth began. They look at the evolution of cosmic life itself, the transformation of our Earth and of other heavenly bodies. If we work with the methods of this spiritual science we must admit on the one hand, that if anything at all can be known concerning such things, these perceptions affect human life most deeply, because they are connected with our innermost nature and being.

On the other hand we must point out that, particularly from the standpoint of so-called modern natural science, we encounter justified skepticism about the possibility of gaining any knowledge in these spheres.

The next question which may be raised in the face of the results of such investigation is the one which will form the subject of this evening's lecture. It is none other than the more than justified question: How do those who advance such statements arrive at their results? How do they set about coming to such conclusions? Needless to say, despite the conscientiousness and sureness of ordinary scientific method (and nobody admires these more sincerely than a serious spiritual scientific investigator), it does not allow us to penetrate into supersensible spheres. But having raised this question, another immediately arises within the human soul, prompted by an indisputable fact: Since there is undoubtedly a deep longing to know such things in every human heart, how does it come about that precisely the most conscientious method of research seems to separate human beings from the world in which they long to look?

If we face this question without prejudice, it soon becomes obvious that the human being is only able to understand certain kinds of facts, when facing them in a particular way. In reality, I can only understand things of which I know the origin and course of development. I can only understand those things in creation in which I can, in a certain way, participate actively through my cognitive capacity. I can only grasp those things at the creation of which I can, in some way, be present. But if I turn my gaze upon the things that surround me in nature, upon the essence of all the kingdoms of nature, I must say to myself: Their form of existence, the way in which they appear finished to me, allows me to see them clearly through my senses and I can know them because I investigate their laws and combine them with my intellect—but when I wish to understand how they have arisen, I cannot penetrate them and my power of observation fails.

The beings and facts of the kingdoms of Nature confront humans as finished acts of creation and at first it appears that we cannot get a hold of things at the moment they are created. But if human beings look into their inner self and survey all that lives in their soul in the form of thoughts, representations, feelings, and impulses of the will, they face a more or less rich inner world, a world whose reality they experience far more vividly than the reality of external objects and the reality of that part of the self which belongs to the external world. Who can deny that the reality of our pains and sufferings, of our impulses and passions, of our thoughts and ideals—in short, of all that surges up and down within our soul from the moment of waking up to the moment of falling asleep, is greater than the reality of the physical and physiological processes within our organism? But even if we do our utmost to gain insight into our soul life—and we find that it is kindled by the external world, that this or that experience affects us, and fills us with joy or sorrow—even if we do our utmost to look into our soul life, we cannot even there take part in, nor penetrate into, the actual genesis of any inner soul process, we cannot be witness to the creative process within us. But bearing in mind that we can only grasp something by participating in its creative process, we can understand what we lose through the two modes of observation explained above.

It is enough to survey what is produced by our fantasy, what we create by means of something lying, so to speak, within our own power, what we form in accordance with our thoughts and ideals; it is enough to remember all that is now accessible to the human being—on the one hand, the sense of satisfaction that arises through an understanding

of creative processes, an understanding gained through
technical knowledge and by the way in which we combine
thoughts dealing with the forces of nature and, on the other
hand, the deep dissatisfaction which makes us feel as if we
were standing before a gate through which we cannot pass,
whenever we survey things around us and within us and
realize that we know nothing whatever of their origin and
of their living process. But might it not be possible, after all,
to find some access enabling us to participate in these creative processes, to penetrate into what we feel to be life's
creative processes, in which we ourselves are placed?

There is one sphere where we can know in a direct way
that we participate in a certain manner in a creative process, but at the same time we know that in ordinary consciousness, observation and cognition do not allow us to
look into the process of creation!

What is meant here can be seen every day, if only we
reflect a little over the strange phenomena which appear in
the alternating states of sleeping and waking. For those
who wish to penetrate more deeply into the essence of life,
these phenomena are of the profoundest significance. They
evoke what we may call a mystery of life. Though it may
not strike our ordinary consciousness that something so
infinitely significant is contained in these alternating conditions of sleeping and waking, this is only due to the fact
that every habitual thing in life has lost the power of making a strong impression upon us. Just because we are accustomed to these alternating states of sleeping and waking
within twenty-four hours, we no longer feel the deep significance, the greatness and power suggested by this everyday phenomenon.

If we wish to characterize the difference between sleeping and waking, it will at first seem trivial and obvious; for
everyone knows that sleep occurs in such a way that all the

emotions filling our soul from the moment of waking up to the moment of falling asleep, the feelings, sensations, impulses, passions, thoughts and ideals, disappear. This whole day world becomes submerged in darkness, in the night of unconsciousness. But everyone is also convinced that even sleep, during the transitory stage between falling asleep and waking up, the activities within our being continue; something occurs, but it is inaccessible to human consciousness.

What can be said, then, concerning the alternating conditions of sleeping and waking is undoubtedly and obviously true; but if we reflect on it, we realize that the reason why a barrier is put up before our knowledge does not lie so far away. If we observe this alternation of waking and sleeping, we must say that our whole daytime conscious life, our whole waking life, must be a kind of destructive process, dissolving deeper processes within our organism. I cannot speak in detail of the physical, chemical and physiological processes of fatigue, for this would lead us too far, and this is not the essential point just now, but what is evident to all is that fatigue is something like a wear and tear, almost a destructive process of deeper forces that are active in our organism. This shows us that, in reality, the peculiarity of our waking daytime life is that it does not participate in our constructive processes, in the creation of our own being, but that it shows symptoms of fatigue, and that, after all, it constantly consumes us, dissolves us. The waking life of day is in fact a process of dissolution and of destruction, and any unprejudiced observer will note that sleep is the very opposite: it is a creative process which restores, reorders and creates anew that which the waking process destroys and decays.

Yet it is only natural that we cannot know anything concerning this creative process within us that takes place during sleep. It concerns us directly, yet we cannot know anything about it, because immediately before this creative process arises, we lose our consciousness, so that we cannot penetrate knowingly into spheres within our being where creative processes take place. But this leads to the immediate conclusion that if only we were able to maintain our consciousness beyond the point where torpor sets in, we could take hold of the creative phenomena in nature and in the universe. When creative forces begin to work in human beings, their consciousness becomes dazed: they fall asleep, become unconscious and this shows us that human nature, as presently constituted, is such that when we wish to penetrate into a creative activity—moreover one that takes place within ourselves—our consciousness vanishes, so that we cannot witness the creative process. The activities within the human organism which are of a creative kind constitute a part of our being into which we cannot penetrate because the activities dull our consciousness and remain a strange world. There is no other path leading to a knowledge of things lying behind the sensory world than that of transcending our ordinary consciousness and penetrating into a creative process which takes place within us, or into some other similar process.

Where do we find something that can teach us how to transcend our ordinary consciousness and to penetrate into something which is estranged from us, without getting dazed, without falling into a kind of sleep? In the large field accessible to our ordinary consciousness there are two things which evidently lead us out of our ordinary consciousness without dazing us or putting us to sleep, as is the case every evening, when we go to bed. These two things in our ordinary consciousness that may serve as a kind of pattern for the way in which our consciousness can transcend its ordinary limits and penetrate into an unknown sphere, these two things must be sought in the moral field. Two moral experiences, permeating the whole life of the human being, supply a prototypical idea for the way in which we can go out of ourselves, without losing our consciousness.

These two things are first *compassion*, and second, *conscience*. If we study the way in which compassion and conscience are related to consciousness, we obtain, to begin with, an idea of how consciousness may go beyond its own limits. When I develop compassion, love or sympathy for another human soul, I experience within myself, according to my capacity, not that which touches me—for that would not be an experience of compassion and of love—but the joys, sorrows, pains and pleasures of the other soul. When I am full of compassion, I can lose myself in the soul of another person, and I actually live (as any unprejudiced observation will show) outside my ordinary consciousness, within the other soul.

Here I am confronted by a deep mystery of life. It is all the deeper because, if our feelings are of a moral nature, our consciousness does not vanish and we are not dazed when passing over into the consciousness of another soul. Indeed, how far I am able to maintain my own consciousness to a full extent, when experiencing the sorrows and joys of another soul, and not my own, is a standard of measure for my morality. It is even a moral defect for my consciousness to be dazed by the joys and sorrows of another soul; for then we have a situation similar to that of facing one's own creative activity taking place during sleep. Consciousness falls asleep, as it were, in the face of another person's sorrows and joys.

The second experience which pertains to the moral sphere and leads us out of our ordinary consciousness, is conscience. If we observe conscience in an unprejudiced way, we can say the following: In life we may love or hate, do or leave certain things undone, under the influence of our instincts and passions, or of sympathy and antipathy, or perhaps we may follow the dictates of education or of social relations—these appear to us from outside. But there is something which never speaks to us from outside, and this we call conscience.

Conscience comes to us from a world—we can feel and experience this—that speaks to us inwardly and can be heard by us inwardly. Conscience influences our ordinary perceptible world, for everything which we can perceive is open to correction when the supersensible demands of conscience impel us to action. Conscience bears witness to the fact that, in the moral sphere, our soul can be told something which transcends our consciousness. And, again, we find that it is a moral defect if our soul falls into a kind of sleep when conscience begins to speak and does not listen to its voice but only listens to what speaks from the physical environment through sympathy or antipathy, so that these promptings govern the soul's impulses to action. If we can thus transcend our ordinary consciousness without feeling dazed, conscience is a phenomenon that speaks to the human soul in such a way that it need not take its impulses from any influence coming from the external world.

In regard to beings outside our own self, in regard to experiences transcending our knowledge and our consciousness, we have in the moral sphere the possibility to penetrate into them through compassion and love. Through conscience we listen, as it were, to truths which do not come from the world of the senses.

If it is possible in this way to penetrate into beings outside our own and to take into our souls truths of the kind uttered by conscience, then there is a prospect of penetrating into a world which is not the one given to us during our waking consciousness from the moment of waking up to the moment of falling asleep. It is possible, and this prospect opens out to us through methods we call the methods of initiation. In regard to thinking, feeling, and willing, these methods of initiation consist in other forms of soul-activity than those to which we are accustomed in our ordinary life for the acquisition of an external knowledge concerning the world.

Why do we acquire concepts and ideas in ordinary life? No one will deny that the reason modern people form concepts and ideas is to gain through these thoughts, and even through their feelings and sensations, certain knowledge concerning what surrounds them in the external world. Today, we designate as truth those concepts and ideas that coincide with something outside, with some phenomenon of the external world, so that these thoughts are, as it were, a reflected image of the external world. For everything that is connected with external life, with the external culture, this form of soul-activity is undoubtedly the right one. But if we wish to penetrate into supersensible spheres of existence, this soul-activity must undergo a complete transformation. In other words (let me use the taboo word!), if we wish to penetrate into occult mysteries, entirely different soul-forces must be used. Our concepts, ideas, thought-pictures, indeed even our feelings and will-impulses, must become quite different from what they mean to us in the external world.

We should not begin by asking: What do these soul-activities mean in regard to this or that in the external world and what is their true value? We should simply take this content of our soul-life as a pedagogical means of self-training. We should let our thoughts and ideas, and even our feelings and sensations work in our soul in such a way as to shut it out from everything coming to us from the external

world, even from the life experiences and memories we
have collected. By a strong effort of the will, we should
eliminate all impressions coming to us from the physical
world, all intellectual thought patterns, and even all anxi-
eties, worries and joys—indeed, anything which may have
accumulated in our memory. We should empty our soul, so
that the same condition sets in which ordinarily arises
through fatigue when we fall asleep in the evening. Doing
so, however, we should reach something entirely opposite
to sleep, namely we should be able to maintain our full
consciousness and direct it towards fruitful thoughts, particularly towards symbolic thoughts, as rich in meaning as
possible. (The essential point is not to ask what value such
thoughts have for the attainment of truth, but to bear in
mind their pedagogical value, when the soul's forces are
directed towards a thought image, or an impulse which is
set in the center of soul-life through a strong effort of the
will.)

This soul activity, purified of everything else, is turned
towards this self-chosen picture and concentrates upon it
more and more until the whole life of the soul, which
remains awake through a strong concentration of the will, is
centered upon this self-chosen content. We then start notic-
ing that something begins to radiate within our soul life and
these rays do not stream from the content we have chosen,
but from the strong concentration of soul forces we have
applied to it. We are now able to experience something
which we generally do not experience, and we obtain the
immediate feeling, the immediate experience: "Now I am
experiencing something which is just as real, important and
essential for life as the things which I see with my eyes and
hear with my ears; it is just as real, yet I could never have
experienced it!" In short, only now do we begin to know
what supersensible experience really is; only now do we

realize that we live within a soul-spiritual core; only now do we begin to understand that it is possible to live within an inner soul being which is quite independent of the bodily being. And this transforms our whole consciousness.

I must point out expressly that the process leading to this inner activity greatly resembles, while also being the very opposite, the trivial process which takes place when our attention is directed towards a shining object, producing a kind of hypnosis. This soul condition, which differs from the normal one, arises through the sharp concentration upon an object, so that other soul activities are kept in the background. The concentration upon an inner, freely chosen content has a certain resemblance with this soul activity, for it is also a kind of concentration; yet it is at the same time the very opposite; for the concentration upon a shining object blots out consciousness, it puts us into a quasi-hypnotic state, whereas when an inner content, and it is strictly an inner thought-content, is placed at the center of our soul life by a strong effort of our will, our consciousness remains intact.

Spiritual science has a technical name for this method of training the soul: *meditation*. This is true meditation. And I wish to emphasize that this kind of meditation is in practice far more difficult then one would think, after hearing it described in such a simple way. It does not suffice to try it a few times. Over and over again we should endeavour to practice such concentration, such meditation, by forming thought-images and pictures, ideas taken from the moral and intellectual sphere—and particularly symbolic representations. This should be done with perseverance, until the decisive moment arises. This simply consists in the inner conviction: "I have within my being a soul-spiritual core, and this lives in a supersensible reality, but in its supersensible reality it cannot be perceived through the ordinary sense-organs, nor grasped through the intellect, bound up with the brain."

From what I have described above, you will be able to deduce one thing—we always remain within our own being. We turn away from the external world by concentrating upon our inner self. The first thing we thus experience is, and only can be, an inner experience, an experience of our inner being, and this leads us practically to a definite point. One who concentrates in this way, or meditates, soon perceives—really does perceive—that his or her field of vision is filled with realities; we may call them, if you like, visions. They appear in the form of pictures, which cannot be compared to anything else, though there may be some external resemblance with what we see in the physical world. Particularly in regard to the way in which they arise and in regard to the effect which they produce, however, these pictures constitute an altogether new experience, and are in no way put together from earlier experiences. This completely new element must be designated as vision, for there is no other apt word to describe it in our ordinary speech. One might say that this new experience exactly resembles the pictures of a dream; yet compared with ordinary dreams, these visions have a far stronger intensity, and possess, so to speak, an obtrusive, almost importunate reality.

At this point, those who practice the methods giving insight into the supersensible world encounter an obstacle, which might be seen as a danger. They incur the danger of taking this visionary world from the outset as something real, as facing them in the same way as the ordinary physical world outside, so that when they perceive this visionary world, they say, "This world is real," in the same way as they would in connection with the sensory world. This danger becomes all the more threatening if all the precautions connected with an occult training, such as the one described above, are not observed. These preventive measures are dealt with in detail in my book *Knowledge of the Higher Worlds* and a person who follows them never for a moment loses the feeling that the world of visions is the self, and that we ourselves produce this world.

It is of the utmost importance that we should never allow our consciousness to be dulled to the extent of having the impression that an external world lies before us in this visionary world. It exactly resembles a world lying outside our own being: it stretches out before us in the manner of a spatial world; it reveals processes governed by time, just like the processes of the external physical world; it calls up altogether the delusion that we are facing a reality, like a dream enhanced to the utmost degree of lifelikeness. People who neglect such precautions and who do not recognize that they themselves have created this visionary world naturally fall prey to dreams and empty fancies. A truly clairvoyant person—allow me to use this word—differs in this point from the fantastic and visionary dreamer who takes such visions for objective realities. Those who have advanced to real clairvoyance are aware at every moment, know and must know, through an intensive self-training, that although they see before them an extensive spatial world, this is merely a world of their own creation. Such things exercise a very suggestive influence, but never for a moment should we lose the consciousness of the fact that they are nothing but our own creation. This consciousness in turn should become the object of meditation and concentration. We should make an effort of the will to concentrate again and again, intensively and for a long time, upon the fact that this new world we have, as it were, conquered is our own work, our own product. And then something strange arises within our consciousness—(this can, of course, only be described as a practical experience). We recognize that in performing this activity we have done quite consciously something which we also do in a normal state of consciousness.

I have already told you that in our normal state of consciousness we really produce a destructive process within us. Ordinarily we do not know this, or at least, we do not pay any attention to it. When we conjure up before us such a visionary world, while maintaining our full consciousness, and at the same time concentrate upon the thought characterized above, we also become fully aware of the fact that the *"imaginative* knowledge" (this is the technical expression used for it) thus reached also produces a destructive process. We observe that we always come to the point where the imaginative world begins to consume us, and if we were to relinquish the full consciousness that can be maintained only through a strong effort of will, if we were not to realize fully that in this visionary world we encounter everywhere our own being, our nervous system would suffer and would become ill. We should never come to the point of overstepping the limit where the real destructive processes would begin. Through the fact that we do not allow things to come as far as the destructive process, but keep it at bay through the intense consciousness that we ourselves are the creators of this imaginative world, through this fact we are able to participate in a creative process. For when we fulfill within ourselves certain creative activities which cannot be perceived through our normal consciousness, we really enter a creative world, and we learn to follow consciously a process resembling that which takes place during sleep. This shows us that in this way we can witness a creative process, understand a process of growth and development within ourselves.

This is, however, connected with something else, though I can only give a brief description of these stages of initiation.

Little by little, the whole process forces us to renounce something the ordinary clairvoyant does not like to renounce. The ordinary clairvoyant is so glad to live in this world of visions, he or she takes such indulgent pleasure in these experiences of a higher world, and they are so suggestive that he or she easily takes them for reality. This can lead to a nervous breakdown. But if through the above effort of will we remain fully conscious that "all this is produced by our own self," if our consciousness never falls asleep, something arises that is a source of regret to many—namely, the power lying at the foundation of that effort of our will falls destructively upon this whole imaginative world, disposes of it and many things which the ordinary clairvoyant holds very precious are thus blotted out. In other words, the following happens. Although in imaginative consciousness we have an element really setting forth the forces constituting a creative process (for we do not let it go beyond the limit where the destructive process would set in)—and we really transcend our ordinary consciousness, as we normally do when we feel compassion or love—the decision, or the effort of will by which we bring destruction (but also structure and order) into our visionary world leads to the development of an activity that does not exist anywhere in the external physical world, and that very soon reveals itself as the creative activity within our own being, lying beyond the reach of our ordinary consciousness. It is the activity which may be seen in our soul-spiritual being when it works upon our organism by drawing regenerating forces out of its spiritual environment; it is the soul-spiritual core which lives in the spiritual cosmos.

In the next stage, which is technically designated as *inspiration*, we learn to recognize the soul-spiritual core of our being, and how it lives within the creative forces of the cosmos. Whereas imagination, the first stage of initiation, only led us into our inner being by conjuring up a merely visionary world, the process of inspiration leads us to a higher stage. A flash of light breaks in upon our whole visionary world, something that really seems to come out of the spiritual cosmos, as does conscience, and we observe that it speaks to us in the same way in which conscience speaks to us in our ordinary consciousness. Conscience may be compared to the way in which inspiration speaks to the imaginative consciousness; but then imagination passes over to the stage of inspiration, and we enter a real, supersensible world.

Through our own development, we have now reached the point where we can glance behind the veil of physical phenomena, so that now we are able to understand the wonderful mystery of human development and also of human death. When we see a human being entering life through birth, when we perceive how the child's undeveloped physiognomy gradually acquires characteristic traits, and its helpless movements gradually acquire strength and sureness, when we observe the development of what lives in the child's soul, we can no longer say: Everything that comes out of the child's soul, that forms its body and its physiognomy, and even the delicate convolutions of the brain immediately after birth, is the result of heredity! No, we are now able to look back upon the child's soul-spiritual core that comes from an entirely different world, and we can see this soul-spiritual part of the child's being unites itself with what comes from father and mother. Now we no longer speak merely of hereditary forces, but of forces from the spiritual world that unite themselves with what is transmitted by father and mother and by ancestors in general. We obtain a real conception of something which was formerly a mere belief, namely, that the human soul-spiritual being comes from the spiritual world and forms the physical-bodily part.

We can then proceed still further. When we study life through the knowledge given by initiation, we see that the human being's soul-spiritual core directs the experiences of life more and more towards its inner center, abstracting them from the external world. We understand and we can see how the soul-spiritual part gradually retreats from the external world. We can see the face getting old and wrinkled, and we obtain the immediate impression: Whereas our physical body begins to fade, after we have reached the climax of life, and even our brain decays, so that the soul can no longer express its own content, and even the soul itself seems to decay, we see on the other hand that the part that can no longer express itself outwardly gradually withdraws to the person's inner being, and concentrates its forces, so that everything which we have experienced, suffered and achieved is gathered within the soul, and is at its strongest, its most powerful, when the body releases our soul-spiritual part. If we follow this process, we find that this strongest force within us becomes united with forces of the supersensible world, forming the prototype of a new incarnation, of a new body for a new life on earth.

If we compare what stands at the beginning of life—the gradual plastic development of the body—if we compare it with what stands at the end of life—the inner concentration of life's experiences within the soul, the emancipation of the soul's forces from the body and the crossing of the threshold of death—if we observe these two things supersensibly, we find that it is like the beginning and the end, say, of a plant's development, where the final process already contains the seed, the beginning of the new plant. But though we see beginning and end thus linked up, supersensible knowledge gained through initiation shows us that what the soul has experienced during life is interwoven with the soul-spiritual core and that when the human being returns, after an intermediate period between death and a new birth, a new body is built. But this soul-spiritual core of the being now forms a new body and a new earthly existence in such a way as to produce the effect of causes that had arisen during a preceding life.

The methods gained through initiation, whose proto-types were compassion and conscience, i.e., experiences of our ordinary consciousness, thus give us an immediate knowledge of processes of the supersensible world connected with the human being. Initiation therefore becomes the path leading us up into the supersensible worlds.

If you delve deeper into what I have described to you just now, in outline form, and if you study it in my book, *Knowledge of the Higher Worlds*, you will find, however, that this kind of initiation has its own characteristics. For its whole development and the way in which it sets forth the events, it follows the requirements of modern human education—the modern requirements of logic, sound common sense and science. Consequently these processes of initiation can be recognized more and more as the description of a path along which every human being may attain knowledge of the supersensible world. In entirely free processes, produced only by the awakening of the soul and the inner forces of the soul, the human being can ascend into the supersensible world and penetrate into processes which reveal the path taken by the soul-spiritual being. Such ideas do not only belong to a world that does not concern us but belong to a world out of which we constantly draw strength and confidence for our ordinary life. The fact that initiation reckons with modern logic and modern scientific requirements is of course a new achievement, one might say, of the process of initiation. People will gradually come to the point of acquiring knowledge in this manner, by following the example of scientific thought, and this will contain truths that penetrate and satisfy religious feeling through knowledge. But this constitutes a revolutionary change, and this change will consist in the process of initiation penetrating visibly and in an evident manner into the civilization of the present and of the future. It is a turning point in the development of humanity which may be designated in regard to supersensible things as the change from faith to knowledge.

But faith (and it will be easier to understand this turning point if we bear this in mind), in the form in which it has arisen and in the light of initiation, is not something that has been thought out intellectually, nor is it a newer form of illumination based upon something unreal; for every kind of faith leads back to results originally gained by initiated persons, to results of initiation. But there is a certain difference between what will more and more become human initiation generally and initiation of past times.

In past times it was a strict rule—and this is still the case today for many initiations which still exist in the world—it was a strict rule that anyone who went in search of the path leading to initiation had to have a kind of guide, who was called in certain circles the spiritual guide, the guru. What is the task of a guru? We have seen that in the course of development described above, we encounter certain dangers, dangers against which we must be warned. In the initiations of the past, which have been handed down traditionally, the guru's chief task was to warn against dangers. A guru may do this even today, if he or she is simply a person whom we consider as a kind of teacher as in ordinary science—a person whom we can trust. But it can easily happen that the new guru wants to be what the old guru had to be, even though the guru today cannot be allowed to have that relationship with the pupil, and this will be increasingly the case the more initiation adapts itself to the progressive course of human development. Initiation really began everywhere in the manner described above. Rules were given, and each person had a personal guide and was told: Now you must concentrate upon this thing, and now upon that; now you must do this exercise, and now that. Under strict guidance, a condition was produced in which the world of imagination appeared. The modern person on the other hand—for that is the very nature of the modern human being—must pass over from imagination to inspiration through a strong effort of his or her own will, where in olden times this task was taken over by the guru who led the pupil from the stage of imagination to that of inspiration by means of certain influences to which the pupil was more easily amenable after having been led up to this stage of initiation. What I have described to you, as something lying concealed in every human being, became an impulse which the guru transmitted to the pupil. This brought the pupil's imaginative, visionary life into order. But, in the process, the guru would gain complete control over the pupil who would become, as it were, an instrument in the teacher's hands. Therefore in all initiations of the past, and they are really the source of every religious faith, there was therefore a strict requirement that the guru, the initiator, should be above the possibility of exercising an immoral or unjust influence over the pupil. In his or her whole inner attitude the guru had to be above every kind of deceit, and success depended upon the guru's having attained to this stage of development. The guru had to use influence only to the extent of transmitting to the pupil the truth-images of the higher world that he or she had gained, thus rendering the pupil's path more easy.

I think that if you wish to understand in an unprejudiced way the development of human consciousness, you will not need to accumulate many proofs showing that in regard to supersensible knowledge as in other things humanity has become more and more independent of personal influences. This is simply a fact of the progress of the human evolution. The gurus who collect their pupils around them, as the founders of religions and sects were wont to do, will gradually disappear from the process of human development, and they will be replaced by men and women of trust, persons in whom the seeker for initiation can have trust and confidence—the same confidence which one has for other teachers. But such a teacher must, so to speak, be one of our own choosing and not a guru assigned to us. We no longer can overcome the perils which beset humanity by founding sects after the manner of ancient adepts. Indeed, in regard to supersensible development, it is good for people not to be too easily inclined to believe but, on the contrary, be hard to convince. It is good if they ask themselves, not only once or twice, but many times, in whom they put their trust, and it is good if they are very skeptical and full of distrust, when any prophet, founder of a sect, or adept, is forced upon them as a great teacher. In the field of which I am speaking, it will always constitute a danger for spiritual streams seeking to bring occultism into the world to base themselves chiefly upon great teachers whose authority is enforced from outside, instead of being founded upon the natural confidence, the inner trust, that rises up in the pupils when they meet the teacher. In a certain connection, we have seen a classic example of this, and it is necessary to mention it. During the last decades, a personality has arisen who revealed to humankind great and significant truths, truths that are not yet recognized by ordinary science but are intrinsic truths, penetrating deeply into supersensible mysteries. Things of this kind are contained in the books of H. P. Blavatsky, who has attained fame in certain circles. Even to those familiar with such things, her books contain truths of extraordinary significance, which, more than anything else, can lead us into the secrets of life. Unfortunately, this occult movement was connected with something which did it great harm. I do not mean to say that in itself it was an error, nevertheless it caused great harm that H. P. Blavatsky referred to her teachers, who were unknown to the world, to her gurus. Those who understand H. P. Blavatsky's capacities know that these capacities would never have enabled her to reach such truths independently. With her own capacities, she could never have reached them. These truths need no recommendation insofar as they are true, for they can be tested, so that it did not harm H. P. Blavatsky if she felt obliged to refer to traditions and exercises derived from gurus—she could never have attained them on her own. But it harmed the movement she called into life that such things were accepted upon the foundation of external authority, and not upon the inner truth of occultism. No matter how much good will might be involved, the fact is that the time is over—the necessities of the times show us, no matter whether this is justified or unjustified—that the possibility of taking in things simply upon the authority of gurus is past, more than past! These things must now be recognized through sound common sense. Truths which can be gained along the paths described, for instance, in my *Theosophy*, are therefore the result of the kind of spiritual investigation of which I have spoken today, but at the same time, these results can be tested and compared with the facts of life itself, and need not be accepted upon any authority.

Initiation can only be recognized and justified today if we take into consideration that it must adapt itself to the modern process of culture—and that it must follow paths and use means which are accessible to every human being.

Of course, for some time yet people having this or that degree of culture, or standing upon this or that stage of scientific training, may need the advice of an occult teacher, so that initiation becomes easier for them through the experience of one who has attained it and who has already taken in the inspirations from a higher world; for only such a teacher can give the right advice in detail. But the relation between pupil and teacher can only be of the kind that otherwise exists in the cultural world between one who wishes to learn something and one who can teach it. Any mysteriousness connected with adept teaching, any form of facing people with the demand—believe in this or that new prophet or founder of religion—all this will be rejected by the modern spirit of civilization, by the modern scientific spirit, and the very fact that it contradicts the modern spirit is a recommendation against it. No matter what people say in regard to teachers who may appear, the only thing which will in future give individuals the right to be teachers will be others' confidence in their achievements, in the way in which they appear and in their whole personality. It must be this confidence that leads a pupil to the teacher from whom advice is asked.

If this is not observed in the occult sphere, where initiation is sought, a danger will arise that is always connected with the delicate and intricate nature of such things: the danger that in this field charlatans will be found beside to conscientious initiates who conscientiously pursue their research into the supersensible worlds and transmit the results thus obtained. Charlatanry easily intrudes itself, and may be found side by side with the conscientious results of occultism or initiation imparted in the spirit of truth. Credulity and sensational curiosity in regard to communications coming from the supersensible world or initiation are just as great today as doubt, for there are just as many people ready to accept things upon this or that authority as there are people who reject everything gained even by the strictest methods of supersensible research. For this reason, a path of investigation, such as the one of initiation described today, must now be shown in addition to the propagation of occult facts. This path of initiation is one that can be followed by every human being; the results obtained along it are accessible to sound common sense as well as any other scientific result; indeed, in the case of scientific truths, one is not always in the position to test them personally, as in the case of clinical facts or other results gained in laboratories. We know that anyone may investigate them if he or she understands the required method; yet it is not possible to test everything, so that we simply accept certain facts that convince us, those our sound common sense recognizes as true.

The same thing can be said of the results of initiation. Not every person will always be in the position to test them, but those who investigate will communicate their results to the world in an ever growing measure, and sound common sense will accept them, in the same way in which it accepts the results of other scientific investigations. There is, of course, a difference, namely that the results of initiation contain truths which every human being needs, in order to gain strength and sureness in the sorrows and joys of life, strength and sureness in work and in one's sphere of activity; so that humans may take hold of the central point of their being that leads them unswervingly along the path of their ideals. The results of spiritual investigation can also give us strength when life becomes crushing, and comfort is needed in sickness and in death, by looking up to the facts of the spiritual supersensible world to which we belong, and from which we gain the true forces which keep us upright. Then into the human soul will penetrate those

results of initiation and occultism that may be recapitulated
in words expressing what has already been said concerning
initiation:

> Es sprechen zu den Menschensinnen
> die Dinge in den Raumesweiten,
> Sie wandeln sich im Zeitenlaufe.
> Erkennend dringt die Menschenseele,
> von Raumesweiten unbegrenzt
> und ungestoert durch Zeitenlauf,
> ins Reich der Ewigkeiten.

> Things in the world's spaces
> Speak to human senses,
> Changing in the course of time.
> By cognizing, the human soul
> Unbounded by the distances of space
> And undisturbed by the course of time
> Penetrates into the kingdom of eternities.

FURTHER READING:

The East in the Light of the West. Blauvelt, NY: Garber Communications, 1986.

The Effects of Spiritual Development. London: Rudolf Steiner Press, 1978.

Genesis: Secrets of Bible Story of Creation. London: Rudolf Steiner Press, 1959.

The Influence of Spiritual Beings Upon Man. Hudson, NY: Anthroposophic Press, 1961.

The Inner Realities of Evolution. London: Rudolf Steiner Press, 1953.

Karmic Relationships: Esoteric Studies. 8 vols. London: Rudolf Steiner Press, 1955–1972.

Man as Symphony of the Creative Word. Sussex, England: Rudolf Steiner Press, 1991.

Man and the World of the Stars; The Spiritual Communion of Mankind. Hudson, NY: Anthroposophic Press, 1963.

An Outline of Occult Science. Hudson NY: Anthroposophic Press, 1972.

The Spiritual Hierarchies and Their Reflection in the Physical World: Zodiac, Planets, Cosmos. Hudson, NY: Anthroposophic Press, 1970.

The Spiritual Guidance of Humanity and the Individual. Hudson, NY: Anthroposophic Press, 1992.

Theosophy of the Rosicrucian. London: Rudolf Steiner Press, 1966.

Universe, Earth, and Man in Relationship to Egyptian Myths and Modern Civilization. London: Rudolf Steiner Press, 1987.

Work of the Angels in Man's Astral Body. London: Rudolf Steiner Press, 1972.

Wonders of the World, Ordeals of the Soul, Revelations of the Spirit. London: Rudolf Steiner Press, 1963.

For a free catalog
containing these and many other related titles,
write or call:

ANTHROPOSOPHIC PRESS
RR4, BOX 94 A-1,
HUDSON, NEW YORK 12534.

518-851-2054.